CONSCIENCE BEFORE CONFORMITY

Conscience before Conformity

Hans and Sophie Scholl and the White Rose
resistance in Nazi Germany

Paul Shrimpton

GRACEWING

First published in England in 2018
by
Gracewing
2 Southern Avenue
Leominster
Herefordshire HR6 0QF
United Kingdom
www.gracewing.co.uk

© 2018 Paul Shrimpton

ISBN 978 085244 843 4

Typeset by Gracewing

Cover design by Bernardita Peña Hurtado

Cover photo: Hans Scholl, Sophie Scholl and Christoph Probst at
Munich's Ostbahnhof (East train station) on 23 July 1942.
(All three were executed on 22 February 1943.)
Photo courtesy of Jürgen Wittenstein/akg-images

CONTENTS

ACKNOWLEDGEMENTS

M Y INTEREST IN the White Rose was aroused by an article by Dr Dermot Fenlon in *Newman Studien* (2010) which linked the name of John Henry Newman to the Munich students: had it not been for him, this book would probably never have been started. Likewise, given my limited German, it would never have reached completion without Inge Jens' and John Maxwell Brownjohn's edition and translation of the letters and diaries of Hans and Sophie Scholl, published as *At the heart of the White Rose* (1987).

I am immensely grateful to my three main readers. Jakob Knab gave me invaluable advice on my first draft, and willingly helped me at other, later stages when I needed to sort out factual matters. Rachael Henry read a second draft in the Easter vacation before her Oxford Finals in English, and gave me feedback as a student who was the same age as Sophie when she was executed. Dr Paul Yowell read my third draft and assisted me enormously by the way he engaged with the story and questioned me on what was unclear. I have also received invaluable editorial assistance from Dr Peter Damian Grint. Obviously, all the infelicities and errors that remain in the text are my very own, not theirs.

Lastly, I wish to thank Tom Longford, Rev. Dr Paul Haffner and the rest of the Gracewing team for all their support and encouragement.

PREFACE

GIVEN THE SUBSTANTIAL and growing literature on Hans and Sophie Scholl and their companions who dared to speak out against Hitler and the Third Reich, any addition to White Rose studies needs to be able to explain what it is saying that is new. This book is not primarily a work of original research: it is the retelling of a familiar story from a new perspective. In presenting the story of the student revolt in the light of the cultural and religious development of the protagonists, chiefly Hans and Sophie, my aim is to give a new context that will enable the reader to make proper sense of the heroic actions of these German students.

Inevitably, the narration of the events leading up to the execution of the Scholls has been influenced by the ideological convictions and interpretations of commentators. Although they often adopt an open attitude to the protagonists' motivation, scholars have nevertheless—at least in studies published in English—tended to downplay the religious dimension of this motivation, and thus, I would argue, unwittingly to misrepresent the students' convictions. Indeed, the religious question at the heart of the White Rose has probably never been fully addressed. The seventy-fifth anniversary of the first White Rose executions provides an opportunity to fill this gap by bringing out the Christian dimension of the story.

My own approach has been to return to the original sources. My main source is the published *Letters and diaries of Hans and Sophie Scholl* (1987), together with the White Rose leaflets themselves. Although the letters and diaries have not been published in their entirety, they bring alive the turbulent times the Scholl siblings lived through and reveal their states of mind. Deeply personal and remarkably expressive, their writings reveal the inner doubts, frustrations and ambitions of these war-time heroes. Both write with a charming frankness. Sophie's writings are often exquisite and touching, though she was rarely writing to an audience of more than one, and in her diary just for herself. Hans is a little strained at times, eager to create an impression when he puts pen to paper, yet he too writes with style and with an honesty that convinces.

The same cannot be said of the interrogation transcripts and court statements from the White Rose trials,[1] since, naturally, the accused felt themselves under no compulsion to utter the truth, and sought rather to protect themselves and others from prosecution. In their correspondence Hans and Sophie and their collaborators deliberately avoided committing details of their seditious activities to paper, so the evidence acquired under interrogation and used in court has to be treated with caution.

More complicated is the case of statements from those who survived the war. It is not easy for modern readers to imagine themselves in the moral chaos of Nazi Germany and to appreciate the overwhelming pressure to compromise one's conscience and settle for an easy life; only a tiny minority had the courage and conviction to withstand this pressure, often at great personal cost. It is, perhaps, inevitable that some of those involved in White Rose activities later tried to present themselves in a better light by passing over deeds and omissions which they later regretted. But with the accumulation of evidence over the years, and the publication of most of the surviving correspondence of those who have now died, a clearer picture has emerged of the sequence of events that led to the White Rose trials and executions in 1943.

Identifying the underlying motives of those who took part in White Rose activities is a difficult enterprise. Yet it is surprising that most researchers have downplayed or even ignored the Christian faith of virtually all those involved. In this context, it is worth drawing attention to the ecumenical composition of the White Rose students: most were Lutheran by upbringing, several were Catholics, and one key figure was Orthodox. While only a minority were regular Church-going Christians, the majority were far more than cultural Christians: they prayed, they read the Bible, and they sought in Christianity the meaning of their lives. But although they drew on their own faith traditions, we should remember that in Bavaria and its environs the Catholic Church provided the dominant cultural and religious influence; and so, as the White Rose students turned to theological and philosophical writings in their attempt to cope with the growing barbarism around them, they were deeply influenced by Catholic culture.

While straining to combat the evil around them and to make sense of so much seemingly meaningless suffering, the students were also inspired by dissident academics and anti-Nazi intellectuals, many of whom were committed Christians. Like the students who gathered together for reasons of fellowship, these cultural dissidents formed their own support networks; and when the two groups—students and academics—came together, each benefitted from the presence of the other. The older generation were given optimism by meeting living specimens of the old Germany and its cultural heritage, and the young were exposed to the wisdom of the ages by hearing the others articulate and apply the thoughts of St Augustine, St Thomas Aquinas, Pascal— and Blessed John Henry Newman.

The last-mentioned is of considerable interest to English-speaking Christians. Four days after attending the beatification of Newman in September 2010, I was asked to speak about the event to around 700 pupils, aged from 11 to 18, at the school where I teach. Struggling to distil two decades of research on Newman into a ten-minute talk and uncertain how to gain the attention of my audience, I opted to speak of the link between the Oxford clergyman academic and Sophie Scholl. It worked. Referring to the nearby University Church of St Mary the Virgin, where Newman had preached numerous sermons in which he developed and illustrated his idea of conscience, I was able to show, through the connection with Sophie Scholl, that these sermons were not just a matter of fine words, but instead showed the power of ideas lived out.

One of the most striking literary references to the power of Newman's words comes from the novelist Aldous Huxley. At a pivotal point in his dystopian *Brave new world* (1932), the Controller of the Western World, Mustapha Mond, unlocks his safe to show the Savage his collection of 'pornographic old books'. Beside the Bible, the works of Shakespeare, and several other books on religion and God, he pulls out a volume of Newman's sermons and reads the Savage an example of the 'smut' that is now forbidden:

> We are not our own, any more than what we possess is our own. We did not make ourselves; we cannot be supreme over ourselves. We cannot be our own masters. We are God's property by creation, by redemption, by regeneration. He has a triple claim upon us. Is it not our happiness thus to view the matter? Is it any happiness, or any comfort, to consider that we *are* our own? It may be thought so by the young and prosperous. These may think it a great thing to have everything, as they suppose, their own way,—to depend on no one,—to have to think of nothing out of sight,—to be without the irksomeness of continual acknowledgment, continual prayer, continual reference of what they do to the will of another. But as time goes on, they, as all men, will find that independence was not made for man—that it is an unnatural state—may do for a while, but will not carry us on safely to the end.[2]

Like Mustapha Mond, Adolf Hitler appreciated the dangerous influence of ideas on his subjects. He despised the university and the 'weaklings' it housed, and from the moment he came to power sought to smother all ideas that were at odds with Nazi doctrine. His attempts to starve his subjects of sustenance for the life of the mind only aggravated the normal human quest for meaning, and failed to eliminate the cultural thirst of a people—some of whom were prepared to go to extraordinary lengths to slake their thirst. Not surprisingly, the unjust laws promulgated and enforced by the Nazi state prompted jurisprudential reflection on the true foundations of law, and on the obligations of the individual who was subject to these laws. And so the line of thinking on conscience articulated by Augustine and Newman, together with that on natural law by Aquinas, addressed a desperate need; and hence the significance of the final words of the fourth White Rose leaflet: 'We will not be silent. We are your bad conscience. The White Rose will not leave you in peace!'

Notes

1   The Gestapo destroyed most of their files at the end of the war, but around 60,000 survived, including the White Rose ones.
2   'Remembrance of past mercies', *Parochial and Plain Sermons* vol. v (London: Longmans, Green & Co, 1840; 1907), pp. 83–4.

INTRODUCTION

SOPHIE SCHOLL MAY not be a household name in Britain, but she is something of a legend in Germany, with two films made about her life and nearly two hundred schools named after her, as well as streets and squares. At the turn of the millennium she was voted 'Woman of the twentieth century' by readers of the German magazine *Brigitte*, and a popular television series called 'Greatest Germans' dubbed her the greatest German woman of all time.

Sophie was a 21-year-old student of biology and philosophy at the time of her execution in February 1943, when she was beheaded along with her brother Hans for urging fellow students at Munich University to oppose the Nazi regime. Brother and sister Scholl belonged to a group of students who spoke out against National Socialism and circulated thousands of leaflets telling other Germans that they had a moral duty to resist Hitler. Adopting the name *Die Weisse Rose* (The White Rose), these students also condemned the persecution of the Jews in the year when Hitler began to implement the Final Solution.

When the police caught Sophie and Hans distributing leaflets at the University they were interrogated by the Gestapo over four days, tried in court, and then, on Hitler's orders, guillotined. We know from the transcripts of the trial that Sophie said she had been compelled by her Christian conscience to peacefully oppose the Nazi regime; the same was true for Hans, for he, like his sister, had found in prayer and reading the Christian resources and inspiration to make sense of the brutal and demonic world around him.

Did Pope Benedict XVI have the Scholls in mind when he opened his four-day visit to Britain in September 2010 with an address to the Queen? The question is not an idle one, as he referred back to the dark days that he and the Queen had lived through, when

> Britain and her leaders stood against a Nazi tyranny that wished to eradicate God from society and denied our common humanity to many, especially the Jews, who were thought unfit to live. I also recall the regime's attitude to Christian pastors and religious who spoke the truth in love, opposed the Nazis and paid for that opposition with their lives.[1]

The Pope could conceivably have had Hans and Sophie Scholl in mind if he had read the latest volume of *Newman Studien*, the German journal on Newman studies, which had appeared earlier that summer, for it revealed that they and their White Rose friends had been deeply influenced by the very man Pope Benedict was to beatify at the end of his state visit to Britain. The journal contains two articles[2] which examine Newman's influence on the White Rose students, and draws on letters between Sophie and her boyfriend; these letters reveal that the heroism of Sophie and her brother was inspired, at least in part, by the sermons and writings of John Henry Newman, sometime Fellow of Oriel College, Oxford and vicar of the University Church of St Mary the Virgin.

When Sophie's boyfriend, a *Luftwaffe* officer called Fritz Hartnagel, was deployed to the eastern front in May 1942, Sophie's parting gift was two volumes of Newman's sermons. Witnessing the carnage in Russia and hearing reports of mass killings of local Jews, he wrote to Sophie to say that reading Newman's words in such an awful place was like tasting 'drops of precious wine'.[3] In another letter, Fritz wrote: 'we know by whom we were created and that we stand in a relationship of moral obligation to our creator. Conscience gives us the capacity to distinguish between good and evil.'[4] These words were taken almost verbatim from a sermon Newman preached in Oxford called 'The Testimony of Conscience'.[5] In this sermon Newman explains that conscience is an echo of the voice of God enlightening each person to moral truth in concrete situations. All of us, he argues, have a duty to obey a good conscience over and above all other considerations.

Pope Benedict encountered these ideas just a few years after Sophie did, when he entered the seminary in 1946 and was placed under a supervisor, Alfred Läpple, who was writing his doctorate on Newman and conscience. These and other thoughts were running through my mind early in the morning of Sunday 19 September as I sat with 50,000 other pilgrims on the slopes of a Birmingham park in the dark and drizzle in our five-hour wait for the arrival of Pope Benedict.

It might seem fanciful to suggest that the sermons and writings of a nineteenth-century Christian humanist could have had much purchase in war-time Germany, for those living under Nazi rule inhabited a world where the old certainties were fast diminishing and ugly alternatives seductively proffered, a world remote from the one Newman had inhabited for nearly four decades in Oxford—but there are two reasons why we should think otherwise. Firstly, we ought not to underestimate the insights of this great Christian humanist: Pope Benedict spoke of the 'modernity of his existence, [...] his great culture, [...] and his constant quest for the truth' as the three elements which give Newman 'an exceptional greatness for our time' and make him 'a figure of Doctor of the Church for us'.[6] Secondly, it is worth noting that Newman's reception in Germany was probably more developed than anywhere else, as translations and studies of Newman abounded in Germany during the inter-war years.

By the early 1940s the questioning students involved in White Rose activities were hungry for answers that might explain the nightmare they found themselves living through, and Newman was one—just one—of the Christian sages who was able to respond to their need to make sense of the cultural and moral chaos around them. For this group of lively students, who frequented the Munich concert halls and coffee bars in term, and the Bavarian lakes and mountains in vacations, Newman's words provided much-needed relief for their spiritual and intellectual hunger.

Before embarking on the White Rose story itself, the next chapter sets the scene by introducing the philosopher and cultural historian Theodor Haecker, the man who brought Newman's writings to the attention of the Munich students and academics who refused to submit to National Socialism. The leading Newman scholar in inter-war Germany discovered that the insights of the Oxford-educated academic were ideally suited to making sense of the catastrophe he was living through, and he sought to share this discovery with others. The story of how Newman's writings reached these students and how they were viewed by intellectuals goes some way to explaining the state of affairs in war-time Germany, where the battle for minds and hearts was raging.

It is possible that some might find the first chapter heavy going, as it deals with Newman's reception in Germany via Haecker, but the chapter is brief, and it will enable the reader to trace this one particular influence—one among many—on the celebrated story of student resistance in Nazi Germany that this book aims to tell. Hopelessly outnumbered and labouring against formidable odds, intellectuals like Haecker refused to bow to tyranny and did their best to serve the cause of truth. His story is one of many that feeds into the White Rose tale, and it illustrates the way in which hope survived at the margins. It begins at the Birmingham Oratory in 1920.

Notes

[1]   Address of Pope Benedict XVI, Palace of Holyroodhouse, 16 September 2010.

[2]   J. Knab, ' "Wir schweigen nicht, wir sind Euer böses Gewissen" Die Newman-Rezeption der "Weißen Rose" und ihre Wirkungsgeschichte', *Newman Studien* xx (2010), pp. 21–43; D. Fenlon, 'From the White Star to the Red Rose. J. H. Newman and the conscience of the state', *ibid.*, pp. 45–73.

[3]   Fritz Hartnagel to Sophie Scholl, 26 June 1942, quoted in Fenlon, 'White Star to the Red Rose', p. 63.

[4]   Fritz Hartnagel to Sophie Scholl, 4 July 1942, quoted in Fenlon, 'White Star to the Red Rose', p. 63.

[5]   *Plain and parochial sermons* vol. v, pp. 237–53.

[6]   *Benedict XVI and Blessed John Henry Newman. The state visit 2010: the official record* (London: CTS, 2010), p. 45.

1 BIRMINGHAM AND MUNICH

THEODOR HAECKER WAS born in 1879 in Esslingen am Neckar, a city in the Stuttgart region of Baden-Württemberg in southern Germany, and raised in a Protestant family. He lost his mother when he was twelve and at sixteen left his *gymnasium* to start working. Through the generosity of a friend, he was able to study at the University of Berlin, where he laid the foundation of his vast knowledge of ancient and modern literature, but he could not afford to remain there long enough to take a degree. After working for three years in a business in the great trading port of Antwerp, he was again rescued by a friend and on this occasion was taken into a small publishing business in Munich, where he remained until he was forced to leave at the end of his life. He lived a regular routine all these years: during the day he worked in his office, and by night, upstairs, he pursued his studies in philosophy and classical literature. His first book *Kierkegaard and the philosophy of inwardness* (1913) was a fairly conventional work about the then little-known Danish philosopher. The articles he wrote over the next seven years—'seven years of darkness', Haecker called them—were published as *Satire und polemic* (1922), and gave full vent to his contempt for the literary and philosophical pundits of the day, including Thomas Mann. There was nothing muted or understated about Haecker's style—he once said that if Jesus returned, Prussian Protestants would not put a crown of thorns on his head, but a *Pickelhaube*, a spiked helmet—and when he turned to other fields, he continued to write with verve.[1] His encounter with Newman's writings in 1917, towards the end of the Great War, was a turning point in his life, though Haecker

never lost his admiration and deep sympathy for Sören Kierkegaard and his passion for the truth.

On 18 November 1920 a letter arrived at the Birmingham
Oratory from Munich asking for permission to translate into
German *An essay in aid of a grammar of assent,* the systematic
study of the genesis of religious belief that Newman had finished
writing in 1870. The letter came from the cultural critic Theodor
Haecker. A fortnight later Haecker wrote again to ask for the
latest edition of the *Grammar of assent,* explaining that until very
recently 'the deep originality' of Newman's thinking would have
been obscured from German philosophers, but that now, mainly
owing to the writings of the phenomenologist Edmund Husserl,
the ground was prepared for understanding Newman's analysis
of the processes leading to religious belief. Haecker expressed his
hope that Newman's account of assent and certitude would be
'fully understood and deservedly appreciated by the educated
class of my country', and so be of 'great religious benefit'.[2]

Between 1920 and 1922 no fewer than ten works of Newman
were sent to Haecker from Birmingham, and over a period of
twenty-five years he translated seven of them, five of which were
published before his death in 1945. Haecker found that Newman
was able to supply him with something lacking in Kierkegaard:
the link between the world of phenomena and the creator. As
Günter Biemer, the leading German scholar on Newman,
explains, it was thanks to Husserl's school of phenomenology,
which provided an alternative to Hegel's school, that Germany
had a special *kairos* for Newman.[3]

Haecker married at the age of 38. On 5 April 1921, six days
after the birth of his second child, his quest for the truth led him
into full communion with the Catholic Church. There is little
doubt that he owed his conversion to reading Newman, and for
the rest of his life Newman was his guiding star. In translating
the *Grammar of assent* for publication in 1921, Haecker was won
over by the subtlety and originality of Newman's description of
the process of religious assent. He explains in the postscript to

his translation that he was persuaded by Newman's distinction between *notional* and *real* assent; by his realism and nearness to the concrete; by his understanding of the individual conscience, which he managed to integrate with other mental acts and knowledge more successfully than Kierkegaard; by his 'masterly clear description of the substantiveness' of the separate acts of the human mind, when contrasted with Locke's *Essay concerning human understanding* (1690); by his personalist epistemology which dealt with the mystery of the individual soul[4] and his use of (what Newman terms) the 'illative sense'; and because he judged Newman's analysis of the act of faith 'the one which is humanly and divinely naturally appointed and normal, while [Kierkegaard's] is only exceptionally allowed by God to individual souls and for certain purposes but otherwise of extreme danger'.[5]

Despite the shortcomings he discovered in Kierkegaard, Haecker did not lose his high estimation for him, as shown by his works *The concept of truth* (1929) and *Kierkegaard the cripple* (1947), and by his translations (into German) of his diaries and sermons which he published until 1838. He regarded Kierkegaard's 'huge error to presume that it is only *fides qua* [i.e. the believing itself] that matters', not the *fides quem* (i.e. the content of that belief); and considered that his 'very greatest disappointment' in the 'great works of the great man' was that he did not find in him the zeal for the 'snowy purity of the true doctrine, of which the Apostles and the Fathers give such intensive testimony and for which Newman was relentlessly buffeted about at the same time until he finally with a bleeding heart left his beloved step-mother the Anglican Church for truth's sake'. In response to Kierkegaard's injunction that we should not talk so much about correct doctrine but do what is right, Haecker responds: 'Both constitute the entirety! Newman is not less in favour of doing, of "realising"—which includes indeed a spiritual doing, love [...]—he had the light of intellect, i.e. truth, and the fire of the heart, i.e. love of God, but both as a unity'.[6]

In 1922 Haecker brought out his translation of the *Essay on the development of Christian doctrine*, Newman's highly original articulation of the way in which truths are both implicitly and explicitly contained in Scripture and dogma is formulated, an account that defended Catholic teaching from the criticisms of other Christians who considered some aspects of Catholic teaching to be corruptions or else innovations. Newman's ground-breaking analysis relied on an extensive study of the early Church Fathers in tracing the elaboration or development of doctrine which he argued was, in some way, implicitly present in Divine Revelation as contained in Sacred Scripture and in the living Tradition which was present from the beginnings of the Church. Newman argued that various Catholic doctrines not accepted by Protestants, such as devotion to the Virgin Mary or Purgatory, had a developmental history analogous to doctrines that *were* accepted, such as that of the Blessed Trinity or the divinity and humanity of Jesus Christ. Such developments were, in his view, the natural and beneficial results of reason working on the original revealed truth to draw out consequences that were not obvious at first.[7]

Although sixteen years were to pass before Haecker published his next translation of Newman (in 1938), he drew on Newman's ideas constantly. In an article in 1926, for example, he argues against the separation of intellect and life in philosophical debate, and invokes not just the thinking but the example of Newman, 'that last unity of genius with holiness [...] one of the most inwardly directed Christians that ever lived'.[8] The early 1930s were Haecker's most productive period, in which he produced a book each year. The first was his *Dialogue about Christianity and culture* (1930) which explained his vision of a new Europe, based on a common Christian heritage; his representative figure is Newman, 'the last unity of a natural flash of genius and holiness in our time'.[9] His *Vergil, Vater des Abendlandes* (*Virgil, father of the West*), was published in 1931 and deals with Virgil's influence on the history of Christianity, in the course of which he refers to Newman as 'the last gentle *anima Vergiliana*'.[10]

In January 1933 the National Socialists seized power under Hitler and began what they called 'the thousand-year Reich'. Haecker was among the first to discern the real character of the Nazi movement and that year published *Was ist der Mensch?* (*What is man?*), which attacked the philosophy of the new movement. He was arrested by the Gestapo on 20 May and interrogated about his article on the *Hakenkreuz* (literally 'crooked-cross' or swastika) which was about to appear in *Brenner*, a periodical published in Tyrolia.[11] He was released only with the help of Carl Muth, the founding editor of the monthly journal *Hochland*, and Cardinal Michael von Faulhaber, the Archbishop of Munich, who had his own Advent sermons (published in book form) banned later that year. From May 1933 Haecker was a marked man; he was forbidden to speak on the wireless (i.e. radio) and banned from delivering lectures. Thomas Mann noted in his diary, 'Haecker is a Catholic thinker and a powerful writer with the manners of a zealot. But although he attacks me several times hard (and unmistakably), I feel a deep sympathy for his Christian humanity (in *What is man?*) and was moved by his brave apology of the spirit'.[12]

In 1934 Haecker published *Schöpfer und Schöpfung* (*Creator and creation*), which dealt with the tragic existence of man in a fallen world. He regarded Kierkegaard as an outstanding example of the tragic figure in this drama, but even more so Newman. Searching for the reasons for God's apparent absence from the German political scene, Haecker turned to Newman's analysis of the course of the world in the *Grammar of assent*:

> What strikes the mind so forcibly and so painfully is, His absence (if I may so speak) from His own world. It is a silence that speaks. It is as if others had got possession of His work. Why does not He, our Maker and Ruler, give us some immediate knowledge of Himself? Why does He not write His Moral Nature in large letters upon the face of

history, and bring the blind, tumultuous rush of its events into a celestial, hierarchical order? Why does He not grant us in the structure of society at least so much of a revelation of Himself as the religions of the heathen attempt to supply? Why from the beginning of time has no one uniform steady light guided all families of the earth, and all individual men, how to please Him? Why is it possible without absurdity to deny His will, His attributes, His existence? [...] On the contrary, He is specially 'a Hidden God'; and with our best efforts we can only glean from the surface of the world some faint and fragmentary views of Him. I see only a choice of alternatives in explanation of so critical a fact: either there is no Creator, or He has disowned His creatures. Are then the dim shadows of His Presence in the affairs of men but a fancy of our own, or, on the other hand, has He hid His face and the light of His countenance, because we have in some special way dishonoured Him? My true informant, my burdened conscience, gives me at once the true answer to each of these antagonist questions: it pronounces without any misgiving that God exists: and it pronounces quite as surely that I am alienated from Him [...] Thus it solves the world's mystery, and sees in that mystery only a confirmation of its own original teaching.[13]

Creator and creation was cited during the White Rose trials in February 1943 because a group of Munich students had listened to Haecker reading extracts from it earlier that month. Indeed, Sophie Scholl herself had struggled to make sense of the book after she discovered it in Carl Muth's library the previous year.

Over the next decade Haecker developed his thesis of the German apostasy; its symbol was the crooked cross (or swastika) and the eagle burying its talons in the Body of Christ.[14] Newman's collection of four Advent sermons on 'The Patristical Idea of antichrist'[15] was the pivotal text for Haecker's thesis about Christianity in the Third Reich. In his view England had bequeathed Newman, a prophet of apostasy, to a Germany deeply in need of a response which was adequate to the prevailing anti-Christian totalitarianism. In these sermons Newman analyses the commentaries and interpretations of the prophetic passages in Scripture about the last days contained in the writings of the Fathers of the Church. The consensus was that 'the [second] coming of Christ will be immediately preceded by a very awful and unparalleled outbreak of evil, called by St Paul an Apostasy, a falling away, in the midst of which a certain terrible Man of sin and Child of perdition, the special and singular enemy of Christ, or Antichrist, will appear'. This will happen 'when revolutions prevail, and the present framework of society breaks to pieces', but for the time being 'the spirit which he will embody' and represent is kept in check by 'the powers that be' until the appointed time, though 'the conspiracy of revolt is already at work' (Thessalonians 2:6–7). Newman asked his Oxford congregation in 1835 whether there was 'reason to fear that some such Apostasy is gradually preparing, gathering, hastening on in this very day?'[16]

Haecker translated these four sermons—they were published posthumously—and could not but notice how Newman sought to detect the signs of such an impending apostasy:

> Surely, there is at this day a confederacy of evil, marshalling its hosts from all parts of the world, organizing itself, taking its measures, enclosing the Church of Christ as in a net, and preparing the way for a general Apostasy from it. Whether this very Apostasy is to give birth to Antichrist, or whether he is still to be delayed, as he has already been delayed so long, we cannot know.[17]

Newman observes that history provides examples of how a falling away precedes the coming of a forerunner or shadow of Antichrist: Julian the apostate 'was educated in the bosom of Arianism', and from the heresies of Nestorius and Eutyches 'the impostor Mahomet sprang, and formed his creed'.[18] Applying the thinking of the Fathers to more recent times, Newman detects the shadow of Antichrist in the French Revolution. All this was grist to the mill for a philosopher trying to make metaphysical sense of the deeds of the Third Reich.

In 1935 appeared *Der Christ und die Geschichte* (*The Christian and history*), Haecker's theology of history, in which he examines the role of divine providence in time. He sides with Newman once again in concluding that, despite wars and mishaps, there are no blind coincidences in the events of history but rather acts of divine providence which form part of salvation history. Haecker used his manuscript for a talk to members of the National Socialist student body in Freiburg on 19 May 1935. The talk caused an outcry. It was denounced in the local press as a manifestation of 'political Catholicism', and was heavily criticised by the philosopher Martin Heidegger. (Heidegger had joined the Nazi Party on 1 May 1933, and remained an enthusiastic member until the end of the war.) As a result Haecker was silenced by the regime: he was prohibited from writing or speaking in public in his native Germany, and thereafter operated under house arrest, subject to occasional raids and searches of his house and papers by the Gestapo. The death of his wife that year left him very much alone, though his two sons and daughter continued to live with him.

In the last of his own books that he saw into print, *Der Geist des Menschen und die Wahrheit* (1937, *The spirit of man and the truth*),[19] Haecker insists on the value of truth for those living in a political system run by those who despise humanity. He takes Newman as a witness for that nothingness which is the 'fate of lie and liars', referring to Newman's poem *The dream of Gerontius*. Though now forbidden to write anything of his own, he was able to translate—and what better way to resist Hitler than by translating Newman? In 1938 he saw to the press *Die Kirche und die Welt* (*The Church and the world*), a collection of Newman's sermons, fifteen of his *Sermons bearing on subjects of the day*, including 'Faith and the world' and 'Sanctity the token of the Christian empire', and some of the *Plain and parochial sermons*, such as 'The religion of the day' (several of which had already appeared in *Hochland*). Haecker added no commentary of his own: Newman's words were sufficient. The first sermon finishes with the words, 'You must either conquer the world, or the world will conquer you. You must be either master or slave. Take your part then, and "stand fast in the liberty wherewith Christ hath made us free".'[20]

Haecker's translation of Newman's *Dream of Gerontius* came out in 1939. In his introduction Haecker explains that the poem 'contains in condensed precious fullness and vividness his [i.e. Newman's] living faith and the dogmatic system and theology of the Catholic Church in inseparable connection'. Haecker argues that for a work of art to be called Christian it should be capable of bringing the person who is open to God nearer to Him. In this sense, Newman's work was 'the poetry of a theologian'; it seems 'to have come into existence by the inspiration of angels'.[21]

The last of Newman's works that Haecker saw through to publication during his own lifetime comprised twelve of the *Plain and parochial sermons* under the title *Das Mysterium der Dreieinigkeit und der Menschwerdung Gottes* (*The mystery of the Trinity and the Incarnation of God*). In the epilogue Haecker draws the reader's attention to the participants of that part of salvation history under consideration: the invincible grace of the Holy Spirit, good and fallen angels, the lowliness of the world, the faithfulness of simple believers, and the pure faith and genius of a chosen bishop, Athanasius (whose principle works Newman had translated into English). Haecker finishes by quoting Newman: 'Christianity gives exercise to the whole mind of man, to our highest and most subtle reason, as well as to our feelings, affections, imagination, and conscience'.[22] Haecker's translations of parts of *Historical sketches* (3 vols) appeared in 1948, after his death.

A letter Haecker sent from Switzerland (outside the reach of Nazi censorship) conveys his feelings in 1939.

> I was able to lecture in St Gallen (in Switzerland) yesterday. The permission was given as a result of an oversight. And in my own country I am not allowed to say one word in public, because my books are having a success and are

beginning to have some influence. I have been declared an enemy of the State, a *Staatsfeind*. My name is starred three times in the books of the Police, our *tscheka* [i.e. Cheka], and my safety is always threatened more and more. I have the feeling and the belief that I am in the hands of God, but I am not on that account freed from anxiety and worry about my children. In a couple of hours I shall be back in Germany, and cannot tell what may not happen. At any rate, once there I shall no longer be able to write the truth.[23]

Banned from publishing in his own name, Haecker found new avenues for speaking the truth, either by working on translations or else by writing in secret. His most intimate thoughts were recorded in the secret diary he kept from October 1939, just after World War II began, to 9 February 1945, exactly two months before his death. Published in 1947 as *Tag- und Nachtbücher* (*Journal in the night*, 1950), the *Journal* is now acclaimed as one of the deepest reflections on fascism to date, showing an intellectual's inner resistance to National Socialism. Written at night, the pages were hidden in an old leather suitcase in Haecker's study. As Alexander Dru comments in the introduction to his translation, the *Journal* was 'written by a man intent, by nature, on the search for truth, and driven, by circumstance, to seek for it in anguish, in solitude, with an urgency that grips the reader'.[24] Haecker sought to interpret the everyday political events of a hellish dictatorship 'in the light of Christian faith and to find in the night the golden thread of salvation history as a consolation for the terror of the day'.[25]

The central theme of the *Journal* is the relationship between Christianity and culture, or, better put, the 'momentous instance of their divorce—the *apostasy* of Germany'.[26] Inevitably, he draws on Newman's four sermons on 'The Patristical Idea of antichrist' for his thesis. An entry in June 1940 conveys the strength of Haecker's conviction and outlines his contention that a cosmic battle was taking place in Germany.

Salus ex Germanis, that is what is meant. Not *salus ex Judaeis*. The history of the world, or rather sacred history, is to be overturned. I am horrified when I see and hear to what an extent people underestimate this apostasy. Their attitude to the Christian religion is not simply Machiavellian, or Napoleonic, or fascist, a purely political attitude, bent upon bringing Christianity under their dominion; no, they mean to destroy and supplant it. *Salus ex Germanis*: A German saviour and bearer of light is to replace Christ. [...] They will bring a moral, a religious, and what is more a material misery upon the world that we can only imagine with difficulty, that only the apocalyptic author on Patmos and here and there one of God's saints has seen in the spirit.[27]

Deeply read in history, as well as philosophy, Haecker compared his own times with previous eras and concluded that he was living through some of the darkest moments in the history of Christianity: 'So much and so great evil has never been committed so consciously. It is the first, definite apostasy in Christendom, or let us say: the second, raised to a new power, if we reckon 1789 as the first in the West.'[28] Though confined to the pages of his secret diary, Haecker's thesis undoubtedly informed the conversations he had with the academics and students he got to know in Munich, and helped them to formulate a spiritual foundation for their opposition to Nazism. Between 1941 and 1943 he would speak to the White Rose students and their close friends in a Munich studio; and on one occasion, 14 December 1942, he would bring a copy of the manuscript of his translation of Newman's sermons on Antichrist.

In meditating on the contemporary crisis in Western civilisation, Haecker had come to believe that its problems were ultimately philosophical in origin, that they were inventions of the West itself, and that they radiated out from its historic centres of high culture: Britain, France, Germany and Italy. It was with increasing gloom that Haecker noted in his *Journal* how Germany, whose scientific research, industry and technological accomplishments had increasingly become the envy and model of the developed world, had descended into a crude national egotism and ethnocentrism that justified itself by means of Darwinian racial science. By Haecker's reckoning, the seeds of destruction lay in its contribution to the modern intellectual tradition. In 1943 he wrote, 'In recent times it seems as though the Germans had chosen madmen, men who quite simply went mad, and consecrated them, raised men like Nietzsche and Hölderlin to the level of prophets, heroes, saints and wise men, and made idols of them. [...] they are mortally sick'. The modern intellectual man, who is no longer spiritual, who is 'the ambiguous fudge of good and evil, wanting in all decision, and incapable of saying "no" to anything', this man 'has a nihilistic, devastating philosophy once away from the privileged philosophy of being of Aristotle and Plato; he has a nihilistic politics, an apostate politics, because his will is nihilistic and does not will the true end, which is God alone'.[29] One reviewer of Haecker's *Journal* made the telling observation that he 'had none of that lingering fondness for German history which softens the heart and dulls the moral sensibility of most Germans';[30] it was a detachment which enabled him to analyse what had gone so badly wrong. Among the 'great minds of the nineteenth century' who possessed 'the spirit of prophecy' that enabled them to discern the signs of the times, Haecker identified just three: Dostoyevsky, Kierkegaard and Newman.[31]

Haecker was by no means the only major influence on the White Rose students, nor was he the sole champion of Newman in Germany. A few months after his letter to the Birmingham Oratory in 1920, another arrived (independently) from a Jesuit priest and philosopher called Erich Przywara; he, too, became an avid Newman scholar and, with the assistance of collaborators and translators, enabled his countrymen to discover in Newman a modern counterpart to St Augustine. Przywara published his six-volume anthology *Kardinal Newman. Christentum. Ein Aufbau* in 1922, and it is regarded by many as the finest Newman anthology.[32] It provided a comprehensive overview of Newman's thought, using excerpts from twenty-four of his books, which

Przywara arranged in twenty-one sections, each prefaced by an 'argument' setting out the plan. But neither Haecker nor Przywara were the first to translate Newman into German, as the enterprise had started eighty years earlier, inspired by the Church historian Ignaz von Döllinger.[33]

Up until the First Vatican Council (1869–70) Newman and his main propagator were generally popular among German Catholics, but that changed when Döllinger refused to accept the declaration on papal infallibility and was excommunicated by the Archbishop of Munich. Newman went out of favour as his writings were considered to be incompatible with scholastic thought, which was now enjoying a revival in the Catholic Church. When his *Prophetical office of the Church* (1837) was published in German in 1878, the leading Ultramontane journal proposed that Newman's works should no longer be published without a scholastic commentary, as they were theologically suspect and tainted with Protestant prejudices. Yet Newman's thought remained an interesting alternative to the resurgent neo-scholasticism, especially after 1879 when he was raised to the cardinalate by the new Pope.

There was notable enthusiasm for Newman within the *Reform-katholizismus* movement which sought to integrate Catholicism in Wilhelmine society and undo the sense of Catholic inferiority in the aftermath of Bismarck's *Kulturkampf* policies (which aimed at Protestant and Prussian dominance) by demonstrating the potential for modernity within it. Newman stood for a culturally acceptable Catholicism, and his Englishness and high church views were advantageous as they distanced him from the fathers of neo-Protestantism, Kant and Schleiermacher, while he was theologically safe, since he had been approved by the anti-Modernist Pope Pius X. Carl Muth entered the debate about the confessional character of literature in 1898 under the pseudonym Vermundus,[34] then in 1903 he started a monthly cultural magazine called *Hochland* which featured all fields of science and literature, and accepted articles from writers regardless of their religious affiliation. It was a risky undertaking from the outset, especially as Muth argued for more literary freedom and considered Schiller and Goethe as literary models, and the journal was nearly put on the Index of Prohibited Books in 1911. Significantly, it was through the pages of *Hochland* that many educated Catholics came to know about Newman. In 1907 a young priest called Matthias Laros published a selection of Newman's Anglican sermons, the first to be translated into German, and from this moment, and for nearly fifty years, Laros championed the cause of Newman. Influenced by Modernist tendencies, Laros considered that Newman had moved beyond both neo-scholastic intellectualism and evangelical voluntarism, and that he had superseded dogmatism and historicism with his higher synthesis of development.

A number of intellectuals in Germany saw their defeat in the First World War as a failure of liberal Protestantism and instead turned to Catholicism for inspiration. In a theological re-orientation which saw the Swiss reformed theologian Karl Barth move away from liberal Protestantism, both disillusioned Ultramontane and Modernist Catholics began to take an interest in Newman and his writings. It is likely that Laros' *John Henry Kardinal Newman, Die* Gesch (1913) and *Kardinal Newman, Ex umbris et imaginibus in veritatem* (1920),[35] attracted the interest of both Haecker and Przywara. Haecker attempted to liaise with Laros over translations, whereas Przywara was wary of him and organised a rival school. This meant that there developed two schools for Newman studies in Germany: both leaders spoke regularly at the Association of Catholic Academics and influenced, with their differing interpretations, leading intellectual figures such as Romano Guardini and Karl Adam.

Przywara accused Laros of having strong Modernist leadings, because of his stress on Newman's supposed opposition to neo-scholasticism, and only agreed to call Newman a 'theologian of conscience' so long as conscience was understood as the echo of God's voice, which called for obedience, especially if it spoke in harmony with the authority of the Church. Przywara saw Newman as an antidote to Kant in the way that he supplemented scholasticism with concepts for the subjective side of thinking and acting. For his own anthology Przywara used translations of Newman by the Jesuit theologian Otto Karrer and sought to show the organic unity of Newman's writings.[36] At Przywara's suggestion, Husserl's pupil Edith Stein (canonised as St Theresa Benedicta of the Cross, and named as a patron of Europe by Pope John Paul II) translated letters and diaries from Newman's Anglican period and his *Idea of a university* (1873).[37]

Laros countered by claiming that Przywara sought to impose a scholastic re-interpretation which altered the true guise of Newman's thought. Competition between the two of them led to independent translations of Newman's works being published in German. In the long run Laros was more successful, as his editions were taken up by the publishing house Grünewald after the Second World War, and they enabled educated Catholics to appreciate Newman and his personalism, that is, his 'Christian existentialism'.

What might appear as just the obscure scholarly pursuits of a few academics, turned out to have important consequences because throughout the Third Reich (1933–45) Newman's translators and commentators were influential in enabling intellectuals to make sense of National Socialism, and they in turn helped to sustain a student resistance group opposed to Nazism which went under the name of the White Rose. Among the students involved, the names of Hans and Sophie Scholl, particularly the latter, have captured the imagination of the world.

Notes

1   A. Dru, introduction to T. Haecker, *Journal in the night*, trans. A. Dru (London: Pantheon, 1950), p. xiii.

2   Haecker to the Birmingham Oratory, 30 November 1920, quoted in G. Biemer, 'Theodor Haecker: in the footsteps of John Henry Newman', *New Blackfriars* 81 (October 2000), p. 415.

3   G. Biemer, 'Theodor Haecker', pp. 414–15.

4   Haecker refers to Newman's sermon, 'The individuality of the soul', where it reads: 'every being in that great concourse is his own centre and all things about him are but shades, but a "vain shadow", in which he "walketh and disquieteth himself in vain". He has his own hopes and fears, desires, judgments, and aims; he is everything to himself, and no one else is really any thing. No one outside of him can really touch him, can touch his soul, his immortality; he must live with himself for ever. He has a depth within him unfathomable, an infinite abyss of existence' (*Plain and parochial* vol. iv (1839; 1869), pp. 82–3).

5   Postscript, *Philosophie des Glaubens* (Munich, 1921), pp. 429–48.

6   *Opuscula* vol. i (Olten, 1949), pp. 223, 257–8, trans. in Biemer, 'Theodor Haecker', pp. 419–20.

7   Modernist intellectuals such as George Tyrrell and Alfred Loisy cited Newman's ideas as an inspiration for their own idea of the evolution of Christian dogmas, which did not so much aim to understand the ancient roots of Church doctrine but to make it evolve according to their own thinking in the liberal spirit of the times; this interpretation was condemned by the Church in the papal encyclical *Pascendi* (1907), and Newman's (apparent) association with the originators of the Modernist heresy was to put him under a cloud for several decades.

8   *Hochland* (1926), trans. in Biemer, 'Theodor Haecker', p. 420.

9   *Opuscula* vol. i, p. 334, trans. in Biemer, 'Theodor Haecker', p. 421.

10 *Vergil, Vater des Abendlandes*, p. 141, trans. in Biemer, 'Theodor Haecker', p. 421.

11 Haecker wrote about that first arrest in his secret diary in May 1940: 'The choice between falling into the hands of God and into the hands of men, costs me no agony of indecision. I wish to fall into the hands of God, however frightful it may be. That is how I have understood every serious sickness, full of thankfulness in suffering. What it means to fall into the hands of men, I tasted for just half a day on 20th May 1933' (*Journal in the night*, p. 50).

12 T. Mann, diary entry, 23 August 1934, quoted in G. Biemer, 'Theodor

Haecker', p. 413.

13   *Grammar of assent* (London: Longmans, Green & Co., 1870; 1903), pp. 396–8, quoted in *Schöpfer und Schöpfung* (Leipzig, 1934), pp. 365–7.

14   'The *German* Red Cross has as its badge an eagle puffed up with pride, a *Hakenkreuz* for a heart, sitting on and digging its claws into—a cross, the red cross' (Haecker, 14 April 1940, *Journal in the night*, p. 44). See also the entry: January 1940 (p. 20), 'Why, when they hate the Cross, do they talk of a crusade against plutocracy, why not a *Hakenkreuzzug*, a crooked-crusade? Why not a new language for a new thing, if it is new?'

15   Besides being included in the series 'Tracts for the times' as Tract 83, the sermons were published as part of *Discussion and arguments* (1872, pp. 44–108).

16   'The times of Antichrist', *Discussions and arguments* (London: Longman, Green & Co., 1872; 1907), pp. 56–7, 60.

17   'The times of Antichrist', *Discussions and arguments*, p. 60.

18   'The times of Antichrist', *Discussions and arguments*, p. 59.

19   It is unclear how he managed to defy the ban and get this published.

20   *Sermons bearing on subjects of the day* (London: Longmans, Green & Co, 1843; 1902), p. 111.

21   *Der traum des Gerontius*, p. 9, trans. in Biemer, 'Theodor Haecker', p. 424.

22   'The mystery of the holy Trinity', *Plain and parochial sermons* vol. xi, p. 353.

23   Dru, introduction to Haecker, *Journal in the night*, p. xiv.

24   Dru, introduction to Haecker, *Journal in the night*.

25   Biemer, 'Theodor Haecker', p. 425.

26   Dru, introduction, *Journal in the night*, p. xxxiii.

27   *Journal in the night*, p. 80.

28   March 1941, *Journal in the night*, p. 159.

29   *Journal in the night*, pp. 202–3.

30   G. Himmelfarb, 'Post Mortems on Germany', *Commentary magazine* (1 September 1950).

31   Summer 1941, *Journal in the night*, p. 171.

32   It first appeared in English under the title *A Newman synthesis* (London, 1930) with a condensed commentary, then was republished as *The heart of Newman* (San Francisco, 1997).

33   My analysis draws heavily from Claus Arnold's 'Newman's reception in Germany: from Döllinger to Ratzinger', Newman lecture at Oriel College, Oxford, 2011.

34   *Steht die katholische Belletristik auf der Höhe der Zeit?* (1898, *Are Catholic belles lettres adequate for today?*)

[35]   This appeared in English as *Selected works* (1922)

[36]   The fourth volume of the German original, Przywara's *Einführung in Newmans Wesen und Werk*, was not included in *A Newman synthesis*, but his analysis of Newman's contribution to Catholic theology can be found in E. Przywara, *Polarity. A German Catholic's interpretation of religion*, trans. A. C. Bouquet (1935). (H. Tristram, 'On reading Newman', *John Henry Newman: centenary essays* (1945), pp. 230, 240).

[37]   *Briefe und Texte zur ersten Lebenshälfte* (1801–46), trans. E. Stein, *Edith Stein Gesamtausgabe* vol. xxii (Freiburg, 2002); *Die Idee der Universität*, trans. E. Stein, *Edith Stein Gesamtausgabe* vol. xxi, introd. H-B. Gerl-Falkovitz (Freiburg, 2004).

2 THE SCHOLL FAMILY AND THEIR FRIENDS

HANS FRITZ SCHOLL was born in 1918 in Ingersheim, a town in Baden-Württemberg, and Sophie Magdalena Scholl in 1921 in nearby Forchtenberg. Their father Robert, mayor first of Ingersheim then of Forchtenburg, had studied law and taxation at the regional capital Stuttgart. During the Great War he had refused to fight in the military as he was opposed to its aims, serving instead as an ambulance driver for a military hospital in the suburbs of Stuttgart, where he met his future wife Magdalena, a nursing sister and dedicated Evangelical Christian who was nine years older than him. The couple had four children in addition to Hans and Sophie: Inge (born 1917), Elisabeth, known as Lisl (born 1920), Werner (born 1922), and Thilde (born 1925, she died a year later). Magdalena raised her children to be Bible-reading, though not regular church-going, Christians, and she instilled in them a strong social conscience. Their father was a self-confident businessman who was in touch with the wider world of finance, politics and current affairs; liberal-minded, he rarely attended church and even fathered a child outside his marriage. While Magdalena nurtured her children so that they would gain strong religious beliefs, Robert instilled in them a regard for the right to free speech. In 1930 the family moved to Ludwigsburg and two years later to Ulm, on the Danube, where Robert became a partner in a business specializing in tax and finance consultancy.

The Scholls were a well-off household, cushioned from the economic hardships of the time, and the children were encouraged by their father to develop as independent thinkers. They read widely, took an interest in music, poetry and art, and were encouraged to take part in outdoor activities. Like so many young

Germans of the time, they developed a great love of nature and imbibed the Romantic longing for proximity to mountains, rivers and trees. Their teachers tried to instil in them a strong sense of patriotism and to discourage them from questioning authority, but, as the restrictions mounted during the Nazi years, the Scholls became increasingly non-conformist. The good-looking and athletic Hans was the family favourite. A born leader, he was impulsive and volatile by nature and could be charming or sullen, depending on the company he was in and his mood; outspoken, reckless and enigmatic, he had little sense of danger. His youngest sister Sophie was quite unlike Hans. She was short of stature and slender, a quick learner and, like her mother, patient and a good listener; she preferred to develop her ideas slowly and cautiously, a trait which masked her strength of character and confidence. Herr Scholl regarded her as the wisest of his children. As a young girl, Sophie acquired a keen sense of justice, to the extent that she was unafraid to challenge authority if she thought it had acted unjustly: when her sister Lisl was demoted in class on her ninth birthday, Sophie felt it was so unfair that she attempted to reinstate her. Despite the marked differences in character, there was a special sibling bond between Hans and Sophie.

Ulm itself was not a Nazi stronghold. When Hitler gave a major speech there in 1933, one of the locals sabotaged the sound system; Hitler never returned. When the Nazi Party came to power in January 1933, they took over everywhere and began to implement their nationwide policy, which was designed to indoctrinate the German people with Nazi ideas and to remove all organized opposition. To deal with political crimes the regime created its own state police, the Gestapo, who worked closely with the ordinary German police and judicial system, while creating its own juridical system comprising regional Special Courts and, from 1934, the People's Court. Gradually all sorts of normal activities were criminalised such as the telling of anti-Nazi jokes, making critical comments about the regime, and listening to foreign radio broadcasts; if these were reported, arrest and interrogation followed, which could lead to prosecution and imprisonment. However, the Gestapo was always smaller than the normal police force and being under-resourced was largely a reactive body which relied heavily on tip-offs from informants.[1]

The process of indoctrinating the German people was a gradual one, though from the outset the authorities targeted education as a crucial means of spreading the new ideology. On 10 May 1933 the ceremonial burning of 'un-German' books took place throughout Germany, organized by the German Student Union, thereby presaging an era of uncompromising state censorship, and in many university towns students marched in torch-lit parades to mark the occasion. Soon libraries were cleared of 'subversive' literature, history books were rewritten, and teachers were strongly encouraged to join the National Socialist Teachers League, if not the Nazi Party itself. It took longer to phase out the established youth groups for boys and girls, which had blossomed in the early decades of the century, and to replace them with the *Hitlerjugend* (Hitler Youth) and the *Bund Deutscher Mädel* or BDM (League of German Girls). There was much talk on the wireless and in the newspapers about the fatherland, comradeship, unity of the *Volksgemeinschaft* (community of German people), and love of country, but it only became compulsory to join the Hitler Youth in December 1936; before then pressure had been mounting on the other youth groups to close down, until they were completely outlawed.[2]

The Scholl children loved the countryside and felt strong ties to their fatherland, the extended home of German-speaking people; they were attracted to the youth groups that were so popular among educated Germans and which involved communing with nature. Belonging to them entailed an element of protest against organised, bourgeois society, but in the early 1930s these youth organisations were hijacked by National Socialism. Like most other youngsters, the Scholls were inspired by Hitler's talk of helping the fatherland achieve greatness and prosperity, and were swept along by feelings of comradeship engendered by the uniforms, songs, marching and waving of banners in the Hitler Youth. It is noteworthy that they all joined when membership was voluntary. Hans joined in May 1933, and within two years he was promoted to the rank of *Fahnleinführer* (troop leader); in charge of around 150 boys, he oversaw their physical training and ran indoctrination sessions such as 'comradeship evenings' when they would listen on the wireless to nationally broadcast Hitler Youth programmes. The Hitler Youth proper catered for boys aged fourteen to eighteen, and had a feeder group for those aged ten and above, the *Jungvolk*; the equivalent for girls was the League of German Girls and its junior section, the *Jungmädelbund*, which Sophie joined when she was twelve, like most of her classmates. Enthusiasm and excitement permeated these groups because the youngsters felt themselves part of the rebuilding of a deeply divided and demoralised country. Sophie and Hans were enthusiastic members and hung on the words of their Führer: 'A violent, masterful, dauntless and cruel younger generation—that is my goal. There must be nothing weak or soft about them. Their eyes must glow once more with the freedom and splendor of the bird of prey'.[3]

On New Year's Day 1934 the young Scholls gathered around the wireless in their living room to listen to Baldur von Schirach, the leader of the Hitler Youth, in his address to the nation's youth. Schirach had become a celebrity for the younger generation on account of his passionate addresses and calls to his young audience to submit their wills to the Führer's. On this occasion Schirach hailed the New Year as the beginning of a period of fearless dedication to the German blood brotherhood and the flag. A graduate of Munich University, Schirach wielded considerable influence in the way he convinced youngsters like the Scholls that they represented the beginning of the thousand-year Reich of National Socialism, assuring them that future generations would benefit from their hard work and sacrifices. At twenty-six, he epitomised the Reich's ideal of youth leading youth, inspiring them with a mission by appealing to their idealism and aspirations.

Across Germany, the tranquillity of countless homes was undermined by the influence of the Hitler Youth, which fostered new allegiances amongst the young and introduced the fear of denunciation into the family circle, thereby widening the generation gap in society. The tensions introduced into the Scholl family erupted into blazing rows between Hans and his father, which the other children witnessed in silence. Herr Scholl disapproved of the Hitler Youth and warned, 'Don't believe them—they are wolves and deceivers, and they are misusing the German people shamefully'.[4] He compared Hitler to the Pied Piper of Hamelin, leading children to destruction, but his best logic could not compete with the emotional enticements offered to his children. Nor did he wish to compel them, in accordance with the premium he set on individual freedom. The young Scholls went on camping trips and long hikes, formed friendships with other young people, sang, played games, and worked at handcrafts. In belonging to a well-organised body with noble aims which offered them a role in an historic process, a movement transforming the masses into a *Volk*, the youngsters felt—says Inge Scholl[5]—that they were being invited to join a great cause. It also helped them through the difficulties and loneliness of adolescence.

The Hitler Youth leaders in Ulm did not have a firm grasp of National Socialist ideology, for they decided to experiment with the free-thinking German Boys League, founded on 1 November 1929 (and known as d.j.1/11), by asking Hans to re-start a group along these lines. The aim was for him to train the future Hitler Youth leaders in Ulm using the last surviving splinter of the disbanded *Bündische* youth organisations. What was revived was a tightly-knit group of boys who recognized each other by dress, songs and even their way of talking. Not only did they go on weekend hikes and sing campfire folksongs, like the Hitler Youth, but they painted, wrote and composed their own songs, took photographs and used them to produce 'excursion books' and magazines. They skied in winter and enjoyed dangerous, daring runs at dawn; they ran through woods, plunged into ice-cold rivers, and then lay on the ground contemplating nature. At times they were solemn and silent, while on other occasions they laughed and joked in their own humorous way, with a good deal of mockery and sarcasm. In contrast to the stifling atmosphere of the Hitler Youth, these boys were encouraged to develop their own tastes in reading, to attend concerts, films and the theatre, and to visit museums and cathedrals. Frau Scholl welcomed the d.j.1/11 boys into her home, baking them pastries and offering them privacy for their meetings.

In the spring of 1935 Hans was ordered to disband the d.j.1/11 group, as the authorities felt it had served its purpose, but Hans ignored the command and kept meeting with them in secret, whilst also acting as a leader in the Hitler Youth. That September, Hans was chosen as the flag bearer for his troop at the annual week-long Party Rally in Nuremberg. Hitler chose Nuremberg as the location for some of the most spectacular youth rallies ever staged because it was regarded as a quintessentially German city, on account of its medieval and Renaissance history; its fame had recently been boosted by Wagner's 'The Mastersingers of Nuremburg'. Though the picturesque city provided a ready-made back-drop for marches and military pageantry, the organisers constructed giant arenas on the outskirts of the city for mass gatherings. The previous year Albert Speer's Zeppelin Field had been enlarged using concentration camp labour to provide a capacity of 400,000, and at night the arena was lit up to operatic effect with 150 spotlights which pointed upwards and seemed to extend the huge structure into one great 'cathedral of light'.

At the 1935 'Rally of Freedom' ('Freedom' referred to the reintroduction of compulsory military service and therefore 'liberation' from the Treaty of Versailles) Hitler insisted that 'the German boys of the future must be slender and supple, swift as greyhounds, tough as leather, and hard as Krupp steel'. Almost all the young people present were swept away by the sheer scale of the spectacle and the ranting speeches of the Nazi officials, but the propaganda had the opposite effect on Hans. At Nuremberg he encountered a Hitler Youth which demanded conformity down to the last detail, and he found the endless marches and incessant talk of loyalty unpalatable and stifling; he also found the atmosphere rough and unsophisticated. Hans returned subdued and pensive, and withdrew into uncharacteristic silence; he was a changed person. The change was a subtle one, but over the coming months it began to manifest itself more openly.

During that Party Rally the anti-Semitic Nuremberg Laws were proclaimed. Introduced under the pretext of stabilizing society, someone with at least three Jewish grandparents was defined as a Jew and had their German citizenship withdrawn, and someone with one Jewish grandparent was defined as being of 'mixed race' and became a second-class citizen. The new attitude to the Jews caused a great deal of discussion among the young people, who were not immediately alive to the sinister intentions of those who promulgated the laws. Fourteen-year-old Sophie was disconcerted when a Jewish girl in her class was not allowed to join the Hitler Youth, but she got over her temporary disillusionment after being told by a troop leader that she would have to swallow some changes for the sake of the greater good. That year Sophie became a troop leader herself, even though, like Hans, she had non-conformist inclinations. On one occasion a BDM leader came from Stuttgart to lead an evening of ideological training; she opened up the meeting to discussion and was aghast when Sophie suggested that the girls read the poems of Heinrich Heine, the Jewish writer who had been banned in 1933.

On 7 March 1936 German troops marched into the demilitarised Rhineland. To a people who felt that so many of their woes had resulted from the punitive terms of the Treaty of Versailles, the Führer's success was met with general rejoicing. But the jubilation did nothing to stifle the growing dissatisfaction of those like Hans and Sophie who experienced the increasing conformity of school and the growing militarisation of the Hitler Youth. The Scholl household gradually became a magnet for kindred spirits who felt disillusioned or alienated, a place of sanctuary where the children could talk openly to trusted friends and relatives. Banned books were read and the regime was criticised over meals, especially by Herr Scholl, who had always been vehemently anti-Nazi. For the young Scholls and their friends, books were a shared hobby and food for the mind, as well as a way to explore the world and themselves. Later, when they found themselves cut off from each other, they continued to exchange ideas about their reading in their letters. One of the most influential figures in the family circle was Inge's friend Ernst Reden, who had jointly organised with Hans the Ulm branch of the banned d.j.1/11. His knowledge and enthusiasm for literature and poetry enhanced their appreciation of Stefan George, Georg Heym, Rainer Maria Rilke and Ernst Wiechert, and sometimes he read with them works by Ernst Jünger.

In May 1936 Hans was stripped of his leadership role in the Hitler Youth for insubordination and only reinstated when he promised to disband the d.j.1/11 group. However, his lengthy exposure to its free-spirited ways had affected him for good. He had learned a repertoire of songs that he sang with a guitar, not only the approved Hitler Youth songs, but the Russian and Norwegian songs he had learned with the d.j.1/11; his light-hearted demeanor altered when told not to sing non-German songs, and when he made light of the prohibition he was threatened with punishment. That summer Hans organised a three-week camping trip for ten of his d.j.1/11 friends, as he wanted to experience the Nordic midnight sun; permission for the trip, which was to take them to Copenhagen and Stockholm, was withdrawn just two days before departure, but Hans went ahead nonetheless. In crossing the Swedish border they broke the currency law by smuggling in more money than was allowed. They also read out aloud from books and discussed them in the spirit of d.j.1/11. On another occasion, a book by his favorite author Stefan Zweig[6] was snatched out of his hands by a Hitler Youth leader, who told him that it was Jewish filth and therefore banned.

Hans was a natural leader who could turn on the charm. Though he was volatile and could suddenly lapse into sullenness and introspection, his qualities had seen him chosen as a troop leader. On one occasion, his troop designed and sewed a handsome banner sporting as its design a mythical beast, instead of the stipulated swastika, and dedicated it to the Führer. The boys pledged their loyalty to the banner as a sign of their fellowship, but when the troop was being reviewed a senior official ordered it to be handed over and replaced with a prescribed one. The twelve-year-old boy holding the banner refused to do so, and when the command was repeated, Hans lost his cool and slapped the leader; for the second time he forfeited his leadership, this time for good.

It is likely that Hans knew that he was defying the system by encouraging his troop to make its own banner and that he wanted to test it to the limit. The result was that, in the words of Inge, 'The spark of tormenting doubt which was kindled in Hans spread to the rest of us.' Other incidents occurred which added to their tally of grievances, such as when a young teacher was taken off to a concentration camp for lack of conformity to Nazi ideology. 'What is a concentration camp?' the children asked their father. 'War in the midst of peace and within our own people', Herr Scholl told them: 'War against the defenceless individual. War against human happiness and the freedom of its children.'[7] Over time, the initial doubts of the young Scholls turned to sadness, then burst into the flame of rebellion. Seeing their world of freedom disappearing round them, they thought at first that their fears would not last and tried to defend their former ideas in the face of what they had seen and heard, but the doubts kept on growing. As Inge describes it, using a homely metaphor, there awoke the feeling of living in a beautiful house where fearful things were happening in the cellar, and from doubt grew fear and horror at what might be taking place there.

Once, when they were on a long hike with their father, the young Scholls had a lengthy discussion with him about what

Hitler was doing, and his explanations of Hitler's methods won them over and at the same time created a new bond between them. He explained how the Great War had brought rampant inflation, great poverty and unemployment, and how in desperation people were ready to accept someone who promised a cure-all, uncritical of his methods. Unemployment had been reduced by the growth of the munitions industry, he pointed out, but peaceful aims should have been pursued instead. Material security alone was not enough to make people happy. 'What I want most of all', he told them, 'is that you live in uprightness and freedom of spirit, no matter how difficult that proves to be.'[8]

The shift of the focus of Hans' teenage rebelliousness from his father towards the enforced conformity of the Hitler Youth was not just the manifestation of a youthful whim, but of a conviction which matured over time. His growing disgust with National Socialism was fueled by his father, whose predictions and warnings bore an uncanny resemblance to what he saw happening in Germany. Like Hans, the other young Scholls, who had sided with youth against their own father, now adopted attitudes in tune with their natural affections. Though both their parents were responsible for this transition, it was Robert who articulated his opposition to the regime most openly. After dinner he would sometimes leave the table early, saying, 'Now, if you will excuse me, I will go and earn a jail sentence'– a euphemism for listening to forbidden radio stations such as the BBC or the Swiss Beromünster.

Hans gained his *Abitur* (school-leaving certificate) in the spring of 1937, but before he could enter university, he needed to complete a six-month stint of *Reichsarbeitsdienst* (National Labour Service); he then spent eighteen months doing military service. He soon found himself engaged in road building and was evidently in good spirits when he wrote home, 'I'm putting my heart and soul into my work [...]. We're forever singing with all our hearts [...] and it's a comfort to be able to vent our innermost feelings, if only in song'.[9]

On Palm Sunday 1937, Sophie was Confirmed at St Paul's Church, Ulm, and during the service was the only girl wearing the brown BDM uniform. That very day the papal encyclical *Mit Brennender Sorge* (*With burning anxiety*) was read from the pulpits of all Catholic churches in Germany. The encyclical, the first to be written in German, not the usual Latin, had been smuggled into Germany and printed locally, for fear of censorship. It condemned breaches of the Concordat signed in 1933 between the German Reich and the Holy See, and the neo-pagan ideology which elevated one race above others and idolized the State.[10] In addition to denouncing the idolatrous cult which replaced belief in the true God with a 'national religion' and the 'myth of race and blood', there was a striking and deliberate emphasis on the permanent validity of the Jewish scriptures.[11]

The encyclical, which took the Nazi government completely unawares, had been drafted in secret by the German bishops, under the leadership of Cardinal Michael von Faulhaber, and had an introduction written by Cardinal Eugenio Pacelli (later Pope Pius XII). Around 300,000 copies were made in the attempt to confront the spreading Nazi ideology and draw attention to the pressures exerted by the Nazi Party, both open and veiled, on Catholic officials to betray their faith, pressures which were lambasted as base, illegal and inhuman. It spoke of a condition of spiritual oppression such as had never been seen before in Germany, of the antagonism against confessional schools and youth organisations, and the constant aggression against Catholic life.[12] In this carefully-crafted document, there was no explicit reference to National Socialism, Hitler or the Nazi Party, but people were under no illusions as to the identity of the 'prophet of nothingness' who aspired to place himself on the same level as Christ.

> None but superficial minds could stumble into concepts of a national God, of a national religion; or attempt to lock within the frontiers of a single people, within the narrow limits of a single race, God, the Creator of the universe,

King and Legislator of all nations before whose immensity
they are 'as a drop of a bucket' (Isaiah, 11:15).[13]

With impressive timing Pope Pius XI issued another encyclical
that month, *Divini Redemptoris* (*The Divine Redeemer*), which
denounced Communism, declaring its principles 'intrinsically
hostile to religion in any form whatever', detailing the attacks on
the Church which had followed the establishment of Communist
regimes in Mexico, Russia and Spain, and calling for the imple-
mentation of Catholic social teaching to offset both Communism
and 'amoral liberalism'. The language was stronger than that used
in *Mit Brennender Sorge*, as Nazi ideology had not been fully
formulated and as its ramifications were not entirely evident, not
to mention hopes that some sort of *modus operandi* between the
regime and the Church might still be possible.

It has been commented that in the 'fascist epoch' (1918–45)
untold numbers of Catholics, Protestants and Orthodox believers
in the most crisis-torn parts of Europe were 'lured into supporting
the politics of ultra-nationalism and authoritarianism by the
spectre of Bolshevism and anarchy, seduced by the fatally flawed
logic that "my enemy's enemy is my friend".'[14] This may be so,
but it is also true that these Christians were no different from
most other citizens in Croatia, Italy and Slovakia, as well as
Germany, where authoritarian rule appeared a timely solution to
political and economic woes in the era after the Great War. In
Germany, few had any idea what lay ahead, though the signs were
ominous for those who had already noticed the Nazis' flagrant
disregard for human dignity and basic human rights.

Mit Brennender Sorge undoubtedly strengthened the resolve
of German Catholics but it provoked the Nazi State to intensify
its oblique assault upon Catholic institutions and brought swift
and long-lasting reprisals. The Gestapo raided Catholic churches
the next day to confiscate all the copies of the encyclical they
could lay their hands on, and the presses that had printed them
were closed down; the bishops' diocesan magazines were banned,
paper for church pamphlets was severely restricted, grants to

theology students and priests in need (agreed upon in the Concordat) were reduced. Not a word about it appeared in the press. There were also numerous vindictive measures against the Church, including a long series of staged immorality trials of the Catholic clergy, given maximum publicity by the Nazi-controlled press, while a film was produced for the Hitler Youth which featured priests dancing in a brothel.[15]

The encyclical caused a sensation, as it was the first major official public document which dared to confront and criticize Nazism, and Hans and Sophie must have heard about it—and may even have read it, since it had been produced in such large numbers.

That summer Hans and Inge visited the opening exhibition at the *Haus der Deutschen Kunst* (House of German Art) in Munich on 'Great German Art', which was intended as a celebration of Nazi art, but the Propaganda Minister Joseph Goebbels made the mistake of organising a parallel exhibition at the nearby Archaeological Institute on 'Degenerate Art'. He had hoped to illustrate the inferiority of modern art, but the public showed its preference for the cubists, the works of the Dada movement and the Bauhaus artists over the heavily stylised scenes of Teutonic knights, muscular storm troopers, German maidens and idyllic rural scenes. Both exhibitions proved popular, but four times as many people visited the modern art exhibition as the Nazi one. Recognising the misjudgement, the authorities closed down the exhibition of modern art. Sophie not only had a growing interest in art but a talent for drawing and painting. At first, she dismissed modern art, but she soon revised her attitude when she came under the influence of a family friend, Wilhelm Geyer, a painter who lived in Ulm, and she became an admirer of expressionism. Geyer was regarded by the regime as a cultural Bolshevist and a 'degenerate' artist.

It was at a school-friend's house that summer that Sophie first met Fritz Hartnagel, a career soldier who had recently graduated from the prestigious military academy at Potsdam (at a time when a career in the *Wehrmacht* was regarded as an honorable one) and was now stationed at Augsburg, 50 miles south of Ulm. Despite the four years between them and their differing backgrounds, there began a romantic friendship which flourished until Sophie's execution five and a half years later. Military duty took Fritz to various parts of Germany and, once war broke out, to areas of conflict in the east and the west, yet the friendship between them continued by means of an assiduous correspondence. The letters of Sophie reveal that at first she craved a great deal of attention, as they were demanding and self-centred, but the tone soon changed as she became more serious and reflective. Those of Fritz were more restrained, if only because he was a soldier and had to watch his words, though in time they became less guarded, as he become fonder of Sophie.

In mid-October Hans began his military service in a cavalry unit near Stuttgart. A few weeks later a nationwide campaign got under way to wipe out the remnants of the genuine youth movements that had sprung up at the start of the century, and in the wave of arrests many young men served weeks or months in prison before they were released. The Gestapo raided the Scholl's house and arrested Inge, Sophie and Werner. Sophie was released as soon as they realised she was just a sixteen-year-old girl (although she had been interviewed by the Gestapo that April), but Inge and Werner spent a week behind bars in solitary confinement at Stuttgart. Although Frau Scholl had managed to hide some of the more incriminating evidence in the house, the Gestapo were able to confiscate diaries, magazines, poems, essays, collections of folk songs, and other items which indicated membership of illegal organisations. Initially exempt on account of his military status, Hans was not arrested until mid-December and then he found himself in deep trouble, as the rest of his unofficial youth group had already been arrested and, under interrogation, had divulged details which implicated him. He was put in solitary confinement at the Gestapo headquarters in Dusseldorf and interrogated; he was not even allowed to open the Christmas present Sophie sent him, and was only released in early January

1938. Herr Scholl lobbied for his son and because of Hans' rapport with his commanding officer the case was transferred to the jurisdiction of the Special Court in Stuttgart. The months leading up to the trial on 2 June were trying ones for Hans and wore out his spirits. The family never forgot the trauma inflicted on them, and it caused attitudes to the regime to harden.

On hearing of the arrest of his siblings, Hans had told his parents, 'We don't have to feel like martyrs, even though we may sometimes have reason to, because we won't let anyone impugn our purity of sentiment. Inner strength is our most powerful weapon.'[16] Nevertheless, Hans felt that he was to blame for the arrests. After his own arrest, he wrote a contrite letter to his parents expressing his desire to make amends: 'Only now am I fully alive to my father's desire, which he himself possessed and passed on to me, to become something great for the sake of mankind.'[17] Once released, he admitted, 'I often forget the whole thing and act carefree and exuberant, but then the dark shadow looms up again and makes everything seem dismal and empty.'[18] Wishing to console his mother, he wrote, 'above and beyond the flickering blaze of my youthful soul, I sometimes detect the eternal breath of Something infinitely great and serene. God. Fate'.[19]

In the mudslinging that resulted from the interrogations, it emerged that Hans had been responsible for smuggling German currency across the Swedish border in the summer of 1936. Under interrogation, Hans spoke of same-sex actions by Ernst Reden, mentioning his advances on his brother Werner, while he himself was accused of same-sex acts with a minor under his command—which he admitted at his trial.[20] In these anxious times Hans took solace in his visits to the Remppis family in Leonberg and their daughter Lisa, who was close to both Sophie and Hans. When the German troops entered Austria on 12 March 1938, Hans had expected to be part of the operation. He wrote home, 'A lot of sabre-rattling goes on here. In general, I refrain from commenting on political developments. My head feels heavy. I don't understand people anymore. Whenever I hear all that anonymous jubilation on the wireless, I feel like going out into a big, deserted plain and being by myself. [...] In Lisa I've found a person I can love wholeheartedly. [...] She's so natural and fresh, and that is just what I need'.[21] He also paid a visit to a fortune-teller, who told him he had nothing to fear.

On 25 April Hans was charged, and in reporting the news to his parents, he told them, 'I am not afraid of going on trial. Even if I can't justify myself in open court, I can justify myself to myself.'[22] At the trial, Hans was fully acquitted and the judge attributed his indiscretions to his youthful exuberance and obstinate character.[23] The judgement was in line with the amnesty announced by Hitler for all those charged with *Bündische* offences following the *Anschluss* (the annexation of Austria), though Hans was very fortunate not to be punished for same-sex acts with a minor under his charge, however mild they were. His co-leader Ernst Reden spent three months in a prison and another three in a concentration camp.

In his despair, Hans Scholl turned for solace to the Virgin Mary and composed a poem, entitled 'Maria—our Queen'. It began,

> You are powerful
> you are the rose from on high
> deeply melted in God
> let us greet you
> hail you.
> Ave Maria
> Gratia plena.[24]

Why did the Protestant Hans Scholl turn to the Virgin Mary for help? Perhaps, in his despair, he felt attracted to Mary's qualities of wisdom and purity, though he may also have been influenced by the talented artist Otl Aicher who had become very friendly with Hans and Sophie earlier that year. A school-friend of Werner Scholl, Otl had refused to join the Hitler Youth and on that account had not been allowed to take the *Abitur* and was therefore barred from entry to university. His refusal had placed him and Hans in opposing camps, but they discovered common ground after they were both detained by the Gestapo for 'subversive activities', that is, for belonging to the d.j.1/11. Hans may have been inspired to write 'Maria—our Queen' after visiting Otl's parish church Mariä Himmelfahrt in Ulm-Söflingen, as the church contains a painting of Mary, Queen of heaven, surrounded by angels holding garlands of roses.[25] Otl was the main Catholic influence on the Ulm group in its early stages and he introduced the teenagers to St Augustine's *Confessions* and told them about the intellectual Catholic monthly *Hochland*. Denied a university education, Otl's teachers and mentors included the editor of *Hochland*, Carl Muth, as well as the courageous parish priest of Ulm-Söflingen, Franz Weiß, and his highly-educated curate, Bruno Wüstenberg.

Hans suffered some ostracism and abuse from his fellow soldiers as a result of his arrest and trial, and Sophie became the target of verbal abuse from her friends at school and was charged by the BDM with disloyalty. The protracted drama ensured that Hans' holiday at Ulm with Lisa, Sophie, Fritz and other friends and siblings was all the more wonderful; there he spent his time reading, swimming, hiking and fencing (the favourite sport of the d.j.1/11). Once back at the barracks, he told Inge:

> I keep a rosebud in my breast pocket. I need that little flower because it's the other side of the coin, far removed from soldiering but not at odds with a soldierly frame of mind. You should always carry a little secret around with you, especially if you are with comrades like mine.[26]

In August 1938 Hitler threatened war unless the 3.5 million German speakers in Sudetenland, the border lands of Czechoslovakia, were granted self-determination. With the aim of meeting what Hitler claimed was his last demand for territory, Britain, France, Italy and Germany signed the Munich Agreement on 30 September which sanctioned the Third Reich's annexation of Sudetenland. German troops marched in on 1 October. After all the excitement, Hans wrote:

I have never been such a patriot, in the true sense, as I was in
the early days of October this year. Only when you're compelled to wonder if the Fatherland still means as much as it
may once have done—only when you've lost your faith in
banners and speeches because prevailing ideas have become
trite and worthless—does true idealism assert itself.[27]

On 1 November Hans completed his basic military service and
was assigned to a hospital in Tübingen in order to complete his
stint in the army medical corps prior to studying medicine.
Unable to spend Christmas at home for the second year running,
Hans wrote to his parents: 'Tending to the sick is a great and
humanitarian occupation, and a healthy person like me should
be glad and grateful for the chance to help others'.[28] He admitted
that he had been 'brooding on the year that has gone by', asking
himself, 'have I really improved? Have all my efforts borne fruit
and resulted in progress? Many things have changed, but there
are times when you feel petty and ridiculous in your human
frame.'[29] Troubled by news that the father of Annelies Kammerer,
a family friend, had been ostracised for continuing to serve Jewish
customers at his shop in Ulm and unsettled by the changes
around him, Hans flung caution to the wind and bought a banned
book by Ernst Wiechert, one of the authors recommended by
Ernst Reden. In his lecture 'The writer and his times' delivered
at Munich University in April 1935, Wiechert had stunned his
audience by arguing that art fabricated by the Nazis was like
'murder of the soul', and he went on to admonish the students
'not to allow yourselves to be seduced, if your conscience orders
you to speak'.[30] Two years later Wiechert was interred in Buchenwald concentration camp for a period of four months.

In April 1939, at the age of twenty, Hans was finally able to
begin his medical studies, which he did by enrolling at Munich's
Ludwig-Maximilians University. As his interests were not confined to medicine, he enlisted on courses in Greek and philosophy, and he began reading Plato and Nietzsche deep into the
night. One of his Ulm friends recalls that their discussions on

Nietzsche centred on three points: his views on friendship as a human virtue; his theory of the duty of great individuals to resist the tendency to lose their individuality in the age of the herd; and the prediction that God would die in a church that backed an inhuman regime.[31] To judge by his correspondence over the following years, it is clear that Hans was influenced by his reading of Nietzsche, particularly the idea of elevating oneself above the herd; and something similar can be said of Sophie.

While Hans was becoming more cerebral, now that he had begun university, Sophie was developing in other ways in her final year at school, where she found the biology classes 'tremendous fun', especially the ones which involved dissection of animal organs and fish.[32] She too aspired to higher education though she would have to endure 18 months of National Labour Service before she was able to follow her brother to Munich. Her letters to Fritz are full of comments which show her wit and playfulness: 'If you have the time and the inclination you can write me some far more boring letters than mine, I will read them just the same. [...] You can write anything you like, absolute rubbish even, and I will read it patiently.'[33] On his part, Fritz told Sophie, 'We are becoming closer and getting to understand each other more'; and he urged her, 'tell me everything and don't hide your feelings'.[34] She was becoming an avid reader, devouring popular books such as Thomas Mann's first novel *Buddenbrooks* (1901), and she urged Fritz to use his time better by improving his knowledge of literature.

Sophie was beginning to take her sketching seriously and she told Inge, 'I don't have a sense of vocation or anything like that, but anyone who wants to be an artist must become a human being first and foremost. From the bottom up. I'm going to try and work on myself. It's very difficult.'[35] She was developing a passion for art and was learning to discriminate and to articulate opinions. 'I'm crazy about Paula Modersohn's work', she told Inge. 'She developed a tremendously original style for a woman, and her paintings aren't derivative of anyone in particular',[36] she remarked about one of the most important representatives of early expressionism. She and Fritz had planned a trip to Yugoslavia in the summer of 1939 but, due a ban on foreign travel by young people, decided to head to the North Sea, where they took in a visit to an artists' colony at Worpswede, near Bremen. While staying at the youth hostel there someone threatened to report them to the police for possessing suspicious books, but nothing came of it. When she returned to Ulm, Sophie continued working on illustrations for a new translation of J. M. Barrie's *Peter Pan* (published as a play in 1904 and a novel in 1911), which had been undertaken by a family friend called Hanspeter Nägele. She was also engaged in illustrating a short story by Georg Heym, at the suggestion of Ernst Reden, who planned to publish it. She wrote about her holiday to her sister Lisl: 'I fell in love with the North Sea all over again. The breakers were simply terrific. I'd feel I was in the seventh heaven, bobbing around on the waves, if only the salt water didn't keep disillusioning me so cruelly.'[37] A fortnight later war broke out.

Notes

[1]   See Frank McDonough's *The Gestapo: the myth and reality of Hitler's secret police* (2015).

[2]   By the end of 1933 the Evangelical youth associations had been absorbed into the Hitler Youth, whereas the Catholic groups continued to operate, protected by the Concordat. The law of 1 December 1936 incorporating all youth organisations into the Hitler Youth was not brought to completion until the *Jungmännerverband* was dissolved on 6 February 1939 (book review of L. D. Walker, *Hitler Youth and Catholic Youth 1933–36: a study in totalitarian conquest* (1970) by A. W. Zeigler in *Journal of Church and State* 16:2 (Spring 1974), 327).

[3]   Quoted in A. Dumbach & J. Newborn, *Sophie Scholl and the White Rose*, (Oxford: Oneworld, 2006) [first published as *Shattering the German night* (1986)], p. 25.

[4]   I. Scholl, *The White Rose: Munich, 1942–1943*, trans. A. R. Schultz (Middletown: Wesleyan University Press USA, 1983), p. 6.

[5]   *The White Rose*, pp. 5–7.

[6]   The book was *Sternstunden der Menschheit* (1927, *The tide of fortune: twelve historical miniatures*, 1940), a collection of essays about great

moments of human achievement which spoke about individuals following their own consciences and the idiosyncratic needs of their creativity (*Sophie Scholl and the White Rose*, p. 33).

7   *The White Rose*, p. 11. Before the war broke out in 1939, around 150,000 people were put in concentration camps, most of whom were socialists or Communists. Around 12,000 of these were convicted of high treason (I. Kershaw, 'Resistance without the people? Bavarian attitudes to the Nazi regime at the time of the White Rose', *Die Weisse Rose: student resistance to National Socialism, 1942–43*, ed. H. Siefken (Nottingham: University of Nottingham, 1991), p. 61).

8   *The White Rose*, p. 12.

9   Hans to his mother, 4 May 1937, *At the heart of the White Rose: letters and diaries of Hans and Sophie Scholl*, ed. I. Jens (New York: Harper & Row, 1987), p. 2.

10   'Whoever exalts race, or the people, or the state, or a particular form of state, or the depositories of power, or any other fundamental value of the human community—however necessary and honorable be their function in worldly things—whoever raises these notions above their standard value and raises them to an idolatrous level, distorts and perverts an order of the world planned and created by God.' (*Mit Brennender Sorge*, section 8).

11   E. Duffy, Saints and sinners, a history of the Popes (London: Yale University Press, 1997), p. 343.

12   A. Rhodes, The Vatican in the age of the dictators, 1922–1945 (London: Hodder & Stoughton, 1973), p. 205.

13   *Mit Brennender Sorge*, section 11.

14   R. Griffin, 'The "Holy Storm": "Clerical Fascism" through the Lens of Modernism', *Totalitarian Movements and Political Religions* 8:2 (June 2007), p. 220.

15   One hundred and seventy Franciscans were arrested in Koblenz and tried for 'corrupting youth' in a secret trial (Rhodes, *Vatican in the age of the dictators, 1922–1945*, pp. 202–10). See also O. Chadwick, *A history of Christianity* (London: Weidenfeld & Nicolson, 1995), p. 254 and J. Vidmar, *The Catholic Church through the ages: a history* (New York: Paulist Press, 2005), p. 254.

16   Hans to his mother, 27 November 1937, *Heart of the White Rose*, p. 3.

17   Hans to his parents, 18 December 1937, *Heart of the White Rose*, p. 5.

18   Hans to his parents, 18 January 1938, *Heart of the White Rose*, p. 7.

19   Hans to his mother, 22 January 1938, *Heart of the White Rose*, p. 7.

20   Section 175 of the German Criminal Code was a provision (dating from 15 May 1871) that made homosexual acts between males a crime.

21   Hans to his parents, 14 March 1938, *Heart of the White Rose*, p. 9.

22   Hans to his parents, 25 April 1938, *Heart of the White Rose*, p. 10.

23   The judge described his youthful failing as that of a normal heterosexual Aryan.

24   12 May 1938, quoted in R. Zoske, *Sehnsucht nach dem Licht, Zur religiösen Entwicklung von Hans Scholl* (Munich, 2013), p. 538. The first stanza reads: 'Maria—Königin /Du Starke /Du tief in Gott verschmolzne Rose der Höh /lass uns dich grüßen /Ave Maria /Gratia Plena.'

25   I owe this observation to Jakob Knab.

26   Hans to Inge, 27 June 1938, *Heart of the White Rose*, p. 12.

27   Hans to Inge, 21 October 1938, *Heart of the White Rose*, p. 13.

28   Hans to his parents, 6 December 1938, *Heart of the White Rose*, p. 16.

29   Hans to his parents, 18 December 1938, *Heart of the White Rose*, p. 17.

30   *Sophie Scholl and the White Rose*, p. 84.

31   Recollection of Otl Aicher, *Heart of the White Rose*, p. 19.

32   Sophie to Inge, 8 July 1938, *Heart of the White Rose*, p. 28.

33   Sophie to Fritz Hartnagel, 21 April 1938, *Heart of the White Rose*, p. 25.

34   Fritz Hartnagel to Sophie, 1 February & 15 March 1939, *Sophie Scholl/Fritz Hartnagel, Damit wir uns nicht verlieren Briefwechsel, 1937–1943*, ed. T. Hartnagel (Frankfurt: S. Fischer, 2006), pp. 74, 79. [Hereafter *Scholl/Hartnagel letters*]

35   Sophie to Inge, 8 July 1938, *Heart of the White Rose*, p. 28.

36   Sophie to Inge, 9 August 1939, *Heart of the White Rose*, p. 34.

37   Sophie to Lisl, 19 August 1939, *Heart of the White Rose*, p. 35.

3 DARING TO BE DIFFERENT: 1939–41

ON 1 SEPTEMBER 1939 Germany invaded Poland, and within a month the *Blitzkrieg* military tactics saw another 23 million Europeans come under Nazi rule. Two days later Britain and France declared war on Germany. On hearing the news, Fritz informed Sophie, 'We will now be separated for long periods, but feel free to write whatever comes into your head and as often as possible.'[1] Later that week Sophie replied, 'You and your men must have plenty to do now. I just can't grasp that people's lives are now under constant threat from other people. I'll never understand it, and I find it terrible. Don't go telling me it's for the sake of the Fatherland.'[2] This was the first of her letters questioning Fritz's military role, which then entailed acting as an adjutant of a signals unit attached to the army staff on the Upper Rhine, and, aged eighteen, it signalled a political awakening in her. Over the next three and a half years she found it increasingly difficult to accept his role as an officer in the *Luftwaffe* because she saw that military obedience could so easily compromise his conscience, and over time she helped him to appreciate the criminal nature of the regime he served.

Not that her letters to him were turgidly moralistic—far from it—but her nagging doubts and uneasiness kept re-surfacing among the more mundane matters she described—such as sketching the old houses in Cathedral Square in Ulm, where the Scholl family had recently moved, and her trips to the theatre and concerts. Sometimes her affection for Fritz seems lukewarm, as when she confided, 'It's nice when two people keep each other company without promising to meet up at such and such a place, or to stay together for ever. They simply travel together awhile, and if their routes happen to diverge, they both go their way in peace.'³ On other occasions she wrote with real feeling. Once she told Fritz about a strange dream in which she found herself in prison for the duration of the war with 'a heavy iron ring around my neck'.⁴ What possibly lay behind these alternations of mood may well have been her doubts over whether she should be romantically attached to an officer in the *Wehrmacht*.

Hans was engaged in harvesting in East Prussia when the war broke out, and was given permission to defer military duties so that he could continue his medical studies. His restlessness, intellectual and emotional, is revealed in a diary entry:

> I feel no desire for 'heroism' in war. What I seek is purification. I want all the shadows to melt away from me. I'm searching for myself, just myself, because this much I do know: I'll only find the truth inside me. We were glad at first that war had finally broken out. It's bound to bring release from the yoke. A yoke Germany had brought upon itself.

> Perhaps this mass murder will go on for a long time. Perhaps the people of Europe are doomed to undergo a profound upheaval. Will we then rise a stage higher?⁵

He had to work hard at his medical studies between October and March, as university courses had been compressed on account of the war. During these six months he became friends with a medical student called Hellmut Hartert. They shared a common interest in modern French writers, such as Georges Bernanos and Paul Claudel, and the two went on cycling trips, visited monasteries, and met monks and bishops. Hans' mischievous sense of humour made their trips great fun: at one monastery Hans pretended that they were publishers hoping to bring out a book on Bavarian woodcarvings, and fooled the archivist into opening up his collection to them. Hellmut later recalled how, among other literary efforts, he and Hans drafted 'appeals to the young people of Germany, prompted by the growth of conscription for military service and an extremely unpleasant speech addressed to young people by a Hitler Youth leader'.[6] Although nothing came of the drafts, they were a precursor to the White Rose resistance leaflets.

In March, Hans suddenly found time on his hands when he was drafted into a students' company based in Munich and made to fritter away his time in the barracks. Frau Scholl was concerned about the spiritual wellbeing of her eldest son, and she regularly reminded Hans of his religious duties. One of his replies, at Easter 1940, reveals the state of mind of the young medic:

> Since your letter was so full of sage exhortation, I'd better tell you how I spent Good Friday. You urged me to take Communion in some church or other. I couldn't, because that gesture doesn't redeem all a person's sins. It's just an outward rite whose significance I think I understand, and of which I approve because so many people derive a measure of relief from it. [...] I heard the St Matthew Passion. I can't find words to convey the impact this work made on me, and anyway, it's a mistake to talk about profound religious emotions. However, you'll have guessed that the music touched me very deeply.[7]

He told her he would celebrate Easter 'in mountain solitude', which meant with the family of Hellmut's girlfriend, Ute Borchers.

In March 1940 Sophie passed her *Abitur* and celebrated by going skiing in the Austrian Alps with Fritz, who had been granted leave.[8] Unable to progress directly to university, Sophie decided to sign up for a practical course in kindergarten teaching at the Fröbel Institute in Ulm thinking this would count for her *Arbeitsdienst* (National Labour Service), and while waiting to begin she helped her father with his accounts and worked long hours at his office. On 9 April, the 'phoney war' came to an end when the panzers rolled into Denmark and Norway. Her reaction to this latest expression of German militarism was to tell Fritz,

> There are times when I dread the war and feel like giving up hope completely. I hate thinking about it, but politics are almost all there is, and as long as they're so confused

and nasty, it's cowardly to turn your back on them. [...] I think I would be happier if I weren't under pressure all the time—then I could devote myself to other things with a far better conscience. [...] It makes me nervous, being on edge all the time.[9]

She warned Fritz, 'whatever you do, don't turn into an arrogant, uncaring lieutenant. It is so easy to become callous'.[10]

Sophie was able to celebrate her nineteenth birthday in the company of Fritz and to see him off at the railway station. The following day, 10 May, Fritz's unit was one of those sent into action when Germany invaded the Low Countries; that same day Winston Churchill replaced Neville Chamberlain as prime minister of the United Kingdom. A week later Sophie wrote begging Fritz for news of his whereabouts and safety:

> Our ideas are so different, I sometimes wonder if it's really so unimportant, when it ought to be the basis of any relationship. But all this must be shelved for now. It really is unimportant at present, because what you and I need now is love, not friendship and companionship. We'll keep things between us that way till we can be by ourselves again. [...] My dearest wish is that you should survive this war and these times without becoming a product of them. All of us have standards inside ourselves, but we don't go looking for them often enough. Maybe it is because they are the toughest standards of all.
>
> Think of me sometimes, but don't dream of me. I am often with you in spirit, wishing you well and loving you.[11]

To cheer him up and take his mind off the war, she shared her impressions of the countryside: 'it's wonderful how nothing throws Nature off course'.[12] On another occasion she encouraged him to see the humorous side to life:

> I pity the people who can't laugh at every trifle, i.e. who can't find something to laugh at in everything, the salt and pepper of daily life. That does not necessarily have any-thing to do with superficiality—in fact I think I could still

find something to laugh at, if I had to, even at the saddest moments.[13]

She was also worried about Hans as he, too, had received his marching orders, though news soon arrived that he had passed through Luxembourg and Belgium and on to France, officially acting as a dispatch rider, unofficially as an interpreter for his unit. Temperamentally, Hans was eager for a new situation which brought excitement and a challenge, but he was not attracted by the prospect of seeing the Third Reich expand. Shielded from the fighting at the front, his letters enthused about the delightful countryside, the cuisine, and the charming locals. After a minor accident had confined him briefly to bed, where he read André Gide, he bumped into Ernst Reden and listened to his thoughts about the war.

In her next letter to Fritz, written the day after Belgium capitulated, Sophie told him,

> It isn't easy to banish all thoughts of the war. Although I don't know much about politics and have no ambition to do so, I do have some idea of right and wrong, because that has nothing to do with politics and nationality. And I could weep at how mean people are, in high-level politics as well, and how they betray their fellow creatures, perhaps for the sake of personal advantage. Isn't it enough to make a person lose heart sometimes? Often my one desire is to live on a Robinson Crusoe island. I'm sometimes tempted to regard mankind as a terrestrial skin disease. But only sometimes, when I am tired, and people who are worse than beasts loom large in my mind's eye. But all that matters fundamentally is whether we come through, whether we manage to hold our own among the majority, whose sole concern is self-interest—those who approve of any means to their own ends. It's so overwhelming, that majority, you have to be bad to survive at all. Only one person has managed to go straight to God, probably, but who still looks for him nowadays? [...]

Don't just think of me as I am, though—think of me also
as I'd like to be. We'll only be completely at one if you like
me as much then. We don't know one another anything
like well enough, and I'm a lot to blame. I always felt that,
but I was too comfortable to change things. You mustn't
think it stands between us, because I try hard to be with
you and support you in spirit. But don't think, either, that
this is unimportant in wartime. Grave events are no
justification for letting oneself go.[14]

The invasion of France through the wooded Ardennes left the
British Expeditionary Force in complete disarray, and they had
little option but to evacuate in haste, leaving behind most of their
equipment. During the evacuation from Dunkirk, which lasted
from 27 May to 4 June, some 340,000 troops reached safety,
assisted by their trusted ally, the weather. Neither Hans nor
Sophie comment on this minor set-back for the German war
effort, but Theodor Haecker saw something miraculous in it, as
he records in his journal:

Newman's theory respecting the strange coincidence of
natural events at particular moments, as signs of divine
providence, came to mind as I read that the weather was
misty. That is how the Cardinal, were he still living, might
have understood it: an angel smoothed the channel which
is normally rough at this time of year, and spread the
darkness of mist and fog over the sea at the same time.
And so ten thousand were saved.[15]

To interpret Haecker's remarks it is sufficient to turn to 'The
powers of nature', the sermon he had published in translation
two years earlier, where Newman asserts that,

as far as the Scripture communications go, we learn that
the course of Nature, which is so wonderful, so beautiful,
and so fearful, is effected by the ministry of those unseen
beings. Nature is not inanimate; its daily toil is intelligent;
its works are *duties*. [...] The fiery lava of the volcanoes,

> which (as it appears) was the cause of Sodom and Gomor-
> rah's ruin, was caused by the two Angels who rescued Lot.[16]

As regards 'those Three Holy Children whom Nebuchadnezzar cast into the fiery furnace [...] the Angels were bid to change the nature of the flame, and make it harmless to them'. Living men and women who are revered as 'oracles of science' appear to know so much about the 'operations of nature', yet God's 'ministering Angels [...] are ever most useful, in enabling us to *apply* the course of His providence, and the ordinances of His will, to the benefit of man'.[17]

The concept of analogy operates in Newman's interpretations of events in the light of Divine Providence, for that Providence,

> is secretly concurring and co-operating with that system
> which meets the eye, and which is commonly recognized
> among men as existing. It is not too much to say that this
> is the one great rule on which the Divine Dispensations
> with mankind have been and are conducted, that the
> visible world is the instrument, yet the veil, of the world
> invisible,—the veil, yet still partially the symbol and index:
> so that all that exists or happens visibly, conceals and yet
> suggests, and above all subserves, a system of persons,
> facts, and events beyond itself.[18]

Haecker's agreement with Newman is shown in his journal: 'The mystical and symbolical interpretation of Scripture is only possible by virtue of the substantial similarity of all being, by virtue of the formal principle of analogy.'[19] He tried to apply this idea of God's Providence, which was evidently at work in salvation history, to the current situation in Europe; while he *could* make sense of it to explain Dunkirk, the greater the number of Nazi military successes, the more difficult he found such an explanation and the more he succumbed to pessimism.

At this juncture in the war Sophie was not depressed by what was happening around her, though she did marvel at the sheer pace of its development. 'I'm pretty unmoved by each new turn of events', she wrote to Fritz. 'All I sometimes wonder is whether people's ideas and lives were as shallow in previous centuries as they are today, or whether, as an era recedes, its bad aspects gradually recede into the background too, and its good ones take on a special lustre.' Such speculations did not last long. Rather than succumb to idle day-dreaming, she focussed instead on day-to-day living and ensuring that the impact of the war on ordinary life was kept to a minimum. But it required a determined effort to avoid superficiality and to swim against the tide.

> However things turn out, I think individuals should be on their guard, and doubly so when people make it hard for them. I'm sure you believe like me that one can never level upward, however desirable that may seem. If any levelling takes place, it is always in a downward direction. Even here, though, fate has offered us a splendid chance to prove ourselves. Perhaps we should not underrate it.[20]

Her thoughts constantly turned to Fritz, as well as to the others she knew on active service, including Hans. 'He is so vulnerable', she told Fritz, for she knew his mood swings, but added, 'Still, I doubt if the war will do *him* much harm'.[21]

Sophie herself was able to block out news of the war and to draw peace and consolation by contemplating nature, and she shared her thoughts with Fritz in order to raise his spirits.

> There are two roses on my bedside table. Strings of tiny beads have formed on the stems and the foliage, which hangs down into the water. What a pure and beautiful sight, and what chill indifference it conveys. To think that it exists. That trees simply go on growing, and grain and flowers, and that hydrogen and oxygen have combined to form such wonderful, tepid summer raindrops. There are times when this comes home to me with such force that I'm absolutely filled with it and have no room left for a single thought. All this exists, although human beings behave so inhumanly, not to say bestially, in the midst of creation. That is a great blessing in itself.[22]

That June, Sophie was working at a kindergarten in Ulm, and though the work gave her a good deal of pleasure, she found dealing with children 'an immensely tiring business' because of the need 'to adjust to them completely. This certainly is not an egotistical profession and I doubt I could stick it indefinitely—I have been brought up too self-centred',[23] she confessed to Fritz. 'It is terribly tiring having to think yourself into the world of children but remain detached from it at the same time. It takes patience and love not to become abruptly, abominably grown-up again.' She could not resist dwelling on the little faces before her and seeing in them what they promised to become—'the kind of people that exist today'—while reflecting that 'they retain the childish charm we love because we mourn its passing'.[24] Towards the end of her time at the kindergarten she realised how superficial her attitude to children had been: 'You need more than the kind of emotion children so readily arouse. I now realise what infinite love for all living things you need to be able to cope with those unpredictable, often spiteful, often heart-warming little childish creatures. Few people possess as much love as that, but one can cultivate it.'[25]

The exchange of letters between Sophie and Fritz that June indicates that Fritz was undergoing a transformation in his attitude to the regime. The very fact that he was willing to respond to Sophie's questions about his role as an officer shows that he was open to persuasion, despite the danger involved in receiving her letters. Sophie found it hard to say things in writing that could only really be resolved 'by conversational to-ing and fro-ing', as she called it. She told him it was not her custom to argue for argument's sake.

> I have always unconsciously made certain allowances for the profession you are tied to, in the hope that you will weigh these things more carefully and perhaps make concessions here and there.
>
> I can't imagine two people living together when they differ on these questions in their views, or at least in their activities.

People should not be ambivalent themselves just because everything else is, yet one constantly meets the view that, because we've been born into a world of contradictions, we must defer to it. Oddly enough, this thoroughly un-Christian attitude is especially common among self-styled Christians.

If it were so, how could one expect fate to make a just cause prevail when so few people unwaveringly sacrifice themselves for a just cause?

I am reminded of an Old Testament story that tells how Moses raised his arms in prayer every hour of the day and night, asking God for victory. As soon as he let them drop, his people forfeited divine favour in battle.

Do people still exist today who never tire of undividedly focusing all their thoughts and desires on a single objective?[26]

Undeterred by concerns that she might appear overly intellectual and uncaring, Sophie continued:

I am sure you find it unfeminine, the way I write to you. It must seem absurd for a girl to worry her head about politics. She's supposed to let her feminine emotions rule her thoughts. But I find that thoughts take precedence, and that emotions often lead you astray because you can't see big things for the little things that may concern you more directly—personally, perhaps. It is the same with children. You can't provide them with all they need to console them when they cry, not right away, because it is often better for their development if you don't give in to your immediate feelings.[27]

As regards her own development, Sophie was aware of the need to struggle on a regular basis to overcome character defects. She had a rare humility which enabled her to spot and admit her shortcomings and then to struggle against her foibles with determination. Her letters to Fritz are peppered with allusions to this other type of 'warfare' which she carried on relentlessly in her domestic situation: 'I have cured myself of something, too:

dreaming about things I find pleasant. It makes you sad'.[28] As if
to console Fritz, she told him, 'very few of my actions correspond
to what I consider right', and added that she was sometimes
tempted to succumb to the wish not to exist, until she realized
this arose from weariness. 'It keeps me silent when I ought to
speak out—when I ought to admit to you what concerns us both.
I put it off till later'.[29] She had heard that the French intended to
lay down their arms, and told Fritz, 'I sometimes feel like laying
down my arms, too. Still, *Allen Gewalten zum Trutz!* [Stand firm
against all the powers that be!]'[30] This, her father's favourite
quotation from Goethe, was a family motto which the Scholls
used to encourage each other in times of difficulty, and which
those close to the family were familiar with.[31]

On 22 June the Franco-German armistice was signed by
Marshal Pétain; the German Ministry of Propaganda maximised
the effect by arranging for the signing to take place in the same
railway carriage and at the same location where the Germans had
capitulated in 1918. Sophie was dismayed that the French were
so quick to surrender, for it seemed to her that they were only
interested in their home comforts. She told Fritz, 'I would have
been more impressed if they had defended Paris to the last round,
regardless of all the art treasures housed there, even if they had
achieved nothing, or nothing of any immediate value. But
expediency is everything these days, and true purpose no longer
exists. Nor does honour, I suppose. Saving your own skin is the
main thing.' She knew that at Ulm most people took the attitude,
'Who cares how the war turns out as long as my son or husband
soon comes home in one piece? [...] I sometimes shudder at the
spirit that governs history today. Now that the mighty lion has
killed, the jackal and hyena are venturing forth to claim their
share.'[32] This was a reference to Italy, which had declared war on
France on 10 June.

'I don't know how much longer I can bear to watch this
butchery of ours', Hans told his parents,[33] though the Franco-
German armistice brought respite to Hans' unit. He visited Paris,

took time off to play tennis and go cycling, spent time improving his French and reading Baudelaire, and, while working in a medical unit there, became good friends with several French nurses. Yet Hans was not blind to the darker side of events. He felt uneasy with being part of the occupying force, witnessing how the army requisitioned the best houses for its troops, and observing the brutal reign of terror that came in wake of the army by which the Nazis hoped to keep the French in subjection. He told his parents,

> you may believe a man should return from the wars wiser and more mature. That applies only in the rarest instance. I think I was more sensitive and receptive before this madness started.
>
> War sets us back a long way. It's unbelievable how absurd human beings have become.[34]

Hans was charmed by the French people he encountered and remarked (naïvely) on their chariness when asked for their opinion about writers such as André Gide, Georges Bernanos and Francis Jammes. Gide had already withdrawn to the unoccupied zone of France and soon became part of the Resistance press; Bernanos' *Lettre aux Anglais* (1942; *Plea for liberty*, 1944) and radio broadcasts were soon to attack Hitler's expansionist policies. All three were part of *Renouveau Catholique*, the philosophical, socio-critical and literary movement which was founded at the end of the nineteenth century and included Paul Claudel, Léon Bloy, Julien Green and François Mauriac, all of whom were on Hans' reading list.

Hans was now half student, half soldier; a medical student during term-time, a medical assistant in military hospitals in vacations. The medical corps to which he was assigned was an ideal place to meet pacifists, fellow dissidents and opponents of the regime, and to exchange ideas and banned literature (which was becoming ever harder to obtain). Hans was disconcerted by having to live a double life, and unable to reconcile the parts; he even toyed with the idea of becoming an officer while the war lasted, because he found it hard to endure his 'subordinate status indefinitely'.[35] His predicament was exacerbated by the atmosphere around him, since he could feel the grip of the authorities tightening and becoming more unbearable. These were insecure times when arrest could be triggered by a trivial remark, when people simply disappeared.

While Hans was serving in a Paris hospital, Hitler visited the city and stayed for the victory parade (in which Fritz Hartnagel took part). Now that Italy had entered the war on the side of Germany, Hitler was at height of his popularity. Even Germans who were anti-Nazis had to concede the brilliance of his tactics and to admire the way so much had been achieved with so few casualties; nevertheless, these same Germans were dismayed at the lack of resolution of the Western powers to stem the tide. It was generally assumed that Britain would soon be invaded once the battle for the skies had been won.

A personal set-back for Sophie was the news that her work in Ulm did not count as National Labour Service, which meant another delay before going up to university. Before embarking on a second spell of teaching practice, she used her summer vacation to go cycling and enjoy the mountains. After a cycle ride with her sister Inge, 'I came home rich', she told Fritz.

> It is so grand to be able to do things, just like that, without depriving anyone. It is so good that the fields and forests and clouds never change, unlike us human beings. [...] And even when you think that everything is about to end, the moon reappears in the sky the following night, the same as ever. And the birds continue to sing as sweetly and busily without worrying whether there is any point in it. Have you noticed the way they tilt their little heads to the sky and sing with complete abandon, and how their little throats swell? It is good that such things are always with us. You have them too. It is enough to gladden the heart, is it not?[36]

She was equally rhapsodic when describing to Hans one of her cycle rides: 'We felt like senior officials of the Almighty who had been sent off to find out if the earth was still good—and we found it very good indeed.'[37] On another two-day cycling trip, she and Lisa Remppis stayed at an inn attached to a castle, where they ate fresh eggs and country sausages with mulled wine. She wrote home:

> It was glorious to be rolling along the highway in the April sunshine, and we seemed to ourselves to be a couple of gods who had blundered onto earth one fine day and liked it there. The one thing that was not very godly about us was our behinds, which were not used to such a long bike ride.[38]

Later that summer she spent another ten days cycling in the mountains with Lisa. She told Fritz that it reminded her, 'What a tonic simple folk can be.' But the future student of biology and philosophy was entranced above all with nature:

> Who would have thought it possible that a tiny flower could preoccupy a person so completely that there simply wasn't room for any other thought, or that I could have turned into earth, I liked it so much, or thrown my arms around the first person I met, I was so happy. What I enjoyed most was lying on the ground, where I was close to all the little creatures and a part of everything. The ants and beetles regarded me simply as a piece of wood.[39]

In mid-August Sophie started work as a trainee kindergarten teacher at a children's sanatorium in the spa town of Bad Dürrheim, in the Black Forest. It was a residential placement and the first time that she had lived away from home. Her day lasted from 7 am to 9.30 pm and involved working as one of the 'aunties' for the eighty children living there, whom she found spoilt and noisy. She noticed the absence of a proper community spirit and felt at a loss how she could 'do anything sensible with the children'. At first she had nothing to do but 'attend to their physical needs and yell for silence',[40] but soon she was able to claim that 'I am gradually coaxing them into displaying their better nature', though 'their philistinism is well developed and remains as unappealing as ever'. The older girls gradually warmed to Sophie and persuaded her to stay up at night and chat, which Sophie found all the more enjoyable for being against the rules. The responsibility suddenly thrust upon her made Sophie aware of her shortcomings: 'I'm often too scatter-brained, and I'm learning here to keep my eye on lots of things at once', she told Inge. 'I am still not good, but I am genuinely proud that I am at least doing a bit better that I was.'[41]

She was learning in other ways too, since she had to share a room with a girl who snored, had 'the brain of a hen and 130 pounds of unappealing flesh to go with it. On top of that, she never washes and considers herself a beauty. The rest you can imagine. I had a spat with her right away, so as to be left in peace.'[42] Her room-mate read frivolous paperback romances, chattered incessantly and was never still. 'Perhaps it is doing me good to sleep near her, so I acquire a certain immunity to such trivia',[43] Sophie wondered.

She continued to exchange letters with Fritz about his profession and views on nationhood. He argued that the role of the armed forces was to teach people to be honest, modest and sincere; it made moral demands on the individual and in that sense its task was not unlike the task of Christian formation overseen by the Church. True, answered Sophie, but a soldier has to swear an oath, so his job is to carry out his government's orders. Tomorrow he may have to comply with a view diametrically opposed to that of yesterday. 'His profession is obedience', so how can he have an honest attitude when compelled to lie? Or is it not lying,

> when you have to swear one oath to the government one day and another the next? You have to allow for that situation, and it has already arisen before now. You weren't so very much in favour of a war, to the best of my knowledge, yet you spend all your time training people for it.[44]

Fritz asked Sophie, 'tell me what the meaning and purpose of a nation is, or at least how you see yourself in relation to it. I believe that is the question that must first be answered before one can stand in judgement on a soldierly career and our modern age'.[45] It was a subject that many Germans wrestled with, and Sophie obliged Fritz by setting out her thoughts. She thought a soldier's position with respect to his country was like that of a son who vows to stand up for his father and family; if the father committed an injustice against another family, his son had to back him regardless. But Sophie felt she could not muster that much family feeling. 'To me, justice takes precedence over all other attachments, many of which are purely sentimental. And it would surely be better if people engaged in a conflict could take the side they consider right.' She considered it wrong for a parent automatically to take the side of their child on principle. In the same way, 'I think it is just as wrong for a German or a Frenchman, or whatever else a person may be, to defend his nation doggedly just because it is his. Emotions can often be misleading.' She told Fritz how roused she was by the sight of soldiers marching to music, and how on occasions she had had to fight back tears at the sound of military marches—but this was letting sentimentality get the better of you. She had been taught at school that a German's attitude was deliberately subjective, but she felt unable to accept this unless the attitude was objective as well. The 'subjective approach' had caught on with a lot of people, and 'many who were looking for a pattern to fit their conflicting emotions have adopted it with a sigh of relief'.[46] Overall she felt that Nazi nationalism was usurping religion for its own cause, whereas a true patriotism 'tolerated spiritual and religious feelings';[47] it seemed that Hitler was intent on turning Nazism into a secular faith, which was at odds with the teaching of the Bible. Evidently, by exploring her own and other people's attitude to the Nazi regime, she was working out her own line of thought.

After the fall of France, Fritz and his unit had been stationed near Calais. Not having heard from him for several months

Sophie took to re-reading and analysing his old letters. Lighting on two of his comments, 'I intend to be quiet and self-effacing' and 'I can sense new ground beneath my feet', she suggested they sprang from the same sentiment.

> And it made me very happy, because a person who senses the ground you mention does not fumble his way aimlessly along anymore. And I think you will know from now on what to do when you hear that voice. This new state of affairs means a lot to us both as well. To me at least it has meant the greatest (and finest) change in our friendship to date. And if I understand you correctly, it must mean the same to you, for the threads of our relationship no longer run between you and me, but between us and something higher. And that is a better state of affairs.[48]

Sophie followed up this letter with an equally remarkable one. Acknowledging the uncertainty over whether her motive for writing was a selfish one or not, she said she assumed,

> that you are all alone in an atmosphere that has nothing in common with the one I would like to win you over to. And at bottom you are already half on my side, and you will never feel entirely easy there again.
>
> The battle I wage with myself will be yours as well: not to subside into a state of well-being, into the warmth of the herd, into philistinism. Isn't it a prop and a consolation, knowing that one is not all alone? Or rather, feeling it.
>
> Although you sound as if you're very lonely, I cannot help you. I mustn't, however much it hurts me not to. You know that yourself.
>
> I can only advise you to brace up (how absurd that sounds). You say yourself you are getting nowhere. If only you would read some books, however much of an effort you found it. If only you had some minor task that demanded concentration. [...]

> Dear Fritz, please don't think me inconsiderate. Being hard
> is far more difficult than turning soft.[49]

Interspersed with the heavier letters were ones of a lighter tone,
though even in these Sophie did not lose the opportunity to make
a more serious point:

> Here on Münsterplatz the wind plays such funny tricks it
> would be silly not to laugh. When I go outside it completely
> ruins my hair (which is no great shakes anyway). One feels
> a regular urge to prance around and join in. A shame I
> cannot spare the time.
>
> I hope it visits you too, the wind, and takes you out of
> yourself a bit, so that you can't help rejoicing in the wind
> and in yourself, because you're the person in whom the
> wind is unleashing such wonderful emotions. [...]
>
> And don't waste time on unproductive things. That is
> something to be calmly (and not always gently) thrust aside.[50]

She asked Fritz to look up Psalm 13:3, one of the favourite texts
of the young Scholls and their Ulm friends, where it says, 'Lighten
my eyes, lest I sleep the sleep of death; least mine enemy say, I
have prevailed against him.' For Advent she sent Fritz a wreath
and candles, and reminded him to re-read the Advent story,
knowing that her mother had sent him a Bible the previous
summer, when he was on duty in France. With Christmas a
fortnight off, she craved for news from him, and wrote to say, 'I
would like to be able to have a far bigger share in you'. She knew
nothing about his professional life, and only shared part of his
non-military life. 'I don't want to be part of that other life, you
understand, but I'd like to share in it, that's to say, look on at it
so as not to fail you in any way.'[51] But she admitted this might be
an unfair, if not impossible, request to make.

Just after Christmas, Sophie went skiing with Inge, Werner,
Otl Aicher (a friend—later the husband—of Inge), Lisa Remppis
and Willy Habermann (a biology student nick-named Grogo or
'cuckoo'). They had the use of a skiing lodge all to themselves,

survived on bread and tea, went to bed late, and got up late. In the evenings they read aloud *The diary of a country priest* (1936), the novel by Bernanos (which was no longer obtainable in Germany because it was by a living French author) which won for him the French Academy's *Grand Prix du Roman*. Written at a time when the Catholic Church in France was riddled with careerism, worldliness and complacency, it is the story of how God works in hidden ways through the weak vessel of a country priest, who is surrounded by people who are hypocritical, lustful, envious and worldly. Both grittily earthy and profoundly spiritual at once, the book was intended to help Christians 'digest' the modern world and experience a foretaste of heaven in the very ugliness and sorrow of this world. The main protagonist is a priest who relentlessly analyzes his faults and weaknesses, such as his tendency to sentimentality, his timidity, and his perceived inability to pray. The diary he keeps strikes the reader as neurotic, yet, as the book continues, it becomes apparent that the sufferings of the priest brings peace to his little flock—and to himself, as he eventually overcomes his self-hatred and accepts his own short-comings. Sophie found it amusing and serious by turns, and urged Fritz to acquire a copy, just as she hoped to obtain one for herself.

Returning home from the mountains Sophie noticed a striking difference between her party and the other skiing groups. As she described it to Fritz,

> I longed so much during the train journey to see a face that bore comparison with those of my brothers and sisters or friends. Know what I mean? It wasn't nostalgia, just the recognition of a difference. Even the hordes of young people I saw on the train were not young anymore—they were simply exploiting their youth for pleasure's sake. But my brothers and sisters and friends, though often more gauche and unsophisticated, were brimming with good-will. Or filled with good intentions.[52]

Thinking of Fritz on his own, she told him, 'I can well imagine how disagreeable it must be to be marooned somewhere in enforced idleness'.[53]

But Fritz was soon able to spend some of his leave at Ulm with the Scholls. By now he had become part of the extended household; any news Sophie received from him she passed on to her mother, who in turn relayed it to Fritz's mother, a Seventh Day Adventist. After Fritz's departure, Sophie found herself longing to have a note from him, something she could carry around unseen by the others—but no sooner had this thought occurred to her than she was unsure whether she approved of her emotions.[54] Soon she told him, 'I am growing fond of you all over again, in a different way. I am fond of you because of the good that is within you—because of what makes you a human being.'[55]

On his return from France at the end of September 1940, Hans had spent a fortnight at Ulm before taking up his medical studies again at Munich, where he lodged with a family outside the city. He spent his time cramming for his preliminary medical exams, which he passed in January 1941. Then he settled down, as best he could, to a routine of lectures and reading until Easter. By now the war had unsettled the students, and Hans found that the fellow medics he knew had all retreated into their shells and lost their enthusiasm for student life. 'If only this God-forsaken war would soon be over', he told his parents, then he would love to leave Germany.[56] He reassured them, 'I shall manage to preserve my inner freedom, even in the army.'[57]

At the time, Hans was becoming friendly with Rose Nägele, the daughter of a Stuttgart doctor whose five children knew the five young Scholls well, and to her he opened up his thoughts. In early February he wrote: 'It is snowing crazily today. There is nothing to do but stew in your cosy room, light your pipe, and ponder on your sin! If you had received all the letters I have written in my head, you would be buried beneath a mountain of verbiage.' He explained that he felt disinclined to write owing to 'a kind of mad melancholy underlying everything', by which he meant an 'internal, private insecurity' unconnected with weakness or instability. 'One feels a bit world-weary at times, and all one's best efforts seem futile and superfluous. Perhaps these are symptoms of the age we live in. If so, we ought to be able to overcome them.'[58]

He was more upbeat three weeks later. 'I have regained my perception of what freedom is. I trudge the highroads once more and leave all else to the Almighty, or my sudden whim, or I set myself a destination and get there if I am so inclined.' He had been reinvigorated by the mountains, and floated the idea of Rose joining him next time.

> The sun is shining. The snowdrops are out, and white clouds are sailing across the sky. Dark earth and bright sky. I feel like saying yes to everything. I feel like saying, Yes, I love you, yes, I know the way, oh yes, it is a bliss to be a human being.
>
> And then someone slams the door on me. It is dark again—night. A little human being, huddled up, crushed by his own misery, cowers in the darkness, thinking, brooding, realising that it is futile, that he will never make it …
>
> What you say in your letters is right: we lack humility. I lack it above all else. I can't weep, so I curse. A lot of it may be imagination, of course. The war may have distorted a lot of things in my brain.[59]

That Easter he went skiing with Rose, having borrowed the money he needed from Inge, and then spent the rest of the vacation with his students' company in a hospital south of Munich. There he took a hotel room to avoid living in communal quarters and in order to read at night. He was developing an aversion to what he termed 'man in the mass', and wanted to restrict his friends to a minimum. Treasuring memories of their holiday, he told Rose:

> How happy I am! However many more storms rage over our souls, we will always regain the equilibrium of our

existence. However much we worship the young and lovely god Eros, too, the basis of our friendship is purely spiritual in the all-embracing sense. This will matter in the future, I know. There are things that far transcend the sexes when two clear-minded people, who are not man and wife, confront one another and say 'Yes'.

I realise how much my hand is trembling, and that all my thoughts are ruled by confusion, turmoil, youthful turbulence, and agitation, but there is a force that is showing me the way, an invisible force born of the fire of love, pure and fresh.[60]

In March 1941, having passed her exam to become a qualified kindergarten teacher, Sophie was eagerly looking forward to starting her degree that Easter and studying alongside Hans in Munich. Her hopes were soon dashed when she received notice that her teacher training was not recognised as National Labour Service and that she would have to complete six months proper service, all of it away from home. Despite the unwelcome news, she bounced back in characteristic fashion. On 6 April 1941, the day the Germans invaded Greece, Sophie began her *Arbeitsdienst* with eighty other young women at Krauchenwies labour camp, some 45 miles south-west of Ulm. She found herself in a dormitory of ten, most of whom were enthusiastic National Socialists, and from the outset did her utmost to keep herself apart from them, though she found herself sucked into their chatter and jokes if she was not careful. The diary she kept at this time records her intimate thoughts and the faults she noticed in herself. 'I am forever catching myself showing off in little ways. It is awful, my craving for recognition. Even as I write that, I am wondering how it will look on paper. It is destructive of mental harmony.' She wondered whether she would be able to get rid of 'the awful little demon that watches you and your potential effect on other people'. It was a conflict 'which spoils a lot of things for me and makes me mean and nasty'. Looking forward to the mail arriving that day, which would help to offset the depressing news about Greece, she wondered if, after all her lectures to Fritz about self-sufficiency (or, better said, 'independence of people and things'), she had often failed to act on them herself.[61]

At night, while the others were chatting and cracking jokes in the dormitory, she read from an anthology of St Augustine compiled by Erich Przywara.[62] She found it hard going and had to read slowly in order to concentrate, but she persevered every night with 'grim determination', even when she did not feel like it. (Fritz, meanwhile, was fighting in Yugoslavia and in his spare time—at Sophie's suggestion—was working his way through St Augustine's *Confessions*.) Not unnaturally, Sophie's reading attracted snide comments from her room-mates, who preferred to indulge in risqué stories. They were ordinary, decent girls, she realised, but vulgar, and 'this poor topic of conversation [their exploits with boys] probably matters most to them'.[63] Some of them were quite unrestrained, and Sophie was grateful that her books kept her out of their conversations, even if it meant her behaviour was put down to haughtiness. She was glad, too, that she found it hard to fit in, as it helped her to 'remain as impervious as possible' to the atmosphere around her, which she felt could all too easily blunt her mind. She wrote in her diary, '*Il faut avoir l'esprit dûr et le coeur tendre*' (One should have a hard spirit and a tender heart).[64] This was a quotation from Jacques Maritain[65] which Otl Aicher had introduced to the Ulm circle and which they had adopted as a motto of their own. Sophie used her lunchtimes for other, non-spiritual reading, and was working her way through Thomas Mann's *Der Zauberberg* (1924, *The magic mountain*), which she considered well thought-out and precisely conceived. She was lucky to be allowed any books at all, as they were strictly forbidden—even the Bible—but Sophie's supervisor made an exception in her case, provided that she kept her books in her locker. She was also allowed to sketch and even to go out of the camp unaccompanied to buy art materials in a local town.

On Good Friday 1941 Sophie's diary records the state of her spiritual life:

> This evening, as I glanced quickly out of the window of our cheerful, bustling room, I saw the yellow skyline through the bare trees. It suddenly struck me then that it was Good Friday. I was saddened by the strangely remote and detached sky. Or by all the laughing people who were so divorced from the sky. I felt excluded, both from the cheerful company around me and from the indifferent sky.[66]

> I would very much like to go to church. Not the Protestant one, where I listen critically to what the preacher says, but the other one, where I tolerate everything and have only to be open and receptive. But is that the right one?[67]

On Easter Sunday, while the other girls were dancing to an accordion, Sophie read the whole Easter story from her Bible before returning to her St Augustine compendium.

Sophie longed for her *Arbeitsdienst* to finish as she so much wanted to join her brother in Munich. All Hans could do was to tell her, 'I will also keep you supplied with books to the best of my ability.'[68] He had been ordered to re-join his student company, and found himself living a bleak existence sharing a room with seventeen others. But he managed to bend the rules and rent a room outside the barracks, where he made for himself a comfortable nest with old-fashioned chairs, a solid oak desk, and art work. 'I feel so much more at ease on my own territory than I do in the eternal drabness of the military environment', he told Inge. There he was able to write letters and read 'my beloved books' in the afternoons.[69] His ambitious reading programme, which dovetailed with his 40 hours of lectures each week, included a re-reading of the poems of Rilke, Herman Grimm's *Michelangelo* (2 vols, 1860–63), Bernanos' *Sous le soleil de Satan* (1926, *Under the sun of Satan*), Romano Guardini's *Hölderlin: Weltbild und Frommigkeit* (1939), Alois Dempf's *Christlichte Philosophie* (1938, *Christian philosophy*) and Pascal's *Pensées*. He found the language of Bernanos superb and the content 'thoroughly exciting',[70] but he read Pascal in translation, and even then found him 'incredibly tough'.[71]

He told Rose, 'I am childishly pleased with every bit of progress I make, but I sometimes peer into the dark pit of our ignorance and long for a complete, well-rounded view of life.'[72] All this general reading did not mean that his heart was not in his medical studies; quite the opposite, to judge from a letter to his mother: 'I am now at a stage when I would like to devote myself entirely to the natural sciences. I am reading a lot and don't regard my work as work, just a Sunday stroll'.[73] He attended performances at the Bach and Mozart festivals as well: 'Art like that is as essential to us as our daily bread. Definitely! What would life be without it?' he told Sophie.[74]

He also found time to share with Rose his impressions of spring.

> A sunbeam pieced a little gap in the dark sea of cloud, and the world laughed and glittered in the light of heaven. I stood there marvelling and thought, Does God take us for fools, that he should light up the world for us with such consummate beauty in the radiance of his glory, in his honour? And nothing, on the other hand, but rape and murder? Where does the truth lie? Should one go off and build a little house with flowers outside the windows and a garden outside the door and praise and thank God and turn one's back on the world and its filth? Isn't seclusion a form of treachery—or desertion? Things are tolerable in succession—the youthful spirit emerges from the ruins and soars toward the light—but simultaneities are anti-thetical, ruins and light at the same time. I am weak and puny, but I want to do what is right.
>
> Goethe says that if a miracle occurs in the world, it does so through the medium of pure, loving hearts. That consolation had been mine since you loved me.[75]

He shared a similar thought with Sophie:

> So spring has come after all! People must have been thinking that every year for thousands of years, and it is true: however much our spirits may rise and fall, we see the light above us in the vale of tears, and when we're up

> again after untold trials and tribulations, we breathe a sigh
> of relief and tell ourselves: it had to be this way—every-
> thing is bound to come right again.[76]

While Hans was studying in Munich, his brother Werner was
undertaking construction work on costal defences in Brittany as
part of his National Labour Service, prior to being drafted into the
army. Hans had not forgotten his own time in France the previous
year when he had observed the effect of devastation on the
indigenous population, and he now wondered about the extent to
which the French were 'clutching the charred and tattered remnants of their attire to them and doggedly surviving'. Or, he asked
Werner, were they 'superficial, vague, futile' as in Germany? 'I hope
you open-mindedly cling to everything good that comes your way,
but that you firmly shun everything sordid and go your own way
without worrying too much about the others. They will only take
your finest pearls and cast them before swine.'[77] It is not clear that
this advice was really necessary, as Werner had already demonstrated he was quite capable of independent thinking and action
by being the first member of the Scholl family to undertake an act
of open opposition to the Nazi regime. This had taken place in the
summer of 1939 when he resigned from the Hitler Youth, knowing
that his act of defiance would bar him from taking the *Abitur* and
hence from going to university. Unbeknown to his family, he had
also climbed to the top of the statue of Justice outside the Ulm
courtroom one night and blindfolded the lady holding the scales
of justice with a swastika flag.

   Having lectured his younger brother (and apologised for doing
so), Hans had no problems with lecturing his girlfriend, though
in a gentler, more indirect manner.

> One ought to spend more time on oneself, not just go
> hunting for novelties. Our impressions are worth nothing
> until they have gradually permeated us and roam on
> through our innermost selves in the form of purified
> images. That takes time—a great deal of time—and people
> complain of boredom. There is no more appalling term

than self-distraction. Far from distracting ourselves, we should do the opposite. We should not complain about the rain, either. I have found that the best time for walking is evenings in the rain. This afternoon I walked a good way along the edge of the woods with my collar turned up, smoking my pipe, through a steady downpour.[78]

His next letter to Rose reads like one of the passages in Pascal's *Pensées*:

> What are doubts, if not doubts about ourselves? Uncertainty seldom resides in others or in our relationship with them, but usually in our own hearts, and we strive to generalise it. Nothing, I know, is more understandable than our environment, which precisely obeys the laws that govern it, provided we explore the nature of things. Man in the midst of his world resembles a fire that flickers relentlessly, inflames us with apparent unpredictability, burns, and dies. Should we blind ourselves to these dangers? Isn't it preferable to die of ever-gnawing pain than to roam the world freely and easily, but falsely? Is there no consolation?

> Love is the only consolation, because love requires no proof. It exists like God himself, whose existence could doubtless be proved but was sensed by mankind long before any evidence could be produced.

> Yes, there is such a thing as love for its own sake. It is unconstrained and exempt from human justification.[79]

While Pascal was the mainstay of Hans, 'my nightly cold shower and my nightly read' of St Augustine were Sophie's. She was also working her way through Francis Jammes' *Ma fille Bernadette* (1910) with the aid of a French dictionary. She thought the story of the visionary of Lourdes worth the effort as it had 'such lovely little bits in it'.[80] What helped Sophie make sense of St Augustine was her use of his writings to answer points that Otl Aicher had raised with her; she was 'immensely pleased' with this research.[81] Otl also sent her an essay to read about the spiritual and intellectual status in Athens of Socrates, Plato and Aristotle; this was a contribution to the round-robin letters which he and Inge composed, and which later developed into a home-produced magazine. Sophie was also reading *The universe around us* (1929),[82] by the British astronomer James Jeans,[83] which Hans had sent her. At the camp they were forcibly deprived of enter-tainment—for which Sophie was thankful, as she did not think she would be 'tempted to fritter my time away'[84] on films, if they had been allowed to see any. It also helped her, by way of solidarity, to appreciate the 'grim and ubiquitous martial spirit'[85] of army life which Hans and Fritz had to endure.

Sophie confessed to feeling shy of reading in front of the other girls, none of whom were remotely cultured, though some kept copies of Goethe's *Faust* with them (hidden from the authorities) so as to give them refined airs. The sole and most frequent topic of conversation was 'men', and this sickened her. 'It is very educational for me, all the same',[86] she admitted to her friend Lisa. Asked about her companions, Sophie told Lisa, 'You have to be wary of people in the mass. They exert a tremendous attraction in many respects.'[87] Fritz was also privy to Sophie's plight and he wrote reassuringly that 'it is always hard for anyone to fit in with a group of rowdy people, as they tend to dominate and lower the tone'.[88] While she had no special friends, she felt she was on good terms with everyone, and was glad 'not having to fritter away my time with this person or that'.[89] From June, Sophie was assigned to a farm and was much happier now that she could escape the camp for part of the day, even though the farm work was physically exhausting. She felt sorely tempted 'to take things easy', but resisted. Now she read a chapter of St Augustine every night and supplemented her evening shower with a morning one. She still struggled to grasp the meaning of much of what St Augustine wrote and hoped that when she was finally able to talk with someone knowledgeable she would be enlightened.[90] Her sister Inge had recommended to her particular sections of the *Confessions* which were included in her Augustine anthology, such as the famous lines: 'Late have I loved you, beauty so ancient and so new, late have I loved you. You were within me, but I was outside in the world and sought you there.'[91]

From the spring of 1941 large numbers of German troops had been moving to the eastern front in preparation for Operation Barbarossa. On 22 June the non-aggression Molotov–Ribbentrop Pact, which had been signed in August 1939, was broken when German forces invaded Russia with three million troops, the largest military attack in history. The German high command reckoned that the campaign would be over in four months, and at first it seemed they might be right, when whole divisions of the Russian army were routed or surrounded by armoured spear-heads. By mid-July the German army had taken Minsk and shortly afterwards Smolensk, in the process taking 400,000 prisoners. On one day alone, 29 July, there were no fewer than a dozen special news bulletins on the wireless, each announcing a separate victory or advance. By the end of July the German generals who had originally opposed the invasion were convinced that success was now all but certain, and there began a three-pronged attack: on Ukraine and the Caucus to the south, on Moscow to the east, and on Leningrad (now St Petersburg) to the north east.

Despite being part of the invading force, Fritz continued to write to Sophie, his letters taking just three weeks to reach her. Sophie, on the other hand, ceased writing for several months when she realised that her letters were not reaching him. The Krauchenwies camp was just like the real war, Sophie mused, but on a smaller scale, and it was easy to become used to, if not unconscious of, it. Yet the offensive against Russia marked a new phase, and Sophie noticed that the war weighed on everyone more than ever before. Once again, her reaction was not to escape by daydreaming but to focus on everyday reality.

> I think we at last have a chance to prove ourselves—and prove our integrity. I often get such a glorious feeling, like the one you get before you do something athletic—an exultant awareness that you are fully in command of all your muscles. I feel strong inside. Not always, but will-

power is what counts, and I am getting to know my own
moods well enough to assess them accurately.[92]

Returning to the camp after a brief visit home, where she
coincided with Hans, she felt fortified and ready 'to repaint the
camp in glaring colours, reinforce my individuality'—not arrogance—'and redefine my position here more clearly'; she was
prepared to pay the price and to suffer the 'sense of alienation'
that afflicted her while at the camp. Realising that the war would
now have 'powerful repercussions in every respect', she wondered: 'Perhaps we are really being presented with scope for direct
outside action, though it seems as if our sole function is to wait.
That is hard, and one's patience often wears thin, and one longs
to set oneself another, more promising and easily attainable
goal.'[93] Sophie was desperately looking forward to finishing her
National Labour Service in October, but that August she learned
that she now needed to complete an additional six months—and
that they intended to organise her leisure time too. She told Hans
she was ready to 'contract any reasonably tolerable disease' that
might spare her this fate![94]

Sophie spent August looking after a baby and doing house-
work, while living at Krauchenwies. To her surprise, she became
friends with a fellow worker called Gisela Schertling, a tall fair
Nordic girl who was interested in art and, significantly, intended
to study at Munich University. Soon afterwards, during a
weekend at home in Ulm, Sophie introduced her pretty friend to
Hans, who immediately took an interest in her; this was to lead
to a romantic attachment between them—and eventually to a
Gestapo cell and the People's Court.

Sophie and Gisela managed to obtain permission to play the
organ in the local church and they enjoyed themselves playing
some four-handed pieces by Handel and Bach. One Saturday they
played and sang in the church until bedtime. Next morning, the
two of them set off for the 6.30 am Mass, early enough not to be
spotted, as church attendance was forbidden, and on their return
they went back to bed; in the afternoon they revisited the church

to play the organ.[95] Another day, she and Gisela smoked a ciga-rette—also forbidden—behind a haystack in a mood of defiance. By now, as she told Hans, she had developed her 'loathing and contempt' for the National Labour Service system to the full. She now felt 'proof against any form of compulsion', and had a 'marvellous sense of strength'; it gave her an 'immense pleasure to bamboozle my superiors and enjoy my freedom in secret'.[96]

The letters and diaries of Hans and Sophie Scholl reveal that, despite their markedly different character traits, they shared a fierce independence and had adopted strikingly similar attitudes to the war and the Nazi regime. During the first two years of conflict they had developed a growing interest in philosophy and theology, which became for them an alternative world to fascist National Socialism. Culturally restless and in search of meaning, they stumbled on Christian writers, ancient and modern, and there they discovered answers to their deepest longings. As Inge describes it, 'The Bible took on a new and startling meaning; a sense of immediacy broke though the old and apparently worn-out words, giving them the authority of persuasive reality.'[97] During this period Hans and Sophie began discussing the big questions of life—with each other and with other trusted friends, by letter and in person—which had been brought home to them by events that were unfolding in Germany and across Europe. In their different ways they each detested regimentation and its accompanying, deadly standardisation, and reacted against being herded in camps by adopting a defiant attitude and assuming a state of continuous resistance. Feeling abandoned in a strange and empty world, which was tearing itself apart, and finding that the conflict was unbearable when separated from friends and family, they sought out solitude and turned to prayer. Books, especially forbidden ones, came to play a more important part in their lives than they had done hitherto.

Reading the works of St Augustine offered answers to some of the deepest questions, for he had been a seeker on questions of the spirit: about authority, free will, belief, knowledge and illumination. Sophie was transfixed by the opening words of the *Confessions*, 'Thou hast made us for thyself, O God, and our hearts are restless until they rest in Thee.'[98] Later she confided to a friend: 'I could not live without Augustine's *Confessions*.'[99] In pursuit of deeper truths, which were absent from the German poets of his time, Hans had tried Nietzsche, before turning to the Socratic dialogues and then Pascal and St Augustine. More concerned with constructing an overarching worldview than Sophie, Hans was inspired by St Augustine's conviction that the barbarians would not prevail against the truth of God, and he was soon to discover St Thomas Aquinas and his unique blend of reason and faith, as well as his luminous common sense. Both Hans and Sophie were fortunate that at the time there was a renaissance of theological literature, from the Church Fathers to the scholastics, which had inspired some bold successors in modern French philosophy and theology in the shape of *Renouveau Catholique*.

Notes

[1]   Fritz Hartnagel to Sophie, 3 September 1939, *Sophie Scholl/Fritz Hartnagel letters*, p. 101.
[2]   Sophie to Fritz Hartnagel, 5 September 1939, *Heart of White Rose*, p. 36.
[3]   Sophie to Fritz Hartnagel, 7 November 1939, *Heart of White Rose*, p. 41.
[4]   Sophie to Fritz Hartnagel, 6 October 1939, *Heart of White Rose*, p. 39.
[5]   Diary of Hans, 29 September 1939, *Heart of White Rose*, p. 42.
[6]   Hellmut Hartert to Inge Scholl, 26 February 1946, *Heart of White Rose*, p. 290.
[7]   Hans to his mother, 22 March 1940, *Heart of White Rose*, p. 45.
[8]   Her mother was unhappy about her going without a chaperone, but nevertheless allowed her to go.
[9]   Sophie to Fritz Hartnagel, 9 April 1940, *Heart of White Rose*, pp. 65–6.
[10]   Sophie to Fritz Hartnagel, April 1940, *Heart of White Rose*, p. 66.
[11]   Sophie to Fritz Hartnagel, 16 May 1940, *Heart of White Rose*, p. 68.
[12]   Sophie to Fritz Hartnagel, 16 May 1940, *Heart of White Rose*, p. 67.
[13]   Sophie to Fritz Hartnagel, 1 February 1940, *Heart of White Rose*, p. 255.
[14]   Sophie to Fritz Hartnagel, 29 May 1940, *Heart of White Rose*, pp. 68–70.

15   Journal entry, 1/2 June 1940, Haecker, *Journal in the night*, no. 270, p. 69.
16   *Plain and parochial sermons* vol. ii, pp. 360–1.
17   *Plain and parochial sermons* vol. ii, pp. 361–4. I owe this reference to G. Biemer, 'Theodor Haecker', p. 425.
18   'Milman's view of Christianity', *British Critic* xxix (January 1841); reproduced in *Essays critical and historical* vol. ii, p. 192.
19   November 1939, *Journal in the night*, no. 21, pp. 4–5.
20   Sophie to Fritz Hartnagel, 14 June 1940, *Heart of White Rose*, p. 71.
21   Sophie to Fritz Hartnagel, 14 June 1940, *Heart of White Rose*, p. 71.
22   Sophie to Fritz Hartnagel, 17 June 1940, *Heart of White Rose*, p. 73.
23   Sophie to Fritz Hartnagel, n.d. [June/July 1940], *Heart of White Rose*, pp. 72–3.
24   Sophie to Fritz Hartnagel, 17 June 1940, *Heart of White Rose*, p. 74.
25   Sophie to Fritz Hartnagel, 8 July 1940, *Heart of White Rose*, pp. 79–80.
26   Sophie to Fritz Hartnagel, 22 June 1940, *Heart of White Rose*, p. 75.
27   Sophie to Fritz Hartnagel, 28 June 1940, *Heart of White Rose*, p. 78.
28   Sophie to Fritz Hartnagel, 28 June 1940, *Heart of White Rose*, p. 78.
29   Sophie to Fritz Hartnagel, 22 June 1940, *Heart of White Rose*, pp. 75–6.
30   Sophie to Fritz Hartnagel, 17 June 1940, *Heart of White Rose*, p. 73.
31   The passage runs: 'Craven thoughts and timid vacillation, unmanly dread and fearful lamentation can avert no affliction nor render you free. Stand firm against all the powers that be, never yield, be strong, summon the arms of the gods to your aid.'
32   Sophie to Fritz Hartnagel, 28 June 1940, *Heart of White Rose*, pp. 77–8.
33   Hans to his parents, 12 June 1940, *Heart of White Rose*, p. 53.
34   Hans to Inge, 1 August 1940, *Heart of White Rose*, p. 56.
35   Hans to his mother, 1 September 1940, *Heart of White Rose*, p. 58.
36   Sophie to Fritz Hartnagel, 19 July 1940, *Heart of White Rose*, p. 80.
37   Sophie to Hans, 21 July 1940, *Heart of White Rose*, p. 81.
38   Sophie to Lisl, April 1940, quoted in R. Hanser, *A noble treason: the revolt of the Munich students against Hitler* (San Francisco: Ignatius, 2012), p. 60.
39   Sophie to Fritz Hartnagel, 8 August 1940, *Heart of White Rose*, pp. 83–4. This quotation appears on gardening websites such as that of Perennial Resource.
40   Sophie to Lisl, 15 August 1940, *Heart of White Rose*, p. 86.
41   Sophie to Inge, 22 August 1940, *Heart of White Rose*, pp. 89–90.
42   Sophie to Lisl, 15 August 1940, *Heart of White Rose*, p. 87.
43   Sophie to Inge, 22 August 1940, *Heart of White Rose*, p. 90.
44   Sophie to Fritz Hartnagel, 19 August 1940, *Heart of White Rose*, p. 88.

[45]   Fritz Hartnagel to Sophie, 3 September 1940, *Scholl/Hartnagel letters*, pp. 209–10.

[46]   Sophie to Fritz Hartnagel, 23 September 1940, *Heart of White Rose*, p. 93.

[47]   Sophie to Fritz Hartnagel, 23 September 1940, quoted in F. McDonough, *Sophie Scholl. The real story of the woman who defied Hitler* (Stroud: History Press, 2009), p. 68.

[48]   Sophie to Fritz Hartnagel, 4 November 1940, *Heart of White Rose*, p. 119.

[49]   Sophie to Fritz Hartnagel, 10 November 1940, *Heart of White Rose*, pp. 120–1.

[50]   Sophie to Fritz Hartnagel, 12 November 1940, *Heart of White Rose*, pp. 121–2.

[51]   Sophie to Fritz Hartnagel, 11 December 1940, *Heart of White Rose*, pp. 122–3.

[52]   Sophie to Fritz Hartnagel, 13 January 1941, *Heart of White Rose*, p. 124.

[53]   Sophie to Fritz Hartnagel, 13 January 1941, *Heart of White Rose*, p. 124.

[54]   Sophie to Fritz Hartnagel, 21 February 1941, *Heart of White Rose*, p. 125.

[55]   Sophie to Fritz Hartnagel, 28 February 1941, *Heart of White Rose*, p. 125.

[56]   Hans to his parents, 8 February 1941, *Heart of White Rose*, p. 99.

[57]   Hans to his parents, 10 February 1941, *Heart of White Rose*, p. 100.

[58]   Hans to Rose Nägele, 3 February 1941, *Heart of White Rose*, p. 99.

[59]   Hans to Rose Nägele, 24 February 1941, *Heart of White Rose*, p. 101.

[60]   Hans to Rose Nägele, 15 April 1941, *Heart of White Rose*, p. 104.

[61]   Sophie's diary, 10 April 1941, *Heart of White Rose*, pp. 126–8.

[62]   *Augustinus, Gestalt als Gefüge* was published in 1934, and appeared in English as *An Augustine synthesis* (1936).

[63]   Sophie to Lisa Remppis, 13 April 1941, *Heart of White Rose*, p. 131.

[64]   Sophie's diary, 10 April 1941, *Heart of White Rose*, p. 127.

[65]   It occurs in *Le paysan de la Garonne* (1966), but must also have featured in some of his earlier writings.

[66]   In the opinion of Jacob Knab, Good Friday 1941 was the turning point for Sophie in her spiritual life. Knab notes that the 'yellow skyline' and the 'detached sky' are reminiscent of a well-known passage of Newman: 'What a veil and curtain this world of sense is! beautiful, but still a veil.' (Newman to his sister Jemima, 10 May 1828, *Letters and diaries of John Henry Newman* vol. ii (Oxford: OUP, 1979), p. 69). For Knab, both 'Newman and Sophie Scholl talk about unveiling and disclosure, for this world we see is a world of appearances pointing towards a deeper, hidden, underlying reality'. Knab points out that *Himmel* is ambiguous in German, meaning either sky or heaven. 'So it is really about all the laughing people on Good Friday who are so divorced from heaven, who on Good Friday do not care

about human misery' (Eulogy at the book launch of Frank McDonough's *Sophie Scholl. The real story of the woman who defied Hitler*, 22 February 2010).

67 Sophie's diary, 11 April 1941, *Heart of White Rose*, p. 130. This entry also contains another of those observations about her shortcomings: 'I am afraid I showed off again for a moment this evening. I did not lie or exaggerate, but it occurred to me while speaking that I was eager to impress.'

68 Hans to Sophie, 24 April 1941, *Heart of White Rose*, p. 109.

69 Hans to Inge, 25 April 1941, *Heart of White Rose*, p. 110.

70 Hans to Inge, 11 May 1941, *Heart of White Rose*, p. 114.

71 Hans to Rose Nägele, 14 May 1941, *Heart of White Rose*, p. 116.

72 Hans to Rose Nägele, 22 May 1941, *Heart of White Rose*, p. 116.

73 Hans to his mother, 8 May 1941, *Heart of White Rose*, p. 113.

74 Hans to Sophie, 14 May 1941, *Heart of White Rose*, p. 115.

75 Hans to Rose Nägele, 2 May 1941, *Heart of White Rose*, p. 112.

76 Hans to Sophie, 14 May 1941, *Heart of White Rose*, p. 115.

77 Hans to Werner, 6 June 1941, *Heart of White Rose*, p. 117.

78 Hans to Rose Nägele, 15 June 1941, *Heart of White Rose*, p. 117. Rose no doubt smiled on reading that one should not complain about the rain, because it was a variant on a stock expression of the Scholl household when minor mishaps occurred: 'Be glad it is raining. If you aren't glad, it'll rain anyway.'

79 Hans to Rose Nägele, 17 June 1941, *Heart of White Rose*, p. 118.

80 Sophie to Inge, 27 April 1941, *Heart of White Rose*, p. 136. One of the gems in *Ma fille Bernadette* reads, 'Le mot *Dieu* comme une rose rogue, au centre de l'arbuste, et la plus haute pour que le parfum de ses soeurs monte vers elle et que tu la voies toujours dominer. Oh! Si saintes que soient les autres roses, méme la blanche Marie' (p. 158).

81 Sophie's diary, 1 May 1940, *Heart of White Rose*, p. 137.

82 *The universe around us* had been translated into German in 1931.

83 According to Otl Aicher, when the Ulm circle read books on science it was generally to discuss their formulation of philosophical problems. In this context he mentions works by the biologist Hans Driesch, physicists Louis de Broglie, Niels Bohr, Arthur Eddington and Werner Heisenberg, as well as James Jeans (*Heart of White Rose*, p. 296, n120).

84 Sophie to Hans, 18 May 1941, *Heart of White Rose*, p. 138.

85 Sophie to Fritz Hartnagel, 18 April 1941 (draft), *Heart of White Rose*, p. 133.

86 Sophie to Lisa Remppis, 27 April 1941, *Heart of White Rose*, p. 136.

87 Sophie to Lisa Remppis, 1 May 1941, *Heart of White Rose*, p. 137.

[88]   Fritz Hartnagel to Sophie, May 1941, *Sophie Scholl/Fritz Hartnagel letters,* p. 307.

[89]   Sophie to her parents and Inge, 25 April 1941, *Heart of White Rose,* p. 135.

[90]   Sophie to Lisa Remppis, 5 June 1941, *Heart of White Rose,* pp. 138–9.

[91]   Inge to Sophie, 2 May 1941, quoted in B. Beuys, *Sophie Scholl. Biografie* (Munich, 2010), p. 282n.

[92]   Sophie to Lisa Remppis, 23 August 1941, *Heart of White Rose,* p. 147.

[93]   Sophie to Lisa Remppis, 11 August 1941, *Heart of White Rose,* p. 145.

[94]   Sophie to Hans, 2 August 1941, *Heart of White Rose,* p. 143.

[95]   Sophie to Lisl, 29 August 1941, *Heart of White Rose,* p. 296, n125.

[96]   Sophie to Hans, 7 September 1941, *Heart of White Rose,* pp. 149–50.

[97]   I. Scholl, *The White Rose,* p. 16.

[98]   I. Scholl, *The White Rose,* p. 23.

[99]   Quoted in S. Hirzel, *Vom Ja zum Nein: eine schwäbische Jugend 1933 bis 1945* (Tübingen: Klopfer & Meyer, 2000), p. 160.

4 MAKING SENSE OF EVIL: 1941–42

FOR INDIVIDUALS OR FAMILIES like the Scholls, the study and practice of Christianity were themselves a form of low-level protest against the regime, as well as a means of immunisation against the ideological contagion that was infecting all Germans. But whilst they drew solace from religion, there was a sense in which they felt unsupported by the leaders of the two main Christian denominations—the Catholic Church and the Protestant (Lutheran) *Landeskirchen*—which, after their initial decision to try to work with the new Chancellor, had maintained a public silence in the face of mounting outrages. In the Concordat of July 1933 between Germany and the Holy See, the Catholic Church had agreed to withdraw from all political activity, and since then had pursued a policy of avoiding confrontation with the regime in the hope of preserving its core institutions.[1] This became increasingly difficult as the state strengthened its grip and became ever bolder in its actions; as the power of the National Socialists waxed in a crescendo of diplomatic, economic and psychological triumphs, the latent contempt in the Party for religion and clerical institutions became more overt and crude. Clerics who spoke out were imprisoned (under the Treachery Act of December 1934), the integrity of the confessional was violated, and publications were censored then closed down.

Though the Catholic Church was the dominant religious body in Bavaria, in Germany as a whole the majority confession was Protestant—and it was an early policy of the Third Reich to create a new national church out of it, by 'cleansing' it of its Jewish heritage and making it subservient to the regime. Clumsy political attempts to Nazify the *Landeskirchen*, assisted by the *Deutsche Christen* (German Christians) who supported this realignment, led to a schism within the *Landeskirchen* and, after the Barmen Declaration of May 1934, the formation of the *Bekennende Kirche* (Confessing Church), whose leading spirits were Martin Niemöller and Dietrich Bonhoeffer. Claiming to be the true Protestant tradition in Germany (composed of the Lutheran, Reformed and United churches), the Confessing Church objected to state interference in ecclesiastical affairs and church doctrine, but attempts to speak out in public led to the arrest of around 700 pastors, some of whom were imprisoned. One of these was Niemöller, who was kept in Sachsenhausen and Dachau from 1937 until the end of the war. By 1945, eighteen Christians from the Confessing Church had been martyred, including Bonhoeffer himself.

Both Catholic and Lutheran leaders protested strongly to the authorities in private against the more outrageous abuses of human rights, but since there was no public echo, on account of press censorship, it gave the impression that the shepherds had abandoned their flocks—though by 1941 everyone knew full well the price for speaking out. 'It is high time that Christians made up their minds to do something', Hans complained to his family in his frustration. 'What are we going to have to show in the way of resistance—as compared to the Communists, for instance—when this terror is over? We will be standing empty-handed. We will have no answer when we are asked, "What did you do about it?"'[2]

In April 1941 the Bavarian Minister of Culture and Education Adolf Wagner ordered that school prayers should be replaced by Nazi songs and that crucifixes and religious pictures be removed from classrooms. The outrage this caused among the general public, as well as among Catholics, was so strong that it forced Wagner to rescind the order, one of the rare instances of successful public opposition to government diktat in Nazi Germany.

Arguably, the policy Hitler had most difficulty in implementing and which provoked the largest revolt among Germans was the euthanasia programme codenamed *Aktion* T4, which had been secretly adopted at the outbreak of the war. It led to the killing of tens of thousands of mentally ill and handicapped adults and children by means of starvation, lethal injections and poison gas. Due to the scale of the programme it proved impossible to keep it secret, despite all official efforts to do so. Rumours of these atrocities reached the Scholl household via one of Magdalena's friends, a religious nurse at a hospital for mentally retarded children. She was distraught, and related that her wards had been emptied by the black vans of the SS. After the first contingent failed to return, the children had asked where the trucks were going; in her confusion, one of the nurses had said, 'They are going to heaven', and from then on the children mounted the strange trucks singing.[3] The spectacle of these children being taken to their doom epitomised for the Scholls the ultimate barbarity of a system that had taken their country out of the community of civilised nations, and it fostered the conviction that the regime had forfeited its claim to the allegiance of its citizens.

In the face of mounting evidence about the killing of inmates of hospitals and asylums it became increasingly difficult to keep silent, and the Catholic bishops, led by Cardinal von Faulhaber of Munich, wrote privately to the government protesting against the policy. Several Lutheran churchmen also protested in private or else secured exemptions from the policy for institutions they oversaw. Then, in July 1941, the Catholic bishop of Münster, Count Clemens von Galen, took the momentous decision to speak about it from the pulpit. It was the first time in the war that the Nazi regime was challenged in public, and it caused a sensation. The Westphalian aristocrat had initially welcomed the regime as a bulwark against godless Communism, but now he was prepared to raise his voice when the only sounds heard were those of conformity and acquiescence.

His first controversial sermon was preached at St Lambert's, Münster on 13 July 1941, and was a reaction to the confiscation of church properties, monasteries and convents by the Gestapo the previous day, and the expulsion of priests and religious brothers and sisters from Westphalia and the Rhineland. The bishop bemoaned the way the Gestapo had, for 'reasons of state policy', dealt with innocent and highly-respected Germans 'without the judgment of any court or any opportunity for defence, depriving them of their freedom' and treating them 'like vermin'. Since the actions of the Gestapo were not subject to oversight, no-one in Germany was safe; no-one could now be sure he would not someday be 'deported from his home, deprived of his freedom and locked up in the cellars and concentration camps of the Gestapo'. In upholding the authority of the law and asserting that the right to life, inviolability and freedom is 'an indispensable part of any moral order of society', he explained that he was 'not talking about a matter of purely Catholic concern but about a matter of Christian concern, indeed of general human and national concern'. No authority could expect to command the loyalty and willing service of others if their actions were arbitrary and beyond the law; the current policy would only serve to engender a 'feeling of legal defencelessness and an attitude of apprehensive timidity and subservient cowardice, which must in the long run deprave the national character and destroy the national community'.[4]

The following Sunday, von Galen spoke of the attacks perpetrated by 'our opponents within the country', which had continued throughout the week, and of the silence in the newspapers about these 'bloodless victories of the Gestapo officials'. It was clear that what lay behind 'the new doctrines which have for years been forced on us' and led to the ban of religious teaching in Christian schools and the exclusion of all Christian influence in other schools, was 'a deep-seated hatred of Christianity, which they are determined to destroy'.

> Become hard! Remain firm! At this moment we are the anvil rather than the hammer. Other men, mostly strangers and renegades, are hammering us, seeking by violent means to bend our nation, ourselves and our young people aside from their correct relationship with God. We are the anvil and not the hammer. But ask the blacksmith and hear what he says: the object which is forged on the anvil receives its form not alone from the hammer but also from

the anvil. The anvil cannot and need not strike back: it must only be firm, only hard! If it is sufficiently tough and firm and hard the anvil usually lasts longer than the hammer. However hard the hammer strikes, the anvil stands quietly and firmly in place and will long continue to shape the objects forged upon it.

The anvil represents those who are unjustly imprisoned, those who are driven out and banished for no fault of their own. God will support them, that they may not lose the form and attitude of Christian firmness, when the hammer of persecution strikes its harsh blows and inflicts unmerited wounds on them. [...]

What is being forged in these days between the hammer and the anvil are our young people—the new generation, which is still unformed, still capable of being shaped, still malleable. We cannot shield them from the hammer-blows of unbelief, of hostility to Christianity, of false doctrines and ethics.[5]

The bishop asked parents to examine their children's school books, especially the history ones, to see how 'in complete disregard of historical truth' their adversaries 'seek to fill inexperienced children with mistrust of Christianity and the Church, indeed with hatred of the Christian faith'. He warned, 'Christian parents, you must concern yourselves with all this. If you do not, you are neglecting your sacred duties; if you do not, you cannot face your own conscience, nor Him who entrusted the children to you that you might lead them on the way to heaven.' As parents they were defenceless to protect their children from the 'hammer-blows of hostility to the faith and the Church', but being the anvil they had a part to play in the forging.

Let your family home, your parental love and devotion, your exemplary Christian life be the strong, tough, firm and unbreakable anvil which absorbs the force of the hostile blows, which continually strengthens and fortifies the still weak powers of the young in the sacred resolve

not to let themselves be diverted from the direction that
leads to God.

He reminded them, 'Through a conscience formed by faith, God
speaks to each one of us. Obey always without any doubt the voice
of conscience.'[6]

Von Galen's third and most vehement criticism of the Nazi
regime came a fortnight later, on 3 August 1941. In this sermon
he spoke out forcibly against the Nazi policy on euthanasia,
condemning the 'monstrous doctrine, which tries to justify the
murder of the innocent, which permits the slaughter of invalids
who are no longer capable of work, cripples, the incurable, the aged
and the infirm'. There were reports, he said, that incurable mental
patients were being removed from hospitals by force under orders
from Berlin, that shortly afterwards relatives were informed that
they had died and been cremated, and that their ashes could be
collected. There was widespread certainty that these deaths were
not due to natural causes and that the authorities 'follow the
precept this it is permissible to destroy "worthless life"—to kill
innocent persons, if it is decided that such lives are no longer of
value to the *Volk* and the state'. The way was open for the murder
of all 'unproductive people', even those disabled as a result of
industrial accidents or the war. The regime was trampling on all
the Commandments, including the first; 'instead of the One, True,
Eternal God, men have created at the dictates of their whim, their
own gods to adore: Nature, the State, the Nation or the Race.'[7]

The sermon hit the regime hard. The policy of purifying the
nation and making it more vigorous, by rooting out the incurably
ill, the crippled or insane, the retarded or senile, had caused
consternation and resulted in many families withdrawing their
relatives from hospitals and care homes. But now, when for the
first time in the war significant numbers of casualties were
returning to Germany, fears were growing that the shortage of
hospital beds would lead to an acceleration of the T4 programme
and that badly wounded soldiers might be targeted next. These
fears now became a threat to national morale.

After speaking out so forcefully, von Galen fully expected to be punished by the Gestapo, but Hitler decided that hanging the popular 'Lion of Münster' risked alienating the people of Westphalia and the Rhineland, thereby undermining the war effort. Instead, he had him put under virtual house arrest and marked for execution after the war; meanwhile, he arranged for 37 priests (24 secular priests from von Galen's diocese and 13 in religious orders) to be taken to concentration camps, most to Block 26 (the *Priesterblock*) at Dachau, where ten of them would lose their lives. Goebbels had attempted to gain public support for the T4 programme by instructing the Nazi Propaganda Ministry to sponsor a feature film called *Ich klage an* (*I accuse*), directed by Wolfgang Liebeneiner, which would promote the idea of assisted suicide. It featured a young German woman with multiple sclerosis who wishes to die and, after long discussions about the rights and wrongs of assisted suicide, is helped to do so by her husband and a friend. But the film, which was released on 29 August 1941, failed to persuade the public sufficiently and the T4 programme was officially abandoned, by which time around 70,000 had been 'granted release' by euthanasia. In practice, official abandonment meant that the programme was carried out with much greater secrecy. The killing of adults resumed after a year-long pause, and between 1942 and 1945 there were a further 87,000 victims; the killing of children continued, but it was decentralized.[8] As a result of the official abandonment of the programme, most of the personnel involved, together with much of the equipment, were moved to the east, where they were used to set up the extermination camps.

Among those who received the full text of von Galen's third sermon were the Scholls; it was delivered anonymously at their apartment on Cathedral Square in Ulm, urging the recipient to make six copies and pass it on. The sermon had in fact been delivered by one of the 'Galen team', a group of Catholic boys and young men in Ulm, led by Heinrich Brenner, whose mentor was the Catholic priest in Ulm, Fr Eisele. They had secretly duplicated the sermons and posted copies anonymously to those they were sure would approve, such as the Scholls.[9] In this way the sermons, or excerpts from them, were disseminated throughout Germany and reached many people. (The sermons also reached the Allies, and millions of copies were dropped over Germany by the RAF; they were also used in BBC radio broadcasts.)

Inge Scholl recalls that Bishop von Galen 'radiated an astonishing aura of courage and integrity'. Hans, too, was deeply impressed by his straightforward but profound act of opposition,[10] and he told Inge, 'Finally a man has had the courage to speak out'. The duplication and dissemination of these sermons seems to have triggered the idea of using pamphlets as a way of expressing non-violent opposition to the regime which would be very hard for the Gestapo to trace, for Inge recalls Hans commenting at this moment, 'We really ought to have a duplicating machine'.[11] Meanwhile Sophie privately copied and circulated the third sermon of von Galen, a whole year before the White Rose pamphlets were written and disseminated.

During the summer of 1941, when the young Scholls and their like-minded friends met up in Ulm, one of their topics of conversation was the right of resistance under a dictatorial regime. Informing their discussion were the arguments of St Thomas Aquinas about just systems of government and legitimate forms of rebellion.[12] At one of these meetings Otl Aicher came up with the idea of launching a clandestine magazine as a way of sharing ideas between friends who opposed the Nazi regime and were scattered across Europe, from Brittany to the Pripet Marshes; it was a natural development of the round-robin letters that he and Inge had started writing. Part literary review, part circular letter, the magazine was to include 'essays (original wherever possible!), poems, personal reflections, and drawings [...] compiled at regular intervals and circulated in a homemade cover among our friends'.[13] Cultural rather than overtly political or critical of the state, the contributions were to be a means to achieve some form of self-expression beyond the reach of the regime, an escape from the suffocating, mindless propaganda of National Socialism, and an assertion of intellectual independence.This group of a dozen or so young men and women—the Ulm circle—were aged between 18 and 23 and comprised the Scholls and their friends who were opposed to National Socialism. To different degrees they were all striving to develop answers to the problems thrown up by life in a totalitarian regime and to ground them on cultural and spiritual foundations. Badly in need of contact with like-minded souls, if they were to survive the dark days of the war, the recipients agreed to take an active share in the enterprise, contributing book reviews, copying out poems which others could not access, or merely commenting on the articles of others. As the magazine would shield them from the storm raging in the soul-destroying environment of the National Socialist system, it would be called *Windlicht (Hurricane Lamp)*.

Windlicht anticipated the White Rose pamphlets, as it was effectively a subversive venture aimed at bolstering young opponents of the regime. It can also be viewed as a successor of the journal *Hochland (Highland)*, which had recently been banned, since it took *Hochland* for its model. The founder and editor of *Hochland* for most of its existence, 1903–41, was the Catholic journalist Carl Muth. Otl had met Muth in March 1941, after submitting an article on Michelangelo's sonnets for publication in *Hochland*, and thereafter saw him frequently, their discussions sometimes becoming quite heated. Otl introduced his young friends to Muth, who soon began to exert a marked influence on the Ulm circle and its magazine *Windlicht*. The encounter with Muth was to open a window onto another world, as he introduced them to scholars and writers who were vehemently opposed to National Socialism, and in a short time it affected a remarkable religious awakening in Hans and his friends.

Carl Muth had been educated in Berlin, Paris and Rome, and had worked as a journalist for ten years before founding *Hochland*. He had embarked on the enterprise with a view to extricating German Catholics from the cultural ghetto in which they had lived since the time of Bismarck's *Kulturkampf* policies, which aimed at Protestant and Prussian dominance. *Hochland* was deliberately broad in its outlook and in the authorship of its articles, and it became the principal Catholic forum for the airing of topical matters of an artistic, literary, social and philosophical nature, in the process inspiring two generations of educated Catholics. A patriot rather than a nationalist, Muth aimed to overcome the party-political and confessional divides of his time by appealing to the power of art and aesthetics, as well as the Christian foundations of European culture. The journal was denounced by the philosopher Martin Heidegger (before he abandoned Catholicism) for venturing too deeply into the waters of modernism, while Rome disapproved on account of Muth's repeated criticism of the Holy See over its stance with Italian fascism. Nevertheless, *Hochland* was critical of theological liberalism and indeed was considered the official outlet in Germany of *Renouveau Catholique*, the French movement of writers and thinkers which had reacted against the Enlightenment, and sought to revive the Church.

Muth managed to preserve *Hochland*'s characteristic independence and critical detachment after the Nazis came to power in 1933, despite carrying articles more or less covertly critical of the regime, but its days were numbered as it was the leading magazine—with a circulation of around 12,000—providing intellectual resistance against Nazi ideology. Despite the Concordat signed by Hitler and Pope Pius XI, the Catholic Church had come increasingly under attack, and most of its newspapers and all its youth organisations were eventually closed down.[14] An issue of *Hochland* had been banned in 1939 after an article in it denounced the limitations placed on the press, and again in April 1941 after Nietzsche was denounced as a killer of God; the invasion of the Soviet Union gave the authorities the excuse to ban it definitively in July 1941. The support and reassurance Muth had given to hearts and minds in the face of fascist ideology were not stifled by the suppression of *Hochland*; they merely took on a different form.

It is unclear when exactly Otl mooted the idea of producing *Windlicht*, but it was probably in July or early August 1941, to judge from a reference to the 'hurricane lamp' in a letter Hans wrote to his girlfriend Rose Nägele on 8 August:

> I must go my own way, and I do so gladly. I am not anxious to avoid a host of dangers and temptations. My sole ambition must be to perceive things *clearly* and calmly. Until I do, many more storms will buffet and shake the roof of my house. But I will light my lamp even so, and however much it flickers and threatens to go out, its warm red glow will serve as a beacon to many a lonely traveller.[15]

Forming part of the Ulm circle, Rose was privy to the inner thoughts of the volatile leader-in-waiting. Hans tried to persuade her that he was not dejected or distracted at heart, and that he saw 'positive values in the midst of a world of brutal negation', recognising 'suffering as the true and supreme value of European man'. He asked Rose about her exhausting farm work, what she felt about her '*labor* [*omnia vincit*] *improbus*', or 'unremitting toil [which conquers all things]', remarking that 'in the sweat of your brow [you shall eat your bread]';[16] and he suggested she read one of the Psalms every night. He insisted that for the likes of themselves leisure mattered a great deal, and that they should fill their leisure time, rather than let it lie fallow. 'One does not dream, either (that I do at night, a great deal), one "contemplates", meditates, reads, learns.'[17]

Hans was now living close to Munich, working as an assistant to a surgeon and learning minor procedures from him. He told Inge that his medical duties were deeply satisfying: 'It's the only time I am really happy—but it's madness just the same'.[18] His reading now included Hans Carossa's *Das Jahr der schönen Täuschungen* (1941, *The year of sweet illusions*), an autobiographical novel based on the author's student days in Munich studying medicine,[19] Pascal's *Pensées*, and Charles Baudelaire's *Les fleurs du mal* (1857, *The flowers of evil*), the latter two sent by Werner. He then moved on to a translation of Etienne Gilson's *Introduction à l'étude de Saint Augustin* (1929), which he offered to send to his mother, once he had finished it, as she was ill and confined to bed; he also offered her his copy of Dante's *Divina commedia* (*Divine comedy*). Comparing his generation with that of Carossa's before the Great War, Hans told his mother that he saw many parallels between the two, but reckoned that his own generation was less preoccupied with superficial matters.

> We were presented early on with the choice between genuine and false, and our better selves opted for the genuine and true. It may also be that we are more receptive to what is true, or more impervious to what is false, than the generation before us and to come.[20]

Now able to choose where to work for his internship, Hans picked the municipal hospital at Harlaching, a suburb in the south of Munich, because his closest friend Alex Schmorell would be there too. Schurik, as Alex was known to his friends, had served as a medical orderly in France and had joined the students' medical company at the end of 1940. He and Hans had met in March 1941 while they were preparing for their preliminary exams, and they soon found themselves discussing philosophical, theological and literary works together. Born to a German father and a Russian mother, who was the daughter of an Orthodox priest, Schurik had been brought up in the Russian Orthodox Church. After his mother's early death, he was raised in Munich by his father, who was a doctor and had remarried, and cared for by a Russian nursemaid who hardly spoke German. Although he was bilingual, Russian remained Schurik's mother tongue and he felt at home in the world of Pushkin, Gogol and Dostoyevsky. Despite being a German national, he had avoided joining the Hitler Youth, and when called up for military service had managed to escape punishment for refusing to take the oath of loyalty to Hitler.[21] Inexplicably, he was still allowed to serve in the *Wehrmacht*.[22]

When Germany invaded the country of his birth, his hatred of National Socialism intensified.

Schurik was an artistically gifted and sensitive young man, full of humour and childlike in his delight in the world, though there was a seeking, questioning side to him, too. Tall and athletic, Schurik might have appeared a typical medic-soldier, but there was a rebellious and bohemian streak to him which fed his dislike for military conditions; to escape, he took refuge in books, music and congenial friends, indulging his sense of the absurd. He and Hans developed a close friendship and the two of them livened up conditions in the barracks with their practical jokes. In the spring of 1941 Schurik had invited Hans to study with him at his father's house in Munich. A committed opponent of the regime, Dr Erich Schmorell was initially wary of Hans, since he might be an informer, but once he got to know him, he allowed Schurik to invite Hans to the literary soirées he organised. These meetings consisted in reading from literary, philosophical and theological works, intended for the 'spiritual relaxation' of like-minded individuals and to help sustain their morale while living under 'spiritual siege'.

Schurik was in touch with many others of the same mind, often meeting them at concerts, attendance at which was a subtle form of protest insofar as being artistic was to proclaim oneself un-Nazi. One night in May 1941, when the Brandenburg concertos were being performed at the Odeon concert hall in Munich, Schurik introduced Hans to Traute Lafrenz, a bright and good-looking medical student who had transferred to Munich from Hamburg, where she and Schurik had started their medical studies. Traute was a vivacious young lady whose cosmopolitan airs, inherited from her Viennese mother, contrasted with Hans' provincial southern German ways and fascinated him. Another point of fascination was that she had belonged to a circle of dissident students in Hamburg for four years, and prior to that had attended a dissident reading group led by a school teacher. She and Hans were soon comparing lecture notes, engaging in spirited discussions on politics, and going to concerts together. And they fell in love.

In September 1941 Hans used his fortnight's holiday to travel with Schurik down the Danube to Vienna. The trip served to cement the friendship between the two medics and to introduce Hans to Russian literature.[23] That month the Proclamation of Police Ordinance for the Identification of Jews in Public came into force, ordering all Jews to wear a palm-size yellow star on their clothing inscribed *Jude* (Jew). It marked another stage in the persecution of Jews in Germany and its occupied territories. West Prussia had been pronounced 'free' of Jews in October 1940, and in November that year 350,000 Jews had been rounded up in the Warsaw ghetto. During 1941 the Nazi regime stepped up measures against Jews in Holland and occupied France, and crushed any resistance they met with. Theodor Haecker wrote in his journal:

> Today 13th September it was announced that as from 19th September every Jew must wear a yellow star on the left side of his coat, the star of David, the great King from whose stock the Son of Man, Jesus Christ, was born according to the flesh. It is not impossible that the day will come when every German abroad will be obliged to wear a *Hakenkreuz* [i.e. swastika] on the left side of his coat, the sign of the anti-Christ. The more they persecute the Jews, the more the Germans resemble them, and their fate. Today they are crucifying Christ *as a people* for the second time. What is improbable about their undergoing similar consequences?[24]

That autumn Hans received confirmation of the rumours circulating about the mass murder of Jews in Russia and Poland, and that the killing was on a truly monumental scale. His source was a young Munich architect called Manfred Eickemeyer, who had been based in Cracow and involved in construction projects in occupied Poland. Eickemeyer described the operations of the SS *Einsatzgruppen*, the Nazi elite corps composed of the most ruthless and fanatical soldiers, who specialised in mass executions of civilians. On entering a village or town, the paramilitary death squad would round up Jews, officials and anyone who resisted occupation, seize their valuables, strip them down to their undergarments, march to them to an execution site—usually an anti-tank trench—line up the victims on the edge, then mow them down with a machine-gun. It later came to light that in the space of a year, *Einsatzgruppe* D had killed as many as 90,000 men, women and children. Hans also heard that Poles and Russians had been herded into concentration camps as slave labour and young women sent to SS bordellos.[25]

Hans was shaken by the sheer scale of the atrocities. Asked in the People's Court in February 1943 about why he felt compelled to write and circulate leaflets against the regime, he was to answer:

> After much agonising deliberation I became convinced that only one course was possible: to bring about a shortening of the war. Along with this was the consideration that for me the treatment by us Germans of the people in the occupied territories was an abomination. I could not imagine that after such methods of domination a peaceful reconstruction of Europe would be possible. Out of such considerations grew my antagonism for this State; and because, as a good citizen, I could not remain indifferent to the fate of my people, I decided to assert my convictions in deeds, not merely in thought. Thus I came to the idea of writing and producing leaflets.[26]

It was Otl who introduced Hans (and later Sophie) to Carl Muth, not long after *Hochland* had been suppressed. The first meeting took place in September 1941 when Hans and Inge visited the 74-year-old scholar, who lived alone in an affluent suburb on the outskirts of Munich, and presented him with a bust of Pascal. From this encounter followed introductions to theologians, philosophers and writers who were opposed to the regime, such as Theodor Haecker, Alfred von Martin, Werner Bergengruen[27] and Sigismund von Radecki. Over time this group helped Hans heighten his awareness of National Socialism's wholesale threat to individual morality and its perversion of human values. Muth was also the link to other former contributors to *Hochland*—the '*Hochland* circle'—some of whom were living outside Germany: Gertrud von le Fort, Sigrid Undset, Romano Guardini, Alois Dempf, Otto Karrer, Joseph Wittig, and Heinrich Lützeler.[28] Although Muth and his circle were vehemently opposed to the Nazi obsession with the nation state and its associated folk-inspired racist ideology, they did not share a common alternative political view.[29]

But Muth was not just an entrée to a circle of opponents of the regime; he had a talent for teaching and a passion for molding people around him to his own way of thinking. No sooner was one outlet for his energies blocked than he encountered kindred spirits in the form of the Ulm circle, and he set to cultivating the young Scholls and their friends, acting as their companion and mentor. Although more than fifty years their senior, he conversed with them, lent them books, tutored them in theology, and introduced them to other writers and thinkers. While editing *Hochland*, he had lavished care and encouragement on the young people who helped him, as much for their sakes as for the journal's; now, despite his advanced age, he was delighted to make the acquaintance of the younger generation, to explore their aspirations, to enlighten and to encourage them by means of serious conversation and correspondence. He also provided ballast for their Christian faith. Under his influence the religious perceptions of Hans and Sophie were to acquire 'greater intensity and firmer expression: the Christian Gospel became the criterion of their thoughts and actions'.[30] In turn, the younger generation helped Muth not to lose hope that the German people would be purified by suffering and regain its conscience; for him they represented a 'secret Germany' who could uphold and pass on the values he cherished and had made his life's work.

There was a special affinity between Muth and Hans, as both had wide-ranging interests, were passionate about what they read, and had a love of literature, especially French literature. In photographs Muth appears as an old-fashioned scholar with his neat white goatee, rimless glasses and winged collars, yet he was a daring and unorthodox thinker who was capable of great passion if the conversation touched on National Socialism— which he called 'Brown Bolshevism' or 'Satanocracy'. Muth was able to help *Windlicht* by offering excerpts from his own translations of contemporary French authors, and by putting Hans in touch with Haecker, von Radecki and other writers for further, mainly unpublished, contributions. He was keen that Hans should know of and read about Catholics of intellectual calibre, and his wish was granted when, at Inge's suggestion, Hans agreed to reorganise and catalogue Muth's vast private library, stocked largely with banned books.[31] This led to long, almost daily conversations between the two that confirmed Hans in the Christian foundation of his opposition to the regime. In December 1941 Muth wrote to Otl to thank him for having 'mobilized for me' so much help; he reported that Hans was 'a frequent visitor and a dear and much appreciated friend of the house. He often stays for meals, too, and comes into contact with a variety of people who interest him'.[32]

While Otl was working on a philosophical essay for *Windlicht*, Hans chose to write on the 'mystery of poverty', a matter which had preoccupied him for some time. Despite being one of the 'haves' who lacked nothing material in life, he had approached the problem via Dostoyevsky before finding his answer in Léon Bloy's *Le sang du pauvre* (1909, *Blood of the poor*), which had been recently translated into German. In the *Windlicht* archive there is a passage copied out from Bloy's diary on the subject of poverty: 'I am the anvil in the deepest abyss, the anvil of God, who causes me to suffer so because he loves me, that I know full well.'[33] It was texts such as this which confirmed Hans in his understanding of the need for 'absolute poverty', though he was confused about how this would work out in political terms. He concluded that the 'basis of this poverty, which leads to "absolute" Christianity, must be primarily spiritual and only secondarily material', though there was a paradox: 'Material poverty becomes the route to spiritual [poverty].' He felt his view of poverty was more 'serene' than Bloy's because it 'lays no claim to the property of the rich, but despises it because it *knows* about real values'.[34]

In his *Windlicht* essay 'On poverty' Hans wrote:

> Love impels me to wish many a man hardship and afflic-
> tion so that he can know poverty! Poverty is stronger than
> wealth. Poverty enables a person to cast former affluence
> to the winds without regret, to prize spiritual values more
> highly than any possession. Poverty confronts a person
> with the ultimate choice.
>
> The war will render us all very poor. We must abandon all
> hope of a happy outcome. Hunger and hardship will at first
> dog our every step [...].
>
> Yet we do not wish the cup to pass from us, even so. It shall
> be drained to the dregs. [...]
>
> The war will subject Europe to dire poverty. Never forget,
> my friends, that poverty is the road to light.[35]

This might seem an extraordinary piece for a twenty-two-year-old medical student to write, but at the time Hans was preoccupied in thinking through a number of important matters. He confided to Rose that he was in a spiritual crisis, the most important in his life, and that he could not find consolation in worldly things, but had found happiness within himself. 'Mine is the happiness of the victor who foresees the end of the battle', he told her.

> This war (like all major wars) is fundamentally spiritual. I
> sometimes feel as if my puny brain is the battleground for
> all those battles. I can't remain aloof because there is no
> happiness for me in doing so, because there is no happiness
> without truth—and this war is essentially a war about
> truth. Every false throne must first crack and splinter, that
> is the distressing thing, before the genuine can appear in
> unadulterated form. I mean that personally and spiritually,
> not politically. I have been presented with the choice.[36]

The task of reordering and cataloguing Muth's library was not only a lengthy task which would take several months, but an absorbing one, and Hans decided to postpone his medical studies that winter in order to focus his attention on philology and philosophy. During this time Hans read Plato's last four Socratic dialogues (in which Socrates chose to honour his commitment to morality in the face of death), various works of Kant, Schiller's panegyric on freedom, and Goethe's *Das Epimenides Erwachen* (*The awakening of Epimenides*).[37] During this time, he and Otl continued to exchange drafts of, and opinions about, their *Windlicht* articles. In late November, Hans told Otl that Muth was ill, supposedly from bronchitis, but according to Hans from psychological problems induced by the anti-Jewish measures, which were preying on his mind.[38] The previous month six synagogues had been destroyed in Paris, and a fortnight later mass deportations had restarted in Germany, where attempts at escape were blocked by an embargo on emigration. In November, Himmler ordered the construction of the Theresienstadt ghetto (which functioned as a holding camp as well as a concentration camp) in occupied Czechoslovakia, as a preliminary step to the 'Final Solution' of the Jewish Question.

Many of the books in Muth's library fascinated Hans, including one on the Turin Shroud, which featured a photograph of the relic that was revered as the burial shroud of Jesus Christ. A picture taken by an amateur photographer in 1898 had caused a sensation when the negative revealed a human body that had been tortured; pictures taken by a professional in 1931 were published in Italy and led to a worldwide debate. The German edition of the volume of plates appeared in 1939 and it was doubtless this edition which Hans found in Muth's library.[39] Hans made copious notes about the relic, which he believed to be genuine, and decided to write an article about it for *Windlicht*. Otl, who was the magazine's editor, asked Muth for a photograph to accompany the article.

When Hans' article on the Turin Shroud appeared in *Windli-cht* it was prefaced with a line by Paul Claudel: 'Night had to be, that this lamp might appear'. In his research Hans had come across a letter written by Claudel in 1935[40] explaining the significance of the image for contemporary Christianity. In the article Hans wrote that Claudel had spoken of 'the "second Resurrection", Christ's resurrection for the twentieth century. The likeness of the Son of God existed unseen, slumbered, and waited for nearly two thousand years, but our own era was privileged to lift the spell and see the reality.' Hans was amazed that it was technology that had revealed the image, 'the technology that has also mechanised the weapons of war and is even now celebrating its triumphs over mankind'.

> For the first time in almost two thousand years, a human eye was seeing that body, that ineffable countenance with the closed eyes, asleep yet awesomely awake, dead yet preserving vivid signs of superhuman suffering, traces of cruel anguish, just as it is written: a spear thrust in the left side, countless twin weals inflicted by a Roman scourge, nail marks in wrists and ankles. The martyrdom of the world in all its actuality, there before our waking eyes! Who would not tremble and call on God anew from the depths![41]

Clearly, a remarkable spiritual transformation had taken place in Hans. The same could be said of Sophie, too. In October 1941 she was assigned by the National Socialist Public Welfare Service to work as a kindergarten teacher at a nursery school in Blumberg, a village near the Swiss border, and there she resumed her practice of keeping a diary. The entries were now more spiritual, reflecting her prayer life and interior relationship with God, and included appeals to God, invocations arising from doubt and self-reproach, and ecstatic professions of faith. Lyrical musings, which of a sudden turned into prayer, were written alongside interior dialogues and tactful character sketches of friends. Spontaneous jottings about everyday events rubbed shoulders with pithy considerations of a spiritual nature or entreaties to God.[42]

I know that life is a doorway to eternity, and yet my heart so often gets lost in petty anxieties. It forgets the great way home that lies before it. Unprepared, given over to childish trivialities, it may be taken by surprise when the great hour comes and find that, for the sake of piffling pleasures, the one great joy has been missed.

I am aware of this, but my heart is not. Unteachable, it continues its dreaming, lulled to sleep by forces that trouble me, wavering always between joy and depression. All that I am left with is melancholy, incapacity, impotence, and a slender hope.

However stubbornly my heart may cling to its treasures, be it only out of love for the sweetness of life, wrest me away against my will, because I am too weak to do so myself; turn all my pleasures sour, make me wretched, make me suffer before I dream my salvation away.[43]

In another entry she writes:

I would love so much to believe in miracles. I would so much like to believe that I can acquire strength through prayer. I can't achieve anything by myself.

Muth wrote that we should pray for Otl. I had never thought of praying for him—he never seemed to need it at all. Who doesn't, though? Even a saint does.

I'm so terribly tired, and I'm always prone to such futile, ridiculous mental digressions.

Though hast created us in Thine image.

I should like, as that Prophet did, to ask God for visible evidence of himself. Or has that ceased to be necessary? I should like to spread myself out like a cloth for him to collect his dew in.[44]

These diary entries have been ignored by some historians, or else attributed to the delirious condition of a young lady who was, on her own admission ,'mixed up' and homesick. But it is surely not fanciful to compare Sophie's diary entries to the jottings of a mystic, and to suppose that her soul was being forged and purified amidst sufferings and distress.

Sophie was now a war-time auxiliary rather than an *Arbeits-dienst* girl, and she found the designation just as awful. The majority of the pupils at her day-nursery had parents with criminal records, 'but they are far too good to merit comparison with my bosses', she told Hans.[45] She visited the local church, where, as she records in her diary, 'I tried to pray. I knelt down and tried to pray, but even as I did so I thought: better hurry, so that you can get up before someone comes.' Afraid to be seen not by strangers but friends, she realised that this reaction was 'probably wrong, probably a false sense of shame. And that is why I hurried through my prayers and got up just the same as I had knelt down. I was not ready—I was simply trying to rush things.'[46] A few days later she records the ups and downs of her interior life:

> If it were only my own affair, everything would be much easier. Sometimes I feel I can forge a path to God in an instant, purely by yearning to do so—by yielding up my soul entirely. If I beseech him, if I love him far above all else, if my heart aches so badly because I am apart from him, he ought to take me unto himself. But that entails many steps, many tiny steps, and the road is a very long one. One must not lose heart. Once, when I had lost heart because I kept backsliding, I did not dare pray anymore. I decided not to ask anything more of God until I could enter his presence again. That in itself was a fundamental yearning for God. But I can always ask him, I know that now.[47]

An exchange of letters with Inge about prayer shows that Sophie had adopted a very simple and touching form of prayer, based on humility and knowledge of her own nothingness. She writes:

> We should simply entrust God with the worries we so arrogantly cling to and allow to depress us or drive us to despair. I don't find that easy, because when I try to pray

and reflect on whom I am praying to, I almost go crazy, I feel so infinitely small. I get scared, so the only emotion that can surface is fear. I feel so powerless in general, and doubtless I am. I cannot pray for anything except the ability to pray.

Do you know, whenever I think of God, it is as if I am struck blind. I can't do a thing. I have absolutely no conception of God or affinity with him aside from my awareness of the fact. And the only remedy for that is prayer.

Prayer.[48]

By mid-December 1941 Sophie was established in her life of prayer, and making further discoveries.

Lighten my eyes, lest I sleep the sleep of death; least mine enemy say, I have prevailed against him. [Psalms, 13:3] I shall cling to him and when all else fails he alone will remain. How terrible to be remote from him. I cannot record my thoughts dispassionately. Everything I once possessed, all my critical discernment has deserted me. But my soul is hungry, and, oh, no book can assuage that hunger. I remain barred from access to the living world of books. My sole sustenance is Nature, the sky and the stars and the silent earth. [...]

I realise that when I love people very much, I cannot do better than include them in my prayers. If I love people in all sincerity, I love them for God's sake. What better thing can I do than take that love to God?

God grant that I come to love Fritz, too, in His name.[49]

Early in September 1941 Fritz had been transferred from Russia to the spa town of Weimar to raise a signals company for deployment in Libya as part of the Afrika Korps, but his marching orders did not arrive, so he remained there in relative idleness until April 1942. Many Saturdays he took the 11 am train from Weimar to Freiburg, where Sophie would be waiting for him at the barrier at around 6 pm; and he would return to Weimar on the overnight train on Sunday night. They frequently visited the Catholic cathedral in Freiburg (which miraculously survived the bombing in 1944), where Sophie felt very much at home,[50] and they also spent a good deal of time discussing and arguing about what they had read, as well as attitudes to the war.

At Inge's suggestion, Sophie had sent Muth some apples, and to her surprise Muth acknowledged the gift with a letter, which she (mistakenly) presumed was intended for Inge. More apples were sent and this time Muth posted Sophie a book by Martin Deutinger, a philosopher who taught in Freising. Deutinger was a religious writer and an incisive and witty critic, who had tried to reconcile his Christian faith with the demands of reason and in particular the idealist Hegelian philosophy of the time. Sophie noted in her diary,

> I am surprised Muth found the time and love to turn to me as well, when he had no need. He must have a very kindly heart to find room in it for lesser people whose only connection with him is quite superficial. I could not appreciate it more. That in itself puts me under an obligation to better myself.[51]

Muth had asked Sophie to pray for Otl, and her diary records her willingness to comply: 'Like Muth, I pray he remains safe and sound. As for me, whose presence can I enter? Only that of him who knows all the bad there is inside me. I am too much of a coward to confess everything. Give me the time to prove myself.'[52]

Sophie was delighted to receive some candles from Otl at the start of Advent. He had asked her to paint the cover for the Christmas issue of *Windlicht*, but she felt drained and lacking in inspiration: 'Even if God won't help me', she wrote in her diary, 'I'll have faith just the same. I'll write and tell Otl I will do the cover.'[53] In the end, she decided to paint the head of little boy whose family lived near the Scholls.[54] Sophie later worked on an essay about the significance of music to mankind; Wilhelm Habermann wrote poems and an essay entitled 'What is life?'; and Otl contributed theological and philosophical essays. Sophie took to questioning Otl about a line in his piece where he had written that 'nature is a stool that mankind climbs on to reach up to God, and that it will revert into nothingness once it has served its purpose'. She found it inconceivable that the mountains, fields and sky that she could see from her window should cease to exist. 'If they are beautiful and good, why should they someday cease to exist?' Even though she sometimes became 'intoxicated with the sight', she felt her delight in nature was good in the long run because 'it restores things to their proper perspective. [...] I think it is awful to create something, only to consign it to Limbo afterward'. Nature was part of God's creation, and possessed a 'hint of spirituality', though she had not always thought this way. She admitted to another change worked within her, when she wrote: 'I realise that one can wallow in the mind (or intellect) while one's soul starves to death.'[55]

Sophie became more demanding, not just with herself, but with her friends. A letter from Lisa Remppis upset her as it contained just 'isolated snippets, disjointed little trains of thought', which frustrated Sophie's effort to assemble a full picture of her friend. But she put a stop to such critical thoughts— 'I must think of her with all the love I can muster'[56]—and wrote to Lisa about their friendship. The two of them had grown apart for all sorts of reasons—and not just because of Lisa's fiancé. Seemingly, 'all that has united us so far is a friendship we have clung to for its own sake, rather than ideas or a common aim, which form a peculiar bond between people even when they seldom write or see each other. I don't know if you are as determined as I am to cling to our friendship.'[57] She proposed that the two of them try to meet up.

With Hans' *Windlicht* article 'On poverty' fresh in her mind, she wrote:

> I still find life so rich and good, in spite of everything, but people fail to make good use of it. Perhaps it would do us good to become really poor, so as to be better prepared for less ephemeral riches. Don't people look for compensation

> when they are deprived of so much, and don't they then
> realise that they let themselves be distracted by affluence
> and set their hearts on unworthy things? Perhaps they first
> have to discover that they possess a heart.[58]

Thinking of both Fritz and Lisa's fiancé, she thought it 'fortunate that, even in the army and much as it makes people suffer, there are people who retain their inner independence because they don't rely on things that others can deprive them of'. And she reminded Lisa that they were 'privileged to number such people among our friends'.[59]

As Lisa had brought up the question of purgatory in her letter, Sophie had to admit she had not given either purgatory or heaven much thought. She had read a passage about purgatory in Sigrid Undset's three-volume historical novel *Kristin Lavransdatter* (1920–22),[60] in which the protagonist had expressed the hope that the fire of purgatory would completely purify her 'stubborn and impure soul'. Sophie interpreted this as 'another form of God's mercy', but felt she could not say more.[61] Sophie had now begun to read the sermons of John Henry Newman,[62] having discovered his writings in October 1941 when she and Fritz visited a non-conformist bookshop in Aulendorf, recommended by Otl. Its founder and owner Josef Rieck had been a novice at the Benedictine Abbey at Beuron, in the upper Danube valley, and was now a courageous anti-Nazi bookseller. Though Sophie does not mention her discovery of Newman in any of her letters, one of her Ulm friends, Susanne Hirzel, recalls how in 1941 she was introduced to Newman by Sophie: 'Sophie read constantly and one day handed me a book by Cardinal Newman. What? You don't know him? There's a wonderful world awaiting you there!'[63]

The second Sunday of Advent 1941 was one of the most momentous days in the Second World War, for it was on that day that the Japanese Navy launched a surprise aerial attack on the United States naval base at Pearl Harbour which drew the US into the war. Now the Axis powers faced a coalition of the Soviet Union, Britain and the US, and it was not long before the Allies demanded unconditional surrender. The effect this had on those involved in subversive activities in Germany cannot be underestimated. Several weeks before Pearl Harbour, to prevent any collapse of public morale, Hitler had instructed the Special Courts and the People's Court to conduct lightening quick trials and deal severely not only with criminals but with 'all those who weaken, undermine or endanger the fighting efforts of our people'.[64]

That December, Hans told Rose Nägele that he was experiencing Advent 'as a wholehearted Christian for the first time in my life'. A number of loose ends had suddenly come together, and there had been a 'fundamental reinforcement of something that has become my mainstay in an age so eagerly searching for new values. I have discovered the only possible and lasting value'. There were things which rational thought could not fathom, which were 'outwardly incomprehensible but inwardly grasped'. While he wanted to travel as far as he could along the road of reason, he realised that he was 'a creature born of nature *and* grace, though a grace that presupposed nature'. He struggled to say more about this 'innermost development', since, as he explained, he was too much in the thick of it. He wished Rose 'hours of genuine contemplation and peace' for Christmas.[65] He wrote this not in a state of euphoria but at a time when he was at a low ebb; he had weathered army life for four years 'with comparative equanimity', but now he felt 'every little thing a drain on my energy' and that he was 'losing enthusiasm for work'.[66]

Hans conveyed his spiritual state even more clearly when he told Rose, 'For me the birth of Our Lord represents the supreme religious experience, because he has been reborn for me. Either Europe will have to change course accordingly, or it will perish!'[67] He realised that culture was no substitute for God, that salvation could only be found in the Gospel, that resistance to the Nazi state had to begin with the discovery of a new order by means of a personal re-enthronement of the creator in the individual. In *Windlicht* he had written of the need to dethrone oneself in order to see that light which had been protected by the storm lantern.[68]

Muth was largely responsible for Hans' spiritual blossoming, and Hans duly thanked him by describing his change of heart and mind.

> It fills me with joy to be able, for the first time in my life, to celebrate Christmas properly and in a Christian fashion, with true conviction.
>
> The vestiges of my childhood, when my carefree gaze dwelled on the lights and my mother's face, were not obliterated, but shadows had fallen across them. I toiled in a barren age along profitless paths that invariably ended in the same sense of desolation and emptiness.
>
> My loneliness was aggravated by two profound experiences of which I must sometime tell you, and last but not least by this terrible war, this Moloch[69] that insinuated itself into the souls of all men from below and strove to kill them.
>
> Then, one day, from somewhere or other, came the answer. I heard and perceived the name of the Lord. My first meeting with you coincided with that period. Thereafter it grew lighter every day, as if scales were falling from my eyes. I am praying. I feel I have a firm background and a clear goal. This year, Christ has been born for me anew.[70]

The skiing trip that Hans, Inge, Sophie and their friends went on at Christmas 1941 made a profound impression on the group. Several accounts of it were written for *Windlicht* and they manage to capture the atmosphere of the occasion. In 'Our days at the skiing lodge' Inge describes the arduous climb which was led by Hans, partly on foot, partly on skis, zigzagging up the side of a valley, then up a steep gorge to reach the mountain hut where they were staying. At one stage the 'ballad of the Emperor Barbarossa made its way along our little snow-caravan', each person in turn playfully adding another line. At the top they found the wind whistling up the snow-blown valley, for the stone hut was perched on an unprotected hillside, high above the tree line, exposed to wind and storm, and surrounded on three sides by rock faces. 'Most of you will know how grand it is to sit around a stove by candlelight with a few friends, in the solitude that reigns at 2000 metres, with wind-driven snow lashing the four walls outside and nothing visible to the eye but a greyish-yellow, swirling, drifting mass.' The purity and peace at the top were all the more enjoyable,

> because the communal exertion and discomfort of such a climb, and its occasional difficulty, create a special bond between us. The 'us' that can be engendered by an outward experience of this kind forms a perfect basis for another, inwardly and invisibly constituted 'us' to which we aspire and on whose account *Windlicht* has been lighted. It isn't that we want to sacrifice our 'I' to this 'us', but rather that we seek the 'us' for the sake of the 'I', so that it may derive sustenance for its continued development and contemplate its reflection in this 'us' as though in a mirror.[71]

After returning from the day's skiing and hanging up their clothing to dry, the party crowded round the stove and took it in turns to read aloud from Dostoyevsky's *The double* (1846). As Inge comments, 'Books lent our days in the hut a very special flavour because they focussed everyone's attention on the same subjects.'[72] The repeated comical turns of phrase of the novel's protagonist Yakov Goldyakin rubbed off on the skiers to the extent that their favourite passages were repeated throughout the stay in the mountains. The Dostoyevsky novella centres on a government clerk, whose identity is crushed by the bureaucracy and stifling society around him, and charts his descent into madness. Advised by his doctor to take some cheerful company as a remedy for his antisocial behaviour, the low-level bureaucrat gatecrashes an office party, is expelled after committing several social blunders, and on his way home in a snowstorm encounters his double—his double in appearance, his opposite in character. The relationship between Goldyakin and his double, and how it evolves, takes up most of the story.

The reading by the stove was resumed in the mornings until the snow cleared, or else the young people passed the time singing. Conversation took a serious turn when it led on to the question of why so many people appeared not to feel hunger for things of the spirit. As Inge records in her article, someone said,

> Don't they ever wake up with a start and ask, Why? Where does it come from, this restlessness within me, this mild ache? Ah, but they always know of an instant remedy. [...] They bury the little voice within them beneath a heap of stuff instead of simply standing still and asking, Why? If they would only start with that 'Why?' it might be the beginning of hunger. But they seem to be asleep—indeed, they seem to have entirely forgotten how meaningless life can really be.[73]

Surely, someone chimed in, this was taking the mystery of spiritual hunger too far. What form does it take? another asked. Do art and literature satisfy this hunger? Or music? Sophie did not speak, preferring to listen and ponder the matter quietly. Her voluble brother, on the other hand, asserted that spiritual hunger could not be assuaged by music or any other art form, since nothing derived from man could; the most it could do was indicate where to find the 'bread' that could assuage this hunger. Inge records that they failed to find an answer to the question, commenting, 'perhaps it is in the nature of many questions that they have to grow like trees, year after year, until we can one day pluck the ripe fruit from their foliage'.[74]

Traute Lafrenz also wrote about the trip for *Windlicht*, describing the last night when Inge and Sophie prepared a splendid communal meal.

> Once again, as on every night, we crowded around the stove; once more we drew closer in readiness of heart; and once more the flickering, restless glow of burning logs mingled with peaceful candlelight. Voices were raised in song. Songs eliminate what separates people, and their harmony pervades those who sing them, so our hearts were receptive to the words of Novalis' *Hymnen an die Nacht*, that great Christian profession of faith.[75]

At midnight they stepped outside the hut to welcome in the New Year in the open, though nothing could be seen, because of a dense mist, except the sulfurous yellow of the moon. At midnight Inge read aloud two Psalms, and then they retired.

Hans told his sister Lisl that the skiing trip was a 'monumental experience'. All the ingredients of previous trips were present: the snug security inside the hut, tea by candlelight, the reading aloud, and the singing. But there was a difference between this gathering and previous ones: 'a focusing of attention on our troubled times, the cross, and salvation'.[76] The bounce in his step after the skiing trip was clearly discernable. He told Rose, 'I have dropped anchor and, come what may, nothing can really trouble me from now on.' Now he was,

> *homo viator* [pilgrim man] in the best sense, a man in transit, and I hope I always will be. After a lapse of many largely wasted years, I have finally learned to pray again. What strength it has given me! At last I know the inexhaustible spring that can quench my terrible thirst.
>
> That is main thing I have to tell you. All else is secondary![77]

He agreed with Rose that grievous sinners were less off-putting than people who were hard-hearted. 'Spiritual harshness is the most abominable human trait. It stems from an extreme incapacity for life and robs people of their essential humanity.' Courage was something altogether different, but its meaning was being utterly distorted at present. 'Wasn't Christ the most courageous of all? Yet he asked for water when he was thirsty. What a lot of harm Kant inflicted with his categorical imperative! Kant, harshness, Prussianism—the death of all spiritual life.'[78]

By now Hans had known Theodor Haecker for two or three months and attended meetings of the *Hochland* circle at which Haecker read aloud from his journal. The medical student must have imbibed the philosopher's criticisms of Kant and his native Prussia, as Haecker's journal entries are peppered with dismissive remarks about Prussian influence on the rest of Germany:

17th December 1939. The Germans too want to be a nation 'like others'. But without success. They can only be much worse than the others. They are the abhorrence of the whole world. The Prussian leaven has soured the whole nation and falsified its mission.[79]

2nd January 1940. In that part of the history of Christian Europe which is the history of Germany, this war might, and I hope will be the end of the hegemony of Prussia, which had in fact reached its height at the beginning of the war.[80]

20th February 1940. How childish it is to want to save Europe from destruction by changing governments and economic policies. Only a complete change of sentiment and conviction and of heart, a Μετανοειν[*metanoein*] can help us. And 'Prussia', certainly, is the great hindrance.[81]

1–2nd June 1940. German idealism, in Kant and Fichte, is a Prussian affair. Schelling belongs elsewhere; he was a spontaneously speculative mind and a gnostic. Hegel too was originally a great speculative mind, but as happened again and again with so many south German minds, he became infected with Prussianism and was corrupted. Prussian idealism took the heart of flesh and blood from the German and in its place gave him one of iron and paper. The German heart is now a material all of its own, of paper and iron, claptrap and act. That is really the 'inhuman' quality of the German as a Prussian product.

The association of duty and claptrap is what really dehumanises man. It is a characteristic Prussian–German discovery.[82]

Haecker thought that the German nation had apostatized on 30th January 1933. 'Since then, as a nation, we have been on the wrong road, on the wrong side. Yet even now there are few among us who suspect what it means'.[83] He was convinced that, 'The leadership of Germany today [...] is consciously anti-Christian—it hates Christ whom it does not name.'[84] Turning to Scripture to make sense of the evil around him, Haecker reckoned that 'there must always have been Nazis, or how would it be possible for the Bible to be so full of warnings against them'.[85] He wrote repeatedly of the redeeming element that would save the wayward nation: 'We shall need very many just people if there is to be anything left of our people that can still bear a "name" before God and the world.'[86] All this amounted to a 'spiritual resistance' which Hans respected and admired, for it chimed in with his own concerns and gave voice to them.

In contrast to her more cerebral brother, who attempted to analyse the war philosophically, Sophie was more inclined to digest events with her heart than with her head. She too felt buoyed up by her 'lovely days in the indescribably beautiful mountains', which were 'not just behind me but inside me as well, like all experiences'. Music, as well as nature, roused her feelings, helped her escape from all the unpleasantness around her, and raised her spirits. After listening to some music on the wireless, which she described to a friend as 'a marvelously lucid, majestic, joyous quartet, utterly unsentimental and wonderfully "hard"', she was reminded of her favourite line from Maritain, *Il faut avoir l'esprit dûr et le coeur tendre.*

> If anything can raise a storm in my stolid heart, it is music.
> And that is essential—a prerequisite for everything else.
> [...] I longed to breathe the same clear air as those who
> had created the piece. And that desire proved sufficient to
> distance me a little from the turmoil around me, with its
> resemblance to glutinous, hostile mush.[87]

On another occasion, after listening to Schubert's 'Unfinished Symphony', she wrote to Inge, 'I felt like a field that had been thoroughly ploughed, ready for sowing'. She told her elder sister that she had reflected a great deal about music; she thought it was essentially immaterial, more so than painting and sculpture, and she had even imagined music among the angels. 'But it is intended solely for human beings, for their senses, and it is wonderful that an assortment of vibrations can conjure up beauty and arouse such emotions. I found it easier to grasp how highly

God values us, even if it is only a stool [for us to climb on]'.[88] On Inge's suggestion, Otl asked Sophie to write a piece for *Windlicht* entitled 'Why do today's concerts have a flavour of their own?' At first Sophie felt the topic so extraneous to her current concerns that she could not make a start; but conversation at the skiing hut about spiritual hunger had steered her thoughts back to the question, above all when someone asked, Can music satisfy spiritual hunger? In the absence of the surviving number of *Windlicht*, her draft of the essay is the nearest thing we have to Sophie's answer.

Anticipating her university studies in philosophy, she had made a serious effort to read widely and deeply, as well as nurturing her writing style by keeping a diary and penning letters. A certain sophistication and maturity is evident in the way the twenty-year-old articulates her ideas on music.

> A word inexperienced by the soul is a dead word, and an emotion that fails to engender a thought is a futile emotion. But music softens the heart; by resolving its confusions and relaxing its tensions, it enables the mind, which has previously knocked in vain on the locked portals of the soul, to operate within it. Yes, music quietly and gently unlocks the doors of the soul. Now they are open! Now it is receptive. This is the ultimate effect that music has on me, that makes it one of life's necessities for me. [...]

> Listening to music properly entails complete self-abandonment to it, a detachment from all that still holds me captive, even now, and a childish heart devoid of sophistication and the quest for ulterior motives. The reward is a liberated heart, an uninhibited heart, a heart that has become more receptive to harmony and things harmonious, a heart that has opened its doors to the workings of the mind.[89]

Addressing the question that Otl had posed, she suggested that people who went to concerts did not really want to listen because their hearts were intent on so many little things they were reluctant to forgo; they closed their ears before the first note rang out. Why, then, did they go? She wondered if,

> people's sense of propriety demands possession of some ludicrous crumbs of knowledge about every subject. They go to concerts as casually as they show off a new hat. They graciously commend what thousands have commended before them—whatever may be commended with impunity—and coldly condemn anything new to them until it has gained universal approbation. They go home as blinkered as they came. [...] Precisely the same applies when music has given them aesthetic pleasure, however great. It fruitlessly fades away unless the whole heart has absorbed and subjected it to its beneficent, liberating power.

Her conclusion was that the 'flavour of today's concerts is the flat, insipid flavour of the bourgeois mentality'. Nevertheless, she could not discount the possibility that music might stir some individuals, and thus acquire meaning. As for herself, pondering the question had made her aware that 'we would starve to death if unsustained by God, and that not only one long thread attaches us to God through the creation, as I used to believe when I still did not know what a life is, especially a human life'.[90]

Sophie's article may not have been circulated as *Windlicht* was wound up after two or three issues, just at the point when Hans was about to involve his Munich friends in the enterprise. The decision to stop was taken after a brush with the Gestapo. In February 1942, when returning home from a visit to Hans in Munich, Inge ran into the Gestapo with the latest copy in her bag, and was taken to headquarters for interrogation. Fortunately the secretary taking notes was a former classmate of Inge's, and when the officer left the interrogation room, Inge asked the secretary if she could remove a page from the magazine in her bag. The secretary diplomatically left the room to make a phone call, allowing Inge to remove an article on Napoleon (probably by Hans) that was intended to be taken as a parallel to Hitler: the article ended with the words, 'Remember what happened to

Napoleon and take hope!'[91] Discovery of it could have led to a prison sentence for Inge, for circulating subversive literature, and to an investigation about its origins. As she summed up the episode, 'That was the end of this innocent creative endeavour to keep our communal lamp alight and shield it from the hurricane.'[92] Not all the articles in *Windlicht* could be styled 'innocent': there was one, possibly by Hans, which heavily criticised the general attitude of the Christian churches to Nazi attacks on religion and especially the failure to speak out against the T4 euthanasia programme. After the incident with Inge and the Gestapo, four months were to elapse before the first of the White Rose leaflets appeared.

That February the young Scholls suffered another blow when their father was arrested by the Gestapo after one of his secretaries reported him for having criticised the regime in his office. In a moment of exasperation Robert had told her, 'This Hitler is God's scourge on mankind', and added, 'If the war does not end soon, the Russians will be sitting in Berlin'.[93] He spent two weeks in jail pending trial before a Special Court in Stuttgart. No wonder that Sophie decided to abandon the idea of beginning her university studies while the war lasted. 'If one can't decide voluntarily to renounce the world's goods, including knowledge (of the sciences, anyway), and to love poverty, the war and years ahead will inflict a lot more pain on us', she explained to Lisa.[94] The war had already made her suffer a great deal, but she tried to regard her afflictions as secondary so as not to forget more important things.

She wrote in her diary:

> I have decided to pray in church every day, so that God won't forsake me. Although I don't yet know God and feel sure that my conception of him is utterly false, he will forgive me if I ask him. If I can love him with all my soul, I shall lose my distorted view of him.
>
> When I look at people around me and also at myself, I feel awed by humanity because God came down to earth for

its sake. Yet, this is what strikes me as most incomprehensible. Yes, what I least understand about God is his love. But what if I didn't know about it!

O Lord, I need so badly to pray, to ask.

Yes, one should always bear in mind, when dealing with other people, that God became man on their account. To think that one feels too good to condescend to many of them! What arrogance! Where on earth did I get it from?[95]

During her six months as a nursery school teacher Sophie realised that she had become quite experienced, though her work consumed all her evenings and left her exhausted. She took her girls walking every day and after a while found that they had grown fond of her, as she had of them. The arrival of spring had given her new hope and helped her to turn to God.

I believe that every little flower and stalk of grass has grown for my sake. I really don't think that is a delusion. Being as richly endowed as we are, should we not rejoice wholeheartedly in spite of all the sorrow we are forever bringing into this beautiful world? I even believe that every star in the sky is there for my sake. [...] Indeed, we have so much additional evidence of all-embracing love that we could really be the happiest of mortals.[96]

She was discharged from her duties on 1 April, which allowed her one month at home before she could finally join Hans at Munich University. Returning home was a joy for her, but also an upheaval as it meant finding her way back into her circle of friends after a solitary and self-reliant way of life.

On Easter Sunday 1942 Sophie rose at 3.45 am to attend the Easter vigil Mass at Söflingen church, the former abbey church of the Poor Clares on the outskirts of Ulm, but did not arrive in time to see the paschal candle being lit from sparks struck from stone.

Much as I need that kind of service—because it is a real service, not a lecture like you get in a Protestant church—I am sure it takes practice or habit to participate in it fully and not be distracted by the spectacle confronting you. If you have faith, that spectacle becomes a profound religious experience in itself. My trouble is this, however: I would like to kneel down because it genuinely accords with my feelings, but I am shy of people seeing, especially people I know. I would like to bow down before an image of God because you should not just experience such feelings but express them as well, but again I am too inhibited. The result is, I am never wholeheartedly involved—or have not been so far, at any rate.[97]

She was clearly at home in a Catholic liturgical setting and anxious to enter into the public prayer life of the Church. The question she faced was whether the Catholic Church was the true Church.

In his own way Hans, too, was gradually coming closer to the Catholic Church. He and Schurik had formed a book-reading group among their friends, and they chose *Le soulier de satin* (1929, *The satin slipper*), regarded by many as the masterpiece of the poet-dramatist Paul Claudel. Designed to be read rather than performed, as it was so difficult to stage (being 11 hours long and involving a vast synthesis of ideas and experiences), the play is an ambiguous and convoluted epic work that celebrates Catholic doctrine. The play is set on four continents during the late 16th and early 17th centuries and concerns the love of a Spanish *conquistador* for a married woman. The two are separated for many years but when they finally meet again, they do not consummate their great passion; instead, they sacrifice their earthly happiness in exchange for God's ultimate grace. It is a love story dominated by the ideas of sin and redemption, and the various characters frequently engage in a dialogue as though between heaven and earth. Taking the Psalms of the Vulgate as his model, Claudel dispenses with traditional metrics, replacing them with free-verse lines of indeterminate length and an intoxicating use of rhythm and imagery, the so-called *verset claudelien*. Using language and imagery that is often lush, mystical and exhilarating, Claudel uses scenes of passionate, obsessive human love to convey with great power God's infinite love for humanity.

Hans described the work 'as the greatest event in modern European literature'.[98] Though he reckoned Claudel's language did not compare with that of Goethe or Dante, he thought Claudel's ideas more profound and comprehensive than those of *Faust*. At the cultural level, Han's reading was a welcome tonic to counter the suffocating atmosphere around him. It was also an escape from the anxiety arising from an incident in his students' company when one of their National Socialist lecturers in medicine was jeered and the company was confined to barracks for four weeks and reported to High Command for mutiny. As the situation became increasingly tense, Hans observed how 'Informers of the most loathsome kind are sprouting in our ranks'. Everyone was interrogated separately, and Schurik was among the accused. 'I hadn't expected the majority to react as they have to the least little threat', Hans told his parents, 'but I have learned a lot'.[99] Hans thought the original incident (in which he played no part) a trifling matter, but in the protracted aftermath he was determined not to allow matters to 'divert us by so much as a finger's breadth from what really matters'.[100]

For some time, Hans had taken to writing in coded language in his correspondence, often using imagery or expressions that were familiar to the recipients. Into this mix he introduced spiritual thoughts, which helped to disguise his real message. 'The higher we climb', he told Lisl,

> the deeper the abysses, and our aim should be to harness the peaks and troughs of the spirit. Those who fail to see the precipice fall into it; but those without a light search in vain, and their weary eyes are useless to them. Our present task is to find the light on our way. It always has been and thus will remain so for all time.[101]

He was less guarded when not writing home, as there was little chance of his other letters being intercepted. Knowing that after his father's arrest the family mail was being monitored, Hans could not resist writing cheeky asides aimed at those reading his letters home: 'The mail here is very irregular. I really sympathise with the Gestapo, having to decipher all that different handwriting, some of which is highly illegible, but that is what they are paid to do, and duty is duty, gentlemen, isn't it!'[102]

Hans told Lisl about one splendid evening he had had at Muth's, where the host read from his own unpublished works to a small circle of friends that he, Hans, had convened. In particular, he liked Muth's essay 'On poverty' which was a response to his own and which was supposed to appear in the next number of *Windlicht.* Muth told Otl he was 'amazed that you manage to accomplish so much in such a thoroughly unintellectual environment', and pointed out that, as Otl had stirred a hornet's nest by raising the question of poverty, he should not be surprised to find complementary and contradictory replies. 'Arguments like these are a good thing, particularly if they benefit all concerned by prompting them to view the question increasingly, and even *exclusively*, in the light of the Gospel.'[103] That summer Muth hoped that *Windlicht* would include his translations of aphorisms of Gustav Thibon, a French philosopher and poet who drew heavily from St Thomas Aquinas and St John of the Cross;[104] it seems that he was unaware that *Windlicht* was no longer a going concern. Through Muth, Hans met Fedor Stepun, the Russo-German cultural philosopher and author who had been barred from teaching at Breslau University in 1937; he advised Hans that in the presence of so much evil, all that mattered was the preservation of fundamentals.

It was at one of Dr Schmorell's soirées that Schurik introduced Hans to his close school-friend Christoph Probst, a dependable and self-deprecating young man, who had married at the age of 21 and now had two children. Schurik had been the best man at Christoph's wedding, and when his son was baptised, Schurik was the boy's godfather. Christl, as he was known, was tall and noble in appearance. His father came from a wealthy family and had lived as a private scholar, specialising in eastern religions, but after divorcing had remarried a Jew; he despaired of the Nazi regime, and in 1936, after a bout of depression, committed suicide. He and Schurik sustained each other in adolescence, both having suffered the premature death of a parent, and became the best of friends. As Christl had attended various boarding schools, he had avoided the Hitler Youth and been spared the worst of Nazi propaganda; indeed, National Socialism had little appeal for him. Christl was knowledgeable about the stars, plants and minerals, and yet was also in search of answers to the deeper questions about life and shared Hans' response to books and intellectuals. He also shared his love of skiing and mountain climbing.

Christl was becoming increasingly agitated about the Nazi euthanasia programme and the escalation of violence towards the Jews, and like Hans was attracted to Catholicism, though wary of the institutional Church. His father-in-law Harald Dohrn had become a Catholic in 1933 and Dohrn's religious views were beginning to exert an influence on Christl. His sister Angelika testifies to his outrage on discovery of the euthanasia programme:

> He showed me that it was not given to any human being, in any circumstances, to make judgements that are reserved to God alone. No one, he said, can know what goes on in the soul of a mentally afflicted person. No one can know what secret inner ripening can come from suffering and sorrow. Every individual's life is priceless. We are all dear to God.[105]

Despite the certainty and serenity of his religious convictions, neither he nor his sister were baptised since their father, though baptised himself, had not brought them up to follow any faith, having decided to allow them to make up their own minds. Yet the madness Christl saw around him enabled him to see the truth at the centre of Christianity: God's love for the world.

> Love is the power of the world: it engenders all life; it protects us; it leads to blessedness; it is the power which has created the world. By contrast see how far hate is bringing us and has brought us: destruction, blood, and

death, and out of which there is nothing either lasting or good. And what has love engendered? Upon love cultures have been built: cathedrals have risen up. Love is the bond between all men. Love makes all happiness possible.[106]

During the Easter vacation, Hans served a hospital internship at St Ottilien am Ammersee, close to the Benedictine monastery he had visited the previous year, then another internship at Schrobenhausen, which was staffed by nuns from the teaching order founded by Mary Ward in the early seventeenth century. There he found so much work dealing with casualties from Russia as almost to 'make us forget about own little cares and concerns. The demands on us differ from those involved in opening other people's letters and prying around in them. I wonder if those gentlemen would be as courageous if they had to slit open dressing sodden with pus and stinking to high heaven?' he wrote home.[107] He was delighted at how well he got on with the nurses and the English order of nuns, who had had their boarding school closed down and been conscripted for hospital work. 'You would not believe how kind these nuns are', he told his parents. 'They read your every thought. They are like that because they draw on another source of strength, one that never fails.'[108] At the human level, the source of strength for families like the Scholls was the expectation that the Allied troops would soon be landing in the west; Hans made a coded reference to this in one of his letters home: 'We inhale the scent of spring in spite of everything. In spite of the west wind, with its renewed threat of cloud.'[109]

Hans described to Rose Nägele his state of mind: 'I doubt if I will ever be able to love anyone happily and contentedly. There is far too much afoot for me to keep a promise at this stage and say that my course is set for good and all.' After his four-week internship had brought him 'much joy and a little, albeit genuine, sorrow', he was now back in Munich and restless. 'My most faithful friend is Carl Muth. I am to be found at his house every day.'[110]

At the homes of Muth and other secret sympathisers, the students who came to form the White Rose gathered to listen, talk and read during the period December 1941 to February 1943. Here they were offered a spiritual foundation for opposing the regime. Besides Muth, the main other, older contributor was 63-year-old Theodor Haecker, philosopher and translator of Newman. Forbidden to publish or speak in public, Haecker's square features and bow tie did not reveal him as the original thinker he was: someone who had come to regard the Second World War as a war about truth, who believed that National Socialism was sent as a plague upon Europe, and that it sought to impose itself as an alternative religion to Christianity.[111] Being a close friend of Muth and visiting him once a fortnight, Haecker got to know Hans and his fellow student friends, most of whom were studying medicine and forced to combine their studies with active service at field stations in war zones. Sophie was not to join the discussions until she moved to Munich to start her degree, but she did coincide with some of the students on skiing or walking holidays.

On returning from the skiing trip in January 1942, Sophie had met Muth and seen his collection of photographs of the Shroud of Turin. Muth noticed how mesmerized she was by the image: 'I never saw anyone as engrossed as Sophie Scholl was today' in gazing at the picture, he commented. 'It made an impression on me. She seems to be a very thoughtful and serious girl.'[112] On receiving a picture of the Shroud from Hans, who had sent copies to all the Ulm circle, Sophie expressed her surprise that 'the picture does not cause more of a stir, considering that Christians cannot but regard it as the face of God, perceptible to their very own eyes. It is marvelous. And to think that it had to be technology, of all things, that brought the picture to light.'[113]

Sophie seems to have suffered bouts of depression, which were triggered whenever she heard news that the Nazis were moving one step closer to total victory. Raised as a Lutheran, she now found Protestant churches cold, whereas she was drawn to the buildings and doctrines of Catholics. God was becoming increasingly relevant to her freedom and she had now turned to prayer on a daily basis. For solace she began writing to Muth and was buoyed up by his replies. First Inge, then Hans and Sophie, and finally the whole family were introduced to Carl Muth. The Scholls took to caring for him when his health was poor, and sent him food parcels to supplement his ration card, and in his turn Muth took in friends of theirs who were visiting Munich. Muth told Inge that he was commending the Scholl family to the patronage of St Thomas More, but did not explain why; Inge merely commented on the coincidence that someone had given her a copy of the letters More wrote while in prison.[114] When Sophie arrived in Munich to begin her studies it was perfectly natural that she should spend her first month at Muth's house.

It was in Munich, the birthplace of National Socialism, not Ulm, the home of the Scholls, that the student movement that sought to oppose Hitler was beginning to form, and Sophie was soon to meet the key members. Munich styled itself as the 'Athens on the Isar', and it was here that the painter Wassily Kandinsky gave birth to a new art form. A decade later Hitler found his first supporters in Munich, having arrived as a penniless drifter and living in a dingy attic room, and it was here that he made his first political speeches. The city also gave its name to the agreement signed in 1938 that ceded Czechoslovakia to Germany, but the hope that it would bring 'peace in our time' proved to be misplaced, as it gave Hitler strategic command of central Europe without a single shot being fired. Known as the 'capital of the movement', Munich contained the 'shrine' of the men who had died in the Hitler putsch in 1923 and for that reason was the destination of a BDM march that Sophie had once taken part in.

Sophie's arrival in Munich meant missing her mother's birthday (5 May) so Hans wrote home with birthday greetings from the two of them.

> However great the turmoil prevailing today—so great that one often has no idea where to turn because of the multitude of things and happenings around me—elemental words of that kind loom up like beacons in a storm sea. That's my conception of poverty, that one should fearlessly

jettison old ballast at such moments and powerfully, freely, head for the One. But how rare such moments are, and how often and repeatedly man subsides into drab uncertainty, into the stream that flows in no direction, and demons are always busy grabbing him by the hair at every opportunity and dragging him down.

Sophie has arrived here safe and sound [...]

Fondest love and best wishes on your birthday,

Hans and Sophie[115]

Notes

1. Cardinal Faulhaber later explained, 'With the Concordat we were hanged; without it we were hanged, drawn and quartered' (M. Burleigh, *Sacred causes: the clash of religion and politics, from the Great War to the war on terror* (New York: HarperCollins, 2007), p. 175). Cardinal Pacelli told the British ambassador to the Holy See, 'I had to choose between an agreement and the virtual elimination of the Catholic Church in the Reich.' He felt that he was negotiating 'with the devil himself' (G. Lewy, *The Catholic Church and Nazi Germany* (New York: Da Capo Press, 2000), pp. 72–3, 101–4).

2. Hanser, *A noble treason*, p. 103.

3. *The White Rose*, p. 48. Like so many of her accounts, Inge Scholl does not provide a date for this story.

4. C. von Galen, sermon preached at St Lambert's, Münster on 13 July 1941.

5. C. von Galen, sermon preached at the Liebfrauenkirche, Münster on 20 July 1941.

6. C. von Galen, sermon preached at the Liebfrauenkirche, Münster on 20 July 1941.

7. C. von Galen, sermon preached at St Lambert's, Münster on 3 August 1941.

8. N. Stargardt, *The German war: a nation under arms, 1939–45* (London: Bodley Head, 2015), p. 151.

9. R. H. Sachs, *White Rose history* vol. i, *Coming together 1933–1942* (Utah: Exclamation, 2002), ch. 28, p. 1. Hans Hirzel, the son of a Lutheran minister in Ulm, was affiliated to the group, and he might have suggested

sending a copy to the Scholls.

[10] In 1940 Albert Einstein told *Time* magazine: 'Only the [Catholic] Church stood squarely across the path of Hitler's campaign for suppressing the truth. I had never any special interest in the Church before, but now I feel a great admiration because the Church alone has had the courage and persistence to stand for intellectual truth and moral freedom. I am forced thus to confess, that what I once despised, I now praise unreservedly' (quoted in Burleigh's *Sacred causes*, p. 213).

[11] I. Scholl, *The White Rose*, p. 20.

[12] A leading question would have been along the lines, 'Whether human law binds a man in conscience?' St Thomas answers: 'Laws may be unjust in two ways: first, by being contrary to human good, either in respect of the end, as when an authority imposes on his subjects burdensome laws, conducive, not to the common good, but rather to his own cupidity or vainglory; or in respect of the author, as when a man makes a law that goes beyond the power committed to him; or in respect of the form, as when burdens are imposed unequally on the community, although with a view to the common good. The like are acts of violence [...] such laws do not bind in conscience [...] Secondly, laws may be unjust through being opposed to the Divine good: such are the laws of tyrants inducing to idolatry' (*Summa theologiae* II.I qn. 96, art. 4).

[13] Memorandum, Inge Scholl, quoted in *Heart of the White Rose*, pp. 163–4.

[14] In 1934 the Catholic press could number 435 periodicals, but by 1943 there were only seven (L. Faulkner Rossi, *Wehrmacht priests: Catholicism and the Nazi war of annihilation* (Cambridge Massachusetts: Harvard University Press, 2005), p. 41).

[15] Hans to Rose Nägele, 8 August 1941, *Heart of the White Rose*, pp. 153–4.

[16] Hans to Rose Nägele, 12 August 1941, *Heart of the White Rose*, p. 154–5. Hans quotes from Virgil, *Georgics*, I, 145, and from Genesis 3:19.

[17] Hans to Rose Nägele, 19 August 1941, *Heart of the White Rose*, p. 157.

[18] Quoted in Hanser, *A noble treason*, p. 112.

[19] As a German novelist and poet, Carossa is known for his 'inner emigration' during the Nazi era.

[20] Hans to his mother, 13 August 1941, *Heart of the White Rose*, p. 156.

[21] Every German soldier was obliged to abjure, 'I swear before God this holy oath to give my unconditional obedience to Adolf Hitler, Führer of the German Reich and the German people, supreme commander of the *Wehrmacht*, and I pledge my word as a brave soldier to observe this oath always, even at the peril of my life.' The problem for those like Schurik was in swearing absolute loyalty not to a nation but to a person, and one whose motives were questionable (Hanser, *A noble treason*, p. 114).

22 Among those who lost their lives for refusing to take the oath of loyalty to Hitler was the Italian office-worker Josef Mayr-Nusser, who lived near the German border. After Italy joined the Allied forces, Mayr-Nusser was conscripted into the SS in September 1944, but refused to take the oath. For this he sentenced to death; he died on the way to Dachau. Mayr-Nusser was beatified by the Catholic Church on 18 March 2017.

23 Hans offered to send Otl books by the Russian philosopher Nikolai Berdyaev, who had abandoned Marxism for mystical Christianity and left Moscow for Paris via Berlin. In one of these books Hans had inscribed the words 'All they that take the sword shall perish with the sword. [Matthew 26: 52] In the wartime year of 1941' (*Heart of the White Rose*, p. 299). Berdyaev emphasised the creative potential of man who, by collaborating with his Creator, could help to mend the world and bring about a healing and unification of the heart and mind.

24 *Journal in the night*, no. 583, p. 173.

25 Hanser, *A noble treason*, pp. 124–5.

26 Quoted in Hanser, *A noble treason*, p. 127.

27 Bergengruen, a neighbour of Carl Muth, had been received into the Catholic Church in 1936. With the help of his wife, he was to make his own copies of the White Rose leaflets and distribute them by bike at night in Munich. Hans Scholl wrote about him: 'Bergengruen, whom I know personally, I value above all other living German authors' (Hans to Rose Nägele, 5 January 1943, Heart of the *White Rose*, p. 270).

28 From the 1920s, Lützeler wrote on Christian art and, as a regular contributor to *Hochland*, was regarded as one of its most important contributors and a representative in Germany of *Renouveau Catholique*.

29 J. Klapper, *Nonconformist writing in Nazi Germany: the literature of inner immigration* ((New York: Camden House, 2015), p. 221. According to Klapper, Gertrude le Fort nurtured the idea of a Christian Reich formed on a Christian social order, which proved popular with the adherents of *Renouveau Catholique*, though in 'dangerous ideological proximity' to Nazi notions of the Reich (p. 221).

30 I. Jens, editorial comment in H. & S. Scholl, *Heart of the White Rose*, p. 161.

31 Carl Muth to Otl Aicher, 24 October 1941, *Heart of the White Rose*, p. 302, n154.

32 Carl Muth to Otl Aicher, 19 December 1941, *Heart of the White Rose*, p. 302, n154.

33 *Heart of the White Rose*, p. 298, n145.

34 Hans to Otl Aicher, 24 October 1941, *Heart of the White Rose*, p. 162. Hans told Otl he was deeply impressed by the phrase 'The pilgrim of the

absolute'. This was the title of an essay about Bloy (taken from the title of the sixth volume of Bloy's diaries) in a collection (in German) with pieces on Péguy, Gide, Chesterton, Dostoyevsky, Soloviev and Berdyaev (*ibid.*, p. 298, n146).

35 Hans, 'On poverty', essay in *Windlicht*, n.d. [November 1941], *Heart of the White Rose*, pp. 164–5.

36 Hans to Rose Nägele, 28 October 1941, *Heart of the White Rose*, p. 163.

37 J. P. Stern, 'The White Rose', *Die Weisse Rose: student resistance to National Socialism, 1942–1943: Forschungsergebnisse und Erfahrungsberichte: a Nottingham Symposium*, ed. H. Siefken (Nottingham: University of Nottingham, 1991), p. 15.

38 Hans to Otl Aicher, 23 November 1941, *Heart of the White Rose*, p. 166.

39 It is possible that Muth had drawn his attention to the volume as an article about the Shroud had appeared in *Eichstätter Klerusblatt* (10 September 1941) which defended its authenticity.

40 Claudel to Gérard-Cordonnier, 16 August 1935, quoted in *Toi qui es-tu?* (Paris, 1936), pp. 11–15.

41 Hans' article on the Turin Shroud in *Windlicht*, reproduced in *Heart of the White Rose*, pp. 167–9.

42 See the editorial commentary of Inge Jens, *Heart of the White Rose*, pp. 170–1.

43 Sophie's diary, autumn 1941, *Heart of the White Rose*, p. 171; quoted in Hanser, *A noble treason*, p. 97.

44 Sophie's diary, 1 November 1941, *Heart of the White Rose*, pp. 171–2.

45 Sophie to Hans, 20 November 1941, *Heart of the White Rose*, p. 176.

46 Sophie's diary, 4 November 1941, *Heart of the White Rose*, p. 173. It should be remembered that kneeling down was not an easy thing for someone like Sophie, who was brought up as a Protestant.

47 Sophie's diary, 10 November 1941, *Heart of the White Rose*, pp. 174–5.

48 Sophie to Inge (draft), n.d. [November/December 1941], *Heart of the White Rose*, pp. 176–7.

49 Sophie's diary, 12 December 1941, *Heart of the White Rose*, pp. 178–9.

50 'Freiburg Cathedral which I have often visited in recent months, is really beautiful. It makes me warm inside to be there' (Sophie to Lisa Remppis, 12 December 1941, *Heart of the White Rose*, p. 179).

51 Sophie's diary, 4 November 1941, *Heart of the White Rose*, p. 173.

52 Sophie's diary, 5 November 1941, *Heart of the White Rose*, p. 173.

53 Sophie's diary, 6 November 1941, *Heart of the White Rose*, p. 174.

54 The cover picture she sent Otl is reproduced in H. Vinke, *The short life of Sophie Scholl* (New York: Harper and Row, 1984), p. 33.

[55]　Sophie to Otl Aicher, 10 December 1941, *Heart of the White Rose*, p. 178.

[56]　Sophie's diary, 12 December 1941, *Heart of the White Rose*, p. 178.

[57]　Sophie to Lisa Remppis, 12 December 1941, *Heart of the White Rose*, p. 179.

[58]　Sophie to Lisa Remppis, 12 December 1941, *Heart of the White Rose*, p. 179.

[59]　Sophie to Lisa Remppis, 12 December 1941, *Heart of the White Rose*, pp. 179–80.

[60]　This was the trilogy of novels which won the Nobel Prize for Sigrid Undset in 1928; she fled to the United States in 1940, when the German army invaded Norway, and returned in 1945. The book was banned and, according to Hans, very hard to obtain.

[61]　Sophie to Lisa Remppis, 12 December 1941, *Heart of the White Rose*, p. 180.

[62]　Sophie bought two volumes of Newman's sermons, translated into German by the Jewish scholar Max Hofmann.

[63]　Quoted in Fenlon, 'From the White Star to the Red Rose', p. 55. Dermot Fenlon attributes this discovery to Jakob Knab, who found it in the autobiography of Susanne Hirzel. 'Sofie hingegen las unaufhörlich und reichte mir eines Tages ein Buch von Kardinal *Newman*. Den *kennst du nicht* ? Da steht dir eine herrliche Welt bevor!' (Hirzel, *Vom Ja zum Nein*, p. 131).

[64]　Justice Ministry circular, 28 October 1941, quoted in McDonough, *Sophie Scholl*, p. 83.

[65]　Hans to Rose Nägele, 7 December 1941, *Heart of the White Rose*, p. 183.

[66]　Hans to his mother, 6 December 1941, *Heart of the White Rose*, p. 182.

[67]　Hans to Rose Nägele, 20 December 1941, *Heart of the White Rose*, p. 305, n175. Inge Jens asserts that Muth and Haecker were primarily responsible for this conversion.

[68]　'On poverty', n.d. [November 1941], *Windlicht*, reproduced *Heart of the White Rose*, pp. 164–5.

[69]　In the first volume of Winston Churchill's history of World War II, Churchill describes Hitler's moment of triumph when he achieved total power in 1933: 'He had called from the depths of defeat the dark and savage furies latent in the most numerous, most serviceable, ruthless, contradictory and ill-starred race in Europe. He had conjured up the fearful idol of an all-devouring Moloch of which he was the priest and incarnation' (*The gathering storm* (Boston: Houghton Mifflin, 1948), p. 64).

[70]　Hans to Carl Muth, 22 December 1941, *Heart of the White Rose*, pp. 184–5. Mention of scales falling from the eyes is an allusion to St Paul in Acts 9:18.

71   I. Scholl, 'Our days at the skiing lodge', *Windlicht*, reproduced in *Heart of the White Rose*, pp. 305–6.

72   I. Scholl, 'Our days at the skiing lodge', *Windlicht*, reproduced in *Heart of the White Rose*, p. 306.

73   I. Scholl, 'Our days at the skiing lodge', *Windlicht*, reproduced in *Heart of the White Rose*, p. 307.

74   I. Scholl, 'Our days at the skiing lodge', *Windlicht*, reproduced in *Heart of the White Rose*, p. 307.

75   T. Lafrenz, 'New Year's Eve', *Windlicht*, reproduced in *Heart of the White Rose*, p. 309. The *Hymns to the night* are a romantic interpretation of life and death, the threshold of which is symbolised by the night. Novalis was the *nom de plume* of Friedrich von Hardenberg.

76   Hans to Lisl, 6 January 1942, *Heart of the White Rose*, p. 186.

77   Hans to Rose Nägele, 25 January 1942, *Heart of the White Rose*, p. 187.

78   Hans to Rose Nägele, 25 January 1942, *Heart of the White Rose*, pp. 187–8. Hans would expand on this later in the year when he served on the Russian front (see his diary entry, 22 August 1942, quoted on pp. 179–80 of this book).

79   *Journal in the night*, no. 49, p. 11.

80   *Journal in the night*, no. 74, p. 18.

81   *Journal in the night*, no. 99, p. 23.

82   *Journal in the night*, nos 275 & 276, p. 72.

83   January 1941, *Journal in the night*, no. 486, p. 142.

84   12 May 1940, *Journal in the night*, no. 217, p. 53.

85   January 1941, *Journal in the night*, no. 501, p. 150.

86   11 September 1941, *Journal in the night*, no. 580, p. 173.

87   Sophie to Lisa Remppis, 14 January 1942, *Heart of the White Rose*, p. 189.

88   I. Scholl, 'Our days at the skiing lodge' (quoting from two letters from Sophie), *Windlicht*, reproduced in *Heart of the White Rose*, p. 307.

89   S. Scholl, draft article for *Windlicht*, n.d. [January 1942], *Heart of the White Rose*, p. 190.

90   S. Scholl, draft article for *Windlicht*, n.d. [January 1942], *Heart of the White Rose*, p. 191.

91   Hanser, *A noble treason*, p. 102.

92   I. Scholl, memorandum, *Heart of the White Rose*, p. 300, n149.

93   Hanser, *A noble treason*, p. 180.

94   Sophie to Lisa Remppis, 12 February 1942, *Heart of the White Rose*, p. 192.

95   Sophie's diary, 12 February 1942, *Heart of the White Rose*, pp. 191–2.

96   Sophie to Lisa Remppis, n.d. [March 1942], *Heart of the White Rose*, p. 192.

[97] Sophie to Lisa Remppis, 5 April 1942, *Heart of the White Rose*, pp. 193–4.

[98] Hans to Lisl, 10 February 1942, *Heart of the White Rose*, p. 195.

[99] Hans to his parents and Inge, 12 February 1942, *Heart of the White Rose*, p. 196.

[100] Hans to Lisl, 10 February 1942, *Heart of the White Rose*, p. 195.

[101] Hans to Lisl, 28 February 1942, *Heart of the White Rose*, p. 197.

[102] Hans to his parents and Inge, 18 March 1942, *Heart of the White Rose*, p. 198.

[103] Carl Muth to Otl Aicher, 18 February 1942, *Heart of the White Rose*, p. 310, n199.

[104] Carl Muth to Otl Aicher, 18 July 1942, *Heart of the White Rose*, p. 310, n199.

[105] Quoted in Hanser, *A noble treason*, pp. 117–18.

[106] Christl Probst to Dieter Sasse, 13 December 1942 (J. Donohoe, *Hitler's conservative opponents in Bavaria, 1930–45* (Leiden: Brill, 1961), p. 159). In the same letter Christl wrote to his stepbrother about the supernatural meaning of suffering. For the ecstatic vision he experienced that Christmas, see J. Knab, 'Die innere Vollendung der Person', *Die Stärkeren im Geiste: Zum christlichen Wilderstand der Weißen Rose*, ed. D. Bald & J. Knab (Essen: Klartext, 2012), p. 145.

[107] Hans to his parents and Inge, 18 March 1942, *Heart of the White Rose*, p. 199.

[108] Hans to his parents, 29 March 1942, *Heart of the White Rose*, p. 199.

[109] Hans to his parents and Inge, 18 March 1942, *Heart of the White Rose*, p. 199. The interpretation of this coded reference I owe to Inge Jens, the editor of the Scholl letters.

[110] Hans to Rose Nägele, 13 April 1942, *Heart of the White Rose*, p. 200.

[111] See Haecker's journal entry, 12 May 1940, *Journal in the night*, p. 53.

[112] Carl Muth to Otl Aicher, 2 January 1942, *Heart of the White Rose*, p. 303.

[113] Sophie to Hans, 20 January 1942, *Heart of the White Rose*, p. 308.

[114] I. Aicher-Scholl, *Verbindung zu Theodor Haecker* (unpubl., n.d.), p. 1, quoted in Sachs, *White Rose history* vol. ii, *Journey to freedom 1942–1945* (Utah: Exclamation, 2005), ch. 2, p. 10.

[115] Hans (and Sophie) to Magdalena Scholl, 4 May 1942, *Heart of the White Rose*, p. 201. Hans headed the letter with a quotation from 'that fervent seeker of God, St Augustine'.

5 THE WHITE ROSE LEAFLETS: SUMMER 1942

O N 1 MAY 1942 Sophie travelled by train to Munich to begin her university studies in philosophy and natural science. She was met at the station by Hans and his former girlfriend, Traute Lafrenz, and taken to Muth's house in the south of Munich, where she was to stay before a room became available in the city centre a month later. That first night Hans and a few close friends marked Sophie's arrival with a celebration, and either that night or the day after Hans told her about the plan that he and Schurik had been hatching over the previous months. The next day Sophie met up with Fritz Hartnagel, and asked him to use his influence as an officer to requisition a duplicating machine. Fritz asked why she wanted one and, when she admitted it was for reproducing subversive material, he told her, 'Do you realise that this could cost you your head?' As Sophie replied, 'Yes, I understand that', Fritz decided he would only lend her money.[1] It was a tense meeting—'unpleasant' was Fritz's description—and when he wrote a few days later to say that he felt like a fraud in the army, Sophie told him of her own lack of peace. All Fritz could do was to reply, 'If only I could do something to give you a peaceable and full heart. But prayer is my only strength.'[2]

Sophie had brought with her a birthday cake and two bottles of wine, courtesy of her mother, and on the evening of Saturday 9 May she marked her twenty-first birthday with several close friends of Hans, including Schurik and Christl. During the birthday party an impromptu game was played in which poems were read out and everyone had to guess who the author was. The poem Hans chose was just six stanzas long and it baffled everyone. It was about a thief who sets off to find things to steal and soon finds better booty, a nation with its banner torn and its people made dull and stupid by material deprivation and spiritual emptiness. The predator-turned-prophet is a master of deceit: 'Mounting the rubbish heap around him/He spews his message on the world', and 'Where before one liar raged/Thousands were soon thus engaged'. Soon the social order is overthrown: 'The good are reduced to none, or few/The wicked are a mighty crew!' Eventually the tyrant is overthrown and later generations look back on the reign as they once did on the Black Death; in memory of it, children set fire to straw effigies: 'To burn joy from out of sorrow/And make light of ancient woe.'[3]

There was a long pause after Hans finished reading; no-one could guess the author. Christl thought the verses were so timely that they might have been written by someone alive; Schurik suggested that they be reproduced with a dedication from Hitler and dropped from a plane over Germany. Then someone asked if Hans was the author. When Hans revealed that the verses were by the nineteenth-century Swiss poet Gottfried Keller,[4] everyone was heartened that a poem which paralleled current events so accurately should contain a positive outcome. The students retired to the Englischer Garten, the sprawling public park along the banks of the River Isar, and sang to the accompaniment of Schurik on his balalaika, while Hans played on the guitar.

While Sophie listened to all their talk of hospital and first-aid work at field stations, Hans commented, 'there's nothing more pleasant than going from bed to bed and having the sense of holding in your hands a life in peril. There are moments when I'm absolutely happy'. But someone asked if it was not preposterous that while *they* were studying how to heal mankind, 'the state every day sends countless young people to their death? [...] Until one day the war is over and all nations point to us and say that we accepted this government without resisting?'[5] Strong words such as these could not be uttered in public, only among close, trusted friends.

Munich University was the largest university in Germany and like the rest had been purged under the official policy of *Gleich-schaltung*, the enforced conformity that brought public institutions into line with Nazi ideology. The Minister for Culture in Bavaria, Hans Schemm, had told the Munich professors that their job was not to determine whether something was true or not, but whether it was in the spirit of National Socialism. He had been the principal speaker at the solemn torchlight procession in May 1933, led by professors and students in academic robes, which had made its way to the big bonfire in Königsplatz, near the 'Brown House', the national headquarters of the Nazi Party, where they set light to disapproved books, symbolising the purging of German culture from corruption.

During the purge of the universities more than 1,200 intellectuals were removed from institutions of higher education, mainly Jews and liberals, among whom were Nobel Prize winners and other men and women of fame; some influential professors left the country, while others went to ground, but the majority simply went along with the new system, or in some cases fully approved of Hitler, as with the poet Gottfried Benn and the philosopher Martin Heidegger. This state of affairs has been described as *la trahison des clercs* after the title of a novel published in 1927 by the French philosopher and novelist Julien Benda, and translated into English as *The betrayal of the intellectuals.* Just like the students who dared to be different, academics who struggled to survive in the toxic atmosphere needed all the support they could muster among themselves, as well as among other intellectuals outside the university. When dissident students and academics came together, there was an extra dimension to the mutual support they could lend each another.

The student body was largely Nazi in attitude and outlook, and Nazi policies were championed in both classroom and corridor. All student groups were strictly supervised by young zealots from the National Socialist Student Union who monitored the words and actions of students and professors alike. The ideological police were ever on the lookout for signs of defeatism, subversion or irreverence for authority.[6] Despite the enthusiasm for National Socialism among students, the regime had deep reservations about the existence of places where books were read and ideas discussed. Indeed, though the authorities attempted to reduce universities from seats of learning to ideological factories, it proved impossible to stifle the passion for knowledge. On entering this world in May 1942 Sophie found that it was possible, by careful choice of subjects, to avoid courses in 'racial hygiene' and to outwit the system. Both philosophy and science contained pockets of comparative latitude, and there were other subjects that offered a haven and were receptive to dissidents.

One such was Greek philosophy with the lecturer Fritz Joachim von Rintelen. A master of the veiled allusion and barbed reference, he was able to use the Greek past to score points against the Nazi present. He attracted many who were uninterested in philosophy but eager to catch his references and decipher the coded messages they contained. Eventually he was reported to the authorities and one day, without warning, he failed to appear in the lecture-room. The authorities assumed that the class would disperse without a fuss, but those present decided to turn up for his next lecture and meanwhile to investigate his absence. Jürgen Wittenstein, a friend of Hans, kept a record of what happened. As no explanation was given for von Rintelen's disappearance, Jürgen and others went to the chancellor's office to ask for an explanation. The chancellor of the University was Dr Walther Wüst, an SS colonel and an authority on 'Aryan culture'. Such a reaction was unheard of, and Wüst was so taken aback that he merely withdrew without a word and locked himself in his inner office. A group of around sixty students then marched round to von Rintelen's house, only to find he had disappeared. As the demonstration of student displeasure went no further, the authorities refrained from confronting the students and let the matter fizzle out of its own accord. (Von Rintelen had been sacked, but no more serious action was taken against him; he left Munich for Deidesheim, where he worked as a private tutor until the end of the war.)

There were strong hints that women would be forced to make up the toll on human life by means of a systematic population policy. At a large student assembly in Munich in January 1943 *Gauleiter* Giesler would proclaim that it was better for women to 'present the Führer with a child' than to hang on at university. It was not a message that Sophie would have welcomed. Though girls at Munich University were outnumbered ten to one at the time, Sophie soon began to make friends with other girls, first with Traute then with Ulla Claudius and Katharina Schüddekopf. Ulla was one of Traute's friends and the daughter of a National Socialist poet. Katharina had studied in Berlin and volunteered as a translator for the Reich propaganda department in Vienna; though older than most of the other students, she was a merry companion. Her father was an enthusiastic Nazi, but Katharina sided with her mother, who was opposed to National Socialism and remained a fervent Catholic. Katharina had moved to Munich in order to pursue her studies in music, philosophy and French, and so had common interests with Sophie.

The friendships that Sophie and Hans formed were inter-twined, and were all the closer for being forged in fraught times. Their friends were not a group aligned merely by political views but by wider interests, for they were seeking an alternative to Nazi ideology through a shared interest in art, literature, philosophy, theology and nature. Their shared activities, such as skiing trips, reading parties, concerts and eating and drinking together, resulted in intense personal relationships; most of their close friends were drawn into the White Rose circle, some remaining on the periphery, others taking a fuller part.

For Hans, a number of his friendships took a romantic turn, and he had a succession of girlfriends over the years, some of whom were connected with the White Rose. His first romance, in 1938, had been with Sophie's friend Lisa Remppis, but did not last long. After another brief attachment, with Ute Borchers in the spring of 1940, Hans befriended Rose Nägele and kept up a steady correspondence with her over the next three years; to judge from his letters, it seems that Rose was well-acquainted with Hans' views on National Socialism, but not involved with any of his resistance activities. When Traute arrived in Munich in May 1941 she soon fell in love with Hans, but that autumn she put an end to their close relationship, because in her view he was too demanding and too possessive. However, they remained good friends, and Traute was to take a leading role in the White Rose.

Hans' next girlfriend was Traute's good friend, Ulla, and in December 1941, Hans invited both Traute and Ulla to the skiing trip in the mountains, much to Traute's discomfort. Ulla continued to meet up with Hans until she left Munich for Hamburg in June 1942, though once Sophie had arrived in Munich (in May 1942), Hans began to spend much of his free time with her instead. Hans' last girlfriend was to be Gisela Schertling, Sophie's friend from her National Service assignment in Krauchenwies. Hans had taken a liking to her when they coincided in Ulm one weekend in August 1941, and when Gisela arrived in Munich in January 1943, he fell for her again. It was not an easy relationship, as Gisela was deliberately excluded from White Rose affairs, on account of her political sympathies. Hans could certainly turn on the charm, both in person and in his correspondence, and did not worry about having a close relationship with two girls at the same time. Sophie was occasionally uncomfortable with Hans' behaviour, but there is no record of her telling him as much. What is clear is that Hans enjoyed female company and, like his fellow soldiers, sought it as a relief from army life.

For the duration of May 1942, Sophie lodged with Professor Muth and during her stay was introduced to members of the *Hochland* circle and other intellectual dissidents, including Muth's close friend Theodor Haecker. As a young man Haecker had wanted to become an actor, but after a long illness, due to an infection of the sinus, he had an operation which left his face badly disfigured. Those who met him for the first time found his reserve and silences disconcerting, and could be unnerved by his penetrating blue eyes which radiated an unusual power, but they warmed to him when they perceived the subtlety of mind and quick sympathy that lay behind the emotionless face. It has been commented that, 'His silence and reserve were in fact the only surface which he presented to the curious, and he was so lacking in affectation or eccentricity that the most that could be said of him was that he made nothing of himself.'[7] He was not someone who would have called attention to himself; he rarely travelled, and took no part in the learned and literary life that had characterized Germany before 1933—what had now became part of the 'hidden' Germany. Nevertheless, he was a deep thinker who strove to make sense of events around him in the light of Christian revelation. And as Sophie got to know Haecker better, she learnt more about Newman.

On 20 May 1942 Sophie and Fritz Hartnagel met in Munich (in fact for the last time) and she gave him a farewell present of, among other things, two volumes of sermons by John Henry Newman (edited by Matthias Laros and translated by Max Hofmann). Evidently she had read enough of Newman by this stage to enthuse about him and want to share her love of his writings with Fritz. Within ten days First Lieutenant Hartnagel had arrived in Mariupol on the Sea of Azov in the Ukraine where he served as a company commander in the offensive between Kursk and Taganrog that began in June. He heeded Sophie's advice and each day made time to read for an hour and to write to her, even though none of her letters reached the front.[8]

In the only letter to survive from her first month at university (perhaps reflecting how busy she was), Sophie gives a glimpse of her new lifestyle. 'There is something new for me to digest here every day', she relates.[9] The previous day she had had tea with Muth and the cultural commentator Sigismund von Radecki, who had been received into the Catholic Church in 1931, after having read Newman's *Essay on the development of Christian doctrine*. Born in Riga and educated at St Petersburg, von Radecki had worked for ten years as an engineer before turning his hand to drawing and acting, then taking up a career as a freelance writer. He was a close friend of Haecker and effectively became one of the sponsors of the White Rose students, regularly meeting up with them. Hans had met him for the first time on 24 April at Muth's house and had already read some of his works.[10]

After tea with Muth and von Radecki, Sophie paid a visit to a friend of Muth's, someone her circle called 'the philosopher'. This was Josef Furtmeier, a former Communist who had resigned from the civil service when the National Socialists took over and taken up legal work instead. He was well-read and erudite, especially in history and archaeology, and influential with the young students because of the way in which he talked about making hard choices. After three intense hours of conversation with Furtmeier, Sophie felt exhausted, though grateful for the opportunity to learn. 'To be honest, I rather hanker to be on my own', she told her friend Lisa, 'because I have an urge to act on what has so far existed within me merely as an idea—as what I perceive to be right. [...] Hans is being a good brother to me. I am growing fonder and fonder of him.'[11]

Besides exerting a marked influence over the young minds, Furtmeier was the link to Manfred Eickemeyer, the architect who had brought the students information about the German atrocities in Poland, and who allowed his studio to be used for discussions, readings and—eventually—the printing of leaflets in the cellar. Furtmeier himself had been introduced to the students by the theologian and sociologist Alfred von Martin, who had invited Hans to his house in the spring.[12] As a Protestant, von Martin had helped to found an ecumenical high-church federation which sought to bring Catholics and Lutherans together in order to exchange ideas about their respective liturgies. He had acted as editor of their journal *Una Sancta*, but the journal was short-lived as in 1927 Catholics were banned from participating. In response von Martin set up an ecumenical task force, but in 1932 this was disbanded. Rather than collude with the regime, von Martin resigned his prestigious teaching position at Göttingen in 1933, as the university had become a Nazi stronghold. In 1940 he decided to become a Catholic along with others from the ecumenical federation, and he asked Rome if he could become a

Byzantine-rite Catholic, that is, a member of the Eastern Catholic Church; Rome replied in the negative as it feared such a move would invalidate the Concordat with Hitler, so eventually von Martin became a Catholic in the Latin rite.

On Sunday 31 May, Sophie and Hans paid a visit to a friend of Muth called Fr Max Schwartz, 'a highly original, most impressive parish priest',[13] who had been banished by the regime for disciplinary reasons to a little village in the Bavarian Forest. Part of the reason for their visit was to procure food supplies for Muth, who was in poor health and staying with Haecker. Sophie also asked her parents to send Muth some white flour and trout.

The next day, Hans moved into Traute's old apartment, and Sophie moved from Muth's house into the one vacated by Hans on Mandl Strasse, close to the central University buildings. A week later Sophie wrote home with news of other encounters. She had been one of twenty students invited by Hans to an evening event hosted by the pianist and singer Dr Gertrud Mertens. The star of the evening was von Radecki, who, at Hans' request, read from his essays, poems and translations; he did so brilliantly and entranced the students with his sweeping gestures and by acting out what he read. 'How we laughed!'[14] Sophie comments. Von Radecki already exerted an influence on Hans and Otl, and now Sophie was to come within the orbit of the man whose talents as a champion alpine skier, among other things, made him an attractive personality to the young.

The evening, however, was chiefly notable for something else that happened. The host read a paper on the theme of religious renewal, but the students present, mostly medics, were unhappy with the abstract nature of the discussion and steered the conversation towards more immediate matters. When Christl suggested that the French had a healthier notion of 'homeland' than the Germans, an animated political discussion ensued, with Christl and Hans arguing against Christl's former schoolteacher Heinrich Ellermann, while Kurt Huber, a 48-year-old professor of philosophy at Munich University, attempted to arbitrate. The confrontation delighted newcomers such as Hubert Furtwängler and Katharina Schüddekopf, but Dr Mertens was deeply uncomfortable with it.

Undoubtedly, what fuelled the animated exchange of opinions was the air raid on Cologne the previous night but one. This was the first of the famous 'thousand-bomber raids' and the destruction was prodigious, with nearly 50,000 people bombed out of their houses. People began to fear that Germany might after all lose the war, and the students desperately wanted to discuss the outcome. In attempting to reconcile the arguments of the opponents, Huber said, 'Something *has* to be done, and the sooner the better'. Hans responded, 'Yes, action *is* necessary. One cannot hold back indefinitely',[15] and the students moved the focus of discussion onto the need to *do* something rather than just weathering out the storm. The conversation touched on the question of whether some form of overt resistance was called for. Afterwards, Sophie and four others continued the discussion with von Radecki in her room until 5 am.

The evening was also notable for being the occasion when Hans and Kurt Huber first met. Huber lectured at Munich University on Gottfried Wilhelm Leibniz and his 'theodicy', Leibniz's term for his philosophical explanation of God's justice in which he shows how a good God can permit evil: his arguments had made a great impact at a time when the Christian students could see that all around them man was trampling on the divine order and seeking to eliminate God. Following Leibniz, Huber argued that everything was arranged at creation in order to work for the ultimate good, despite many appearances to the contrary, such as the horrors and injustices around them. It might seem incredible that Huber could get away with this, but it needs to be remembered that, unlike schoolteachers, German lecturers and professors were not sent on indoctrination courses and that, after the earlier purges, most of them were left alone, provided they were not Jewish, Communist, or openly anti-Nazi. Some academics read out banned literature in their lectures or else criticized the regime for its over-simplification of complex ideas and its anti-intellectual stance, though they had to be on their guard, since most students had passed through the Hitler Youth and were, in general, more committed to the Nazi cause than themselves.

Despite being lame, prone to tremors, and having a speech impediment, due to contracting rickets and diphtheria in childhood, Huber was a highly popular lecturer. His style was dry, but his shy charm took the edge off his formality, and he occasionally joked. He spoke with clarity of thought, as well as passion, and punctuated his lectures with satirical remarks and provocative insights which hinted at his hostility to Nazi ideology; he even managed to refer to Jewish philosophers such as Spinoza. It was because he was a master of coded language that he was able to get away with so much and to bamboozle the thought-police. Less guarded and occasionally outspoken when he was among his fellow lecturers, Huber would eventually be arrested and stand before the People's Court for taking part in the White Rose activities.

Huber had become the leading expert on German folk music, but his academic career was ruined when he refused to compose marching songs for the regime or become a musical propagandist for it; he even contradicted a superior who insisted that the major scale was the only natural scale for the Teutonic people! Huber was one of those academics who take an interest in young people and their problems, despite the disparity of age, and he happily joined students who wished to carry on discussing matters raised in his lectures. He lived so close to poverty that in desperation his wife secretly enrolled him as a member of the National Socialist German Workers' Party, which saw his salary double, but his spartan existence was no barrier to his associating with the young and regularly inviting them home.

Another intellectual who fraternized with and befriended students was 42-year-old Josef Söhngen, who ran a large bookshop at Maximiliansplatz, near the Gestapo headquarters. Like many devout Catholics, he was not easy to pin down politically; he voted for the National Socialists, yet refused to join them, even though this meant he could not become the official bookstore of the University and so harmed his business. He was interested in art, literature and religion, and enjoyed spending time with his customers; one room in his bookshop was off-limits to most of them and this contained his banned books. Hans had met him in 1940, when he first took an interest in religious books, and discussed with him the differences between Lutherans and Catholics. Söhngen invited Hans upstairs, where he lived with his mother, and the two of them would stay up late chatting over wine, Söhngen explaining with passion and conviction some aspect of Catholic teaching, such as the Blessed Trinity, which Hans could not get his head round. It was around this time that some Lutheran students told the Scholls about 'changes' to the Christian faith that were being prepared at the behest of the regime and which were to be promulgated after victory.

Another addition to the small circle of like-minded friends that formed around Hans and Schurik was their fellow medical student Willi Graf, a tall blond boy from the Saar region (which had become part of Germany again in 1935). He was someone in search of deep and lasting friendships, and demanding in them. At the age of fifteen, when Hitler came to power, he made a list of all his friends and crossed out those who had joined the Hitler Youth as he did not want to associate with them again. He had joined the Catholic youth group *Neudeutschland* in 1929 and after 1933 had seen at first-hand how the authorities tried to squeeze the life out of such groups. They were not permitted to make any public displays of solidarity, but since they could gather for religious festivals and pilgrimages, Willi was able to attend one of the annual *Neudeutschland* Easter pilgrimages to Rome. Pope Pius XI met the young German pilgrims in 1934 and told them, 'always speak the truth, and defend the truth, and defend therewith your rights, which are the rights of conscience';[16] the Pope's message was posted on church doors around Germany, but was ripped down by the Nazi authorities. When the *Neudeutschland* pilgrimage returned from Rome the following year, the sixty buses carrying over a thousand youths were met at the German border by guards, who confiscated rosaries, prayer books, musical instruments and cameras.

In 1934 Willi joined the newly-formed *Grauer Orden* (Grey Order), an underground youth group whose members managed to meet in secret and escape detection for several years. In the purge of illegal youth groups in 1938 Willi was taken into custody with seventeen of his comrades and subjected to hours of interrogation; he was released three weeks later, when Hitler announced an amnesty. After six months' National Labour Service, Willi began his medical studies at the University of Bonn which he had to combine with placements in field hospitals. These took him to France and the Balkans, as well as Poland and Russia, where he witnessed at first hand the unspeakable cruelty and brutality of his fellow soldiers. These horrors merely fuelled his hatred for National Socialism, which stemmed from the regime's attitude to Christianity in general and the Catholic Church in particular. He was haunted by the scenes he witnessed, and tormented as to how he should react.

The son of a businessman who was an active member of the Party, Willi was taciturn, thoughtful and reserved: 'precise, genuine and wholly reliable' was Sophie's impression of him. His diary entries are laconic and point to a certain perfectionism and inarticulate anguish. 'To be a Christian is perhaps the hardest thing to ever become in life', he writes: 'We never are Christians, and only in death perhaps can we become Christian to a small degree.'[17] Willi was a regular attender of Mass on Sundays and an avid reader of books on philosophy and theology, especially those by Romano Guardini on the liturgy. He had other interests, too. He was a long-distance runner and as a student had joined the Munich Bach choir and taken up fencing, which brought him into contact with other dissident students, such as Christl.

Hans, Schurik, Christl and Willi were all studying medicine (though Christl was attached to the *Luftwaffe*, not the army), and after attending concerts would meet at a wine bar before moving to one of their rooms, where they would share ideas, read aloud to each other, hold discussions—and, when in high spirits, talk all sorts of clever nonsense. The four—who within nine months would stand before the People's Court accused of high treason— were part of a larger, loosely-formed group who discussed politics in the barracks and were unhappy with the current state of affairs; they decided among themselves that the best way to foment unrest was to engage in one-to-one discussions with other soldier–students and air the defects of the system. One of them, Jürgen Wittenstein, later recalled a joke going the rounds that in ten years' time a sign would hang from the entrance to the barracks saying, 'The resistance movement was launched here'.[18]

The circle of friends that formed around Hans and Schurik was not a formal club with its own rules and membership list, yet it had a well-defined identity and its unspoken standards were recognised by all within it. Those belonging could sense whether someone else should be allowed to join them; as Willi wrote in his diary, 'we felt each other out'. Sophie was immediately welcomed into the circle, thanks to Hans, but others were accepted only with the utmost caution and over time. Fellow dissenters recognised each other when they withheld consent to remarks which were meant to attract approval; they used the term 'Nazi' because of its derogatory connotation, rather than digni- fying it with the label 'National Socialism'; they avoided, if possible, giving the 'Heil Hitler' salute. In conversation, if a wary exchange continued, code words were offered and deciphered on both sides until the moment came when, as Willi said, 'we understand each other'.[19]

They were united politically in the sense that they were deeply opposed to Nazi ideology and practice, but otherwise there was no shared alternative political perspective. The discussion about what should replace National Socialism was a frequent topic of conversation, when it was safe to speak about it, and views varied according to their political leanings; some of the soldier–students had strong nationalist inclinations, whilst others were attracted to the policies of the left. A similar range of views is evident among the intellectuals who befriended these students. Only on one occasion, at a meeting on 9 February 1943, did political differences threaten to undermine the harmony among the students.

Ridicule was one thing that enraged the Nazis and the penalty for indulging in anti-Nazi jokes was often imprisonment. Yet the disgruntled as well as the dissident enjoyed passing them on, or else hatching new ones to keep pace with developments. It was said, went one joke, that Germany was once the land of *Dichter und Denker* (poets and thinkers) but now under Hitler it had become the land of *Richter und Henker* (judges and hangmen). Another asked, 'What is the difference between Christianity and National Socialism?' 'Simple', ran the answer; 'in Christianity one person died for everyone else; in National Socialism everybody dies for one man'. One of the most popular jokes ran, 'What is an Aryan?' The reply was, 'Blonde like Hitler, tall like Goebbels, and slender like Goering!'

While dangerous, humour served the important function of releasing tension, and wherever Hans and Schurik were there was plenty of it around. Despite the darkness and prohibitions around them, their relish for life did not disappear. They and their circle met up for reasons of solidarity: to feel sustained and secure, and to leave replenished—and they often stayed up late. In Willi's diary there are entries of the sort: 'it was already getting light when we broke up'.[20] Hans, Schurik and their friends all came from stable families and bourgeois backgrounds; none of them was a political radical (in the peacetime sense of the term), yet they rejected the prevailing values, deliberately cut themselves off from the society of their peers, made themselves aliens in own land, and put their lives in jeopardy rather than conform. The comradeship that formed between them was pure and strong, relatively untainted by the world around them. In fact, because their friendships were confined to a small closed group, as Traute later said, 'We "negated" the many, and built on the few, and believed ourselves strong'.[21]

Jürgen Wittenstein was on the periphery of the group that came to be known as the White Rose, as was Hubert Furtwängler; both of them regularly covered for Hans, Willi and Schurik when they were missing from the barracks at roll-call. Repelled by the charged atmosphere at university, where the only social life revolved around Nazi rallies and meetings, they and others provided support for each other by gathering to chat and exchange ideas. They often met in public places, such as wine bars, but it was dangerous to meet there for long, especially if they had drunk deeply, as a loose word picked up by those reading newspapers or playing cards at nearby tables could be reported. So, for serious discussions, they met in private: in Hans' room in the city centre for impromptu meetings, or else for prearranged meetings at Dr Schmorell's house in Harlaching, in the south of Munich, or at Eickemeyer's studio, close to the University buildings. When Manfred Eickemeyer first met Sophie his impression of her was of 'a quiet girl much concerned with religion'; she was serious, but had a radiant smile.[22]

Writing to Fritz, Sophie was eager to challenge his view that nature was unredeemed and tried to persuade him of her view of the world and man's place in it.

> I have always felt that I can hear the most consummate harmony resounding from field and forest. Last Sunday, as I made my way into a big, peaceful mountain valley bathed in warm evening air that was already obscuring little details and throwing big, clear-cut outlines into relief, all my usual worries seemed to fall away from me like useless leaves, and I began to judge my preoccupations by an entirely different criterion. It seemed to me that man alone had disrupted this wonderful harmony, which I can also detect in a Bach fugue. I felt as if man had set himself apart from this harmony, and that it was lingering on, without him. That is why I found it inconceivable that Nature should stand in need of redemption.[23]

But while walking home in the early hours of the morning after a group reading of Claudel's *Le soulier de satin*, it occurred to her that, after all, nature *might* have to be redeemed by death, as even animals have to die, however innocently. But 'the roaring of the offended earth—of things that have been displaced and become demonic, of machines that ought to serve mankind and are destroying it—soon seemed to swamp every vestige of peace', as she returned to her room.[24] These musings reveal an earnest searching of the student in philosophy and biology to marry the two parts of her degree course.

In June 1942, Hitler's *Wehrmacht* began its great summer offensive between Kursk and Taganrog, and towards the end of July, Hans and his friends from the medical company in Munich were ordered to move to the Russian front. It was in the build-up to their departure that the four White Rose leaflets were written, duplicated and distributed. By the time Sophie had arrived in Munich to begin her university studies, plans for mounting a non-violent resistance campaign had been amply discussed and settled on by Hans and Schurik—nobody else, at this stage. Even though the intention to distribute leaflets through the postal system was a relatively mild form of opposition, they knew that they were risking their careers and freedom, if not their lives. For this reason they left no written record of their discussions and avoided all mention of the plans in their correspondence. The scarcity of information about their movements even extended to the name they adopted for their campaign: the White Rose. The origin of the name is unclear, and many suggestions have been made to explain its provenance, including the explanation that the name was chosen precisely because it did not have any special connotations.[25] More poetic and artistic than political, the name White Rose matched the content of the four leaflets bearing that name.

Copies of the first White Rose leaflet were posted on 27 June 1942. The leaflet had been typed up on a portable Remington typewriter acquired by Schurik and duplicated by Hans on a machine he had purchased, along with stencils and paper, from an obscure shop selling second-hand office supplies. The funds came from the 250 Marks the medical students earned each month, supplemented by the generous allowance Schurik received from his father.[26] Wilhelm Geyer, an artist from Ulm, showed them how to make stencils, though he had no idea what they wanted them for. Around one hundred copies of the leaflet were made and they were posted to addresses copied out from a Munich telephone directory; in this way they would have reached the educated classes. Besides friends and relatives known to be sympathetic, the recipients were academics, head teachers, writers, doctors and owners of bookshops, as well as those working in cafes and restaurants. Hans and Schurik deliberately targeted the academic intelligentsia because it was they, not the masses, who had failed politically. Under the influence of Muth, the students had imbibed the critique that National Socialism had resulted from a crisis of liberalism; it was a consequence of an apostasy of faith and a turning to an empty economic liberalism.[27]

The leaflet was 800 words in length and double-spaced, written in the style of a magazine article rather than as a rousing summons to the barricades. Hans and Schurik had each composed their own text for the leaflet, setting about the task as if it were a creative writing assignment to be judged for style, form and content, then they argued through the respective merits of their compositions, before Hans drew up the final version. The language was stilted and the structure smacked of cut-and-paste, but the earnest convictions of Hans and Schurik shone through unmistakably.

The authors were idealists who knew that the regime could not be toppled by anything but force, yet they wanted to make a start at eroding the faith of their fellow Germans in the leadership and to let other dissidents know that they were not alone, and that the monolith of public support for the regime was a mere propaganda exercise. Essentially, they wanted to shake up and arouse their fellow Germans. They were convinced that the system would collapse at some stage and though there were no signs of collapse at the time—quite the opposite, to judge from the victories in the east and in North Africa—they were determined to take huge risks in order to open up a crack. The banner under which they operated was signified by the headline across the top:

[First] 'Leaflet of the White Rose'

Nothing is so unworthy of a civilized nation as allowing itself to be 'governed' without opposition by an irresponsible clique that has yielded to base instinct. It is certain that today every honest German is ashamed of his government. Who among us has any conception of the dimensions of shame that will befall us and our children when one day the veil has fallen from our eyes and the most horrible of crimes—crimes that infinitely outdistance every human measure—reach the light of day? If the German people are already so corrupted and spiritually crushed that they do not raise a hand, frivolously trusting in a questionable faith in lawful order in history; if they surrender man's highest principle, that which raises him above all other God's creatures, his free will; if they abandon the will to take decisive action and turn the wheel of history and thus subject it to their own rational decision; if they are so devoid of all individuality, have already gone so far along the road toward turning into a spiritless and cowardly mass—then, yes, they deserve their downfall.

Goethe speaks of the Germans as a tragic people, like the Jews and the Greeks, but today it would appear rather that they are a spineless, will-less herd of hangers-on, who now—the marrow sucked out of their bones, robbed of their centre of stability—are waiting to be hounded to their destruction. So it seems—but it is not so. Rather, by means of a gradual, treacherous, systematic abuse, the system has put every man into a spiritual prison. Only now, finding himself lying in fetters, has he become aware of his fate. Only a few recognized the threat of ruin, and the reward for their heroic warning was death. We will have more to say about the fate of these persons. If everyone waits until the other man makes a start, the messengers of avenging Nemesis will come steadily closer; then even the last victim will have been cast senselessly into the maw of the insatiable demon. Therefore every individual, conscious of his responsibility as a member of Christian and Western civilization, must defend himself as best he can at this late hour against the scourges of mankind, against fascism and any similar system of totalitarianism. Offer passive resistance—*resistance*—wherever you may be, forestall the spread of this atheistic war machine before it is too late, before the last cities, like Cologne, have been reduced to rubble, and before the nation's last young man has given his blood on some battlefield for the hubris of a sub-human. Do not forget that every people deserves the regime it is willing to endure.

From Friedrich Schiller's 'The Lawgiving of Lycurgus and Solon' [1789]:

Viewed in relation to its purposes, the law code of Lycurgus is a masterpiece of political science and knowledge of human nature. He desired a powerful, unassailable state, firmly established on its own principles. Political effectiveness and permanence were the goal towards which he strove, and he attained this goal to the full extent possible under the circumstances. But if one compares the purpose Lycurgus had in view with the purposes of mankind, then a deep abhorrence takes the place of the approbation which we felt at first glance. Anything may be sacrificed to the good of the state except that end for which the state serves as a means. The state is never an end in itself; it is important only as a condition under which the purpose of mankind can be attained, and this purpose is none other than the development of all of man's powers, his progress and improvement. If a state prevents the development of the capacities which reside in man, if it interferes with the progress of the human spirit, then it is reprehensible and injurious, no matter how excellently devised, how perfect in its own way. Its very permanence in that case amounts more to a reproach than to a basis for fame; it becomes a prolonged evil, and the longer it endures, the more harmful it is ...

At the price of all moral feeling a political system was set up, and the resources of the state were mobilized to that end. In Sparta there was no conjugal love, no mother love, no filial devotion, no friendship; all men were citizens only, and all virtue was civic virtue.

A law of the state made it the duty of Spartans to be inhumane to their slaves; in these unhappy victims of war humanity itself was insulted and mistreated. In the Spartan code of law the dangerous principle was promulgated that men are to be looked upon as means and not as ends—and the foundations of natural law and of morality were destroyed by that law ...

What an admirable sight is afforded, by contrast, by the rough soldier Gaius Marcius in his camp before Rome, when he renounced vengeance and victory because he could not endure to see a mother's tears! ...

The state [of Lycurgus] could endure only under the one condition: that the spirit of the people remained quiescent. Hence it could be maintained only if it failed to achieve the highest, the sole purpose of a state.

From Goethe's *The Awakening of Epimenides,* Act II, Scene 4 [1815][28]

Spirits: Though he who has boldly risen from the abyss
Through an iron will and cunning
May conquer half the world,
Yet to the abyss he must return.
Already a terrible fear has seized him;
In vain he will resist!
And all who still stand with him
Must perish in his fall.

Hope: Now I find my good men

Are gathered in the night,
To wait in silence, not to sleep.
And the glorious word of liberty
They whisper and murmur,
Till in unaccustomed strangeness,
On the steps of our temple
Once again in delight they cry:
Freedom! Freedom!

Please make as many copies of this leaflet as you can and
distribute them.

Most loyal 'national comrades' would have dutifully handed in
the leaflets to the Gestapo, as it was an offence not to do so. The
Gestapo immediately put agents on the case, but they had no idea
where the leaflets came from or how many people were involved
in their production. A report the Gestapo commissioned from a
language expert was to conclude that the leaflet was the work of
a romantic idealist who was deeply influenced by Christian ideas,
rather than the leader of an organized resistance movement; it
noted that no plan of action was offered for the 'passive resistance'.[29] Some of the recipients of the White Rose leaflets were
students and as a result the leaflets were passed around the
University, where they caused intense excitement within the
student body. Not since the early days when Hitler came to power
had there been anything anti-Nazi like this.

According to the historian of the German resistance, Joachim
Fest, the production of the first White Rose leaflet was a new
development in the struggle against Adolf Hitler. 'A small group
of Munich students were the only protesters who managed to
break out of the vicious circle of tactical considerations and other
inhibitions. They spoke out vehemently, not only against the
regime but also against the moral indolence and numbness of the
German people.'[30]

It is not fully clear when it was that Sophie became involved
with the White Rose leaflets, as her testimony under interrogation
was designed to protect others rather than help future historians.

It has been argued that she only got to know about the leaflet production after 12 July 1942—or even as late as 23 July, when Hans and his friends left for the Russian front. After the war, Inge asserted that Sophie had not been privy to plans for the first leaflet, though Inge had suspected that Hans was involved when she found in his room a book by Schiller with the quotation about the ancient Greek lawgivers marked in it. Sophie might have recognised the extract from Goethe's poem, as Hans had cited this before in his letters home.[31] In her third interrogation Sophie claimed that she had confronted Hans by asking him, 'Do you know where the leaflets come from?', and that he had replied, 'These days it is best not to know about certain things, so as not to endanger the lives of others.'[32] Her response was to tell him that he could not act alone. But Lisl and Fritz were convinced Sophie became aware of the campaign as soon as she arrived in Munich, or even earlier—and other evidence, such as her conversation with Fritz about a duplicating machine on 2 May, seems to confirm this.

Sophie's diary entry for 29 June makes no explicit mention of the momentous event which had taken place two days earlier, but read in the context of the first White Rose leaflets having been sent out, her entry takes on a different tone and suggests, at least in the final section, that the author has just taken a decisive step in life:

> My God, I can only address you falteringly. I can only offer you my heart, which is wrested away from you by a thousand desires. Being so weak that I cannot remain facing you of my own free will, I destroy what distracts me from you and force myself to turn to you, for I know that I am happy with you alone. Oh, how far from you I am, and the best thing about me is the pain I feel on that account. But I am often so listless and apathetic. Help me to be single-hearted and remain with me. If I could only once call you Father, but I can hardly address you as 'YOU'. I do so to a great Unknown. I know that you will accept me if I am sincere, and that you will hear me if I cling to you. Teach me to pray. Better to suffer intolerable pain

than to vegetate insensibly. Better to be parched with thirst, better to pray for pain, pain, and more pain, than to feel empty, and to feel so without truly feeling at all. That I mean to resist.[33]

That same day the second leaflet was composed, co-written by Hans and Schurik, and the following day it was sent out by post. It was more strident and polemical in tone than the first, though the public who received it were not offered any concrete suggestions for action. The leaflet stated that the regime was engaged in genocide on a large scale in Eastern Europe—confirmed by the medical casualties from the east that Hans and his friends had been treating and by reports from Eickemeyer and others—and challenged the German people for offering blind allegiance to a criminal regime. This was one of the most sweeping indictments of the German people to go on record inside Germany by Germans, and it unambiguously confronted Hans' countrymen with their collective guilt. (By the end of the war it became apparent that this was the only resistance leaflet to record details of the Holocaust while it was taking place.) As if reluctant to end on a violent note, it concludes with two quotations from the founder of Taoism, whose philosophy taught the futility of violence and passion.

[Second] 'Leaflet of the White Rose'

It is impossible to engage in intellectual discourse with National Socialism because it is not an intellectually defensible programme. It is false to speak of a National Socialist philosophy, for if there were such an entity, one would have to try by means of analysis and discussion either to prove its validity or to combat it. In actuality, however, we face a totally different situation. At its very inception this movement depended on the deception and betrayal of one's fellow man; even at that time it was inwardly corrupt and could support itself only by constant lies. After all, Hitler states in an early edition of 'his' book [*Mein Kampf*] (a book written in the worst German I have ever read, in spite of the fact that it has been elevated to the position of the Bible in this nation of poets and thinkers): 'It is unbelievable, to what extent one must betray a people in order to rule it.' If at the start this cancerous growth in the nation was not particularly noticeable, it was only because there were still enough forces at work that operated for the good, so that it was kept under control. As it grew larger, however, and finally in an ultimate spurt of growth attained ruling power, the tumour broke open, as it were, and infected the whole body. The greater part of its former opponents went into hiding. The German intellectuals fled to their cellars, there, like plants struggling in the dark, away from light and sun, gradually to choke to death. Now the end is at hand. Now it is our task to find one another again, to spread information from person to person, to keep a steady purpose, and to allow ourselves no rest until the last man is persuaded of the urgent need of his struggle against this system. When thus a wave of unrest goes through the land, when 'it is in the air', when many join the cause, then in a great final effort this system can be shaken off. After all, an end in terror is preferable to terror without end.[34]

We are not in a position to draw up a final judgment about the meaning of our history. But if this catastrophe can be used to further the public welfare, it will be only by virtue of the fact that we are cleansed by suffering; that we yearn for the light in the midst of deepest night, summon our strength, and finally help in shaking off the yoke which weighs on our world.

We do not want to discuss here the question of the Jews, nor do we want in this leaflet to compose a defence or apology. No, only by way of example do we want to cite the fact that since the conquest of Poland *three hundred thousand* Jews have been murdered in this country in the most bestial way. Here we see the most frightful crime against human dignity, a crime that is unparalleled in the whole of history. For Jews, too, are human beings—no matter what position we take with respect to the Jewish question—and a crime of this dimension has been perpetrated against human beings. Someone may say that the Jews deserved their fate. This assertion would be a monstrous impertinence; but let us assume that someone said this—what position has he then taken toward the fact that the entire Polish aristocratic youth is being annihilated? (May God grant that this programme has not fully achieved its aim as yet!) All male offspring of the houses of the nobility between the ages of fifteen and twenty were transported to concentration camps in Germany and sentenced to forced labour, and the girls of this age group were sent to Norway, into the bordellos of the SS! Why tell you these things, since you are fully aware of them—or if not of these, then of other equally grave crimes committed by this frightful sub-humanity? Because here we touch on a problem which involves us deeply and forces us all to take thought. Why do the German people behave so apathetically in the face of all these abominable crimes, crimes so unworthy of the human race? Hardly anyone thinks about that. It is accepted as fact and put out of mind. The German people slumber on in their dull, stupid sleep and encourage these fascist criminals; they give them the opportunity to carry on their depredations; and of course they do so. Is this a sign that the Germans are brutalized in their simplest human feelings, that no chord within them cries out at the sight of such deeds, that they have sunk into a fatal consciencelessness from which they will never, never awake? It seems to be so, and will certainly be so, if the German does not at least start up out of his stupor, if he does not protest wherever and whenever he can against this clique of criminals, if he shows no sympathy for these hundreds of thousands of victims. He must evidence not only sympathy; no, much more: a sense of *complicity* in guilt. For through his apathetic behaviour he gives these evil men the opportunity to act as they do; he tolerates this 'government' which has taken upon itself such an infinitely great burden of guilt; indeed, he himself is to blame for the fact that it came about at all! Each man wants to be exonerated of a guilt of this kind, each one continues on his way with the most placid, the calmest conscience. But he cannot be exonerated; he is *guilty, guilty, guilty!* It is not too late, however, to do away with this most reprehensible of all miscarriages of government, so as to avoid being burdened with even greater guilt. Now, when in recent years our eyes have been opened, when we know exactly who our adversary is, it is high time to root out this brown horde. Up until the outbreak of the war the larger part of the German people were blinded; the Nazis did not show themselves in their true aspect. But now, now that we have recognized them for what they are, it must be the sole and first duty, the holiest duty of every German to destroy these beasts.

If the people are barely aware that the government exists, they are happy. When the government is felt to be oppressive, they are broken.
Good fortune, alas! builds itself upon misery. Good fortune, alas! is the mask of misery. What will come of this? We cannot foresee the end. Order is upset and turns to disorder, good becomes evil. The people are confused. Is it not so, day in, day out, from the beginning?
The wise man is therefore angular, though he does not injure others: he has sharp corners, though he does not harm; he is upright but not gruff. He is clear-minded, but he does not try to be brilliant.

                                                    Lao Tzu

Whoever undertakes to rule the kingdom and to shape it according to his whim—I foresee that he will fail to reach his goal. That is all.
The kingdom is a living being. It cannot be constructed, in truth! He who tries to manipulate it will spoil it, he who tries to put it under his power will lose it.
Therefore, some creatures go out in front, others follow, some have warm breath, others cold, some are strong, some weak, some attain abundance, other succumb.

The wise man will accordingly forswear excess, he will avoid arrogance and not overreach.

Lao Tzu

Please make as many copies as possible of this leaflet and distribute them.

Like the other leaflets, the second was composed on the assumption that their message would get through by appealing to the conscience of the reader, and for that reason they included fluctuations in tone, alternating between 'we', 'I' and 'they' (*wir, ich* and *ihr*) and between the formal and the informal (*Du* and *Sie*).[35]

The third leaflet followed hard on the heels of the second and contrasted the evil of Nazism with the good of Christianity. Although it again recommended 'passive resistance', it was distinctly provocative by suggesting different ways of 'sabotage' so as to topple the Führer.[36] It was effectively urging high treason.

[Third] 'Leaflet of the White Rose'

Salus publica suprema lex

All ideal forms of government are utopias. A state cannot be constructed on a purely theoretical basis; rather, it must grow and ripen in the way an individual human being matures. But we must not forget that at the starting point of every civilization the state was already there in rudimentary form. The family is as old as man himself, and out of this initial bond man, endowed with reason, created for himself a state founded on justice, whose highest law was the common good. The state should exist as a parallel to the divine order, and the highest of all utopias, the *civitas dei*, is the model which in the end it should approximate. Here we will not pass judgment on the many possible forms of the state—democracy, constitutional monarchy, and so on. But one matter needs to be brought out clearly and unambiguously. Every individual human being has a claim to a useful and just state, a state which secures the freedom of the individual as well as the good of the whole.

For, according to God's will, man is intended to pursue his natural goal, his earthly happiness, in self-reliance and self-chosen activity, freely and independently within the community of life and work of the nation.

But our present 'state' is the dictatorship of evil. 'Oh, we've known that for a long time,' I hear you object, 'and it isn't necessary to bring that to our attention again.' But, I ask you, if you know that, why do you not bestir yourselves, why do you allow these men who are in power to rob you step by step, openly and in secret, of one domain of your rights after another, until one day nothing, nothing at all will be left but a mechanized state system presided over by criminals and drunks? Is your spirit already so crushed by abuse that you forget it is your right—or rather, your *moral duty*—to eliminate this system? But if a man no longer can summon the strength to demand his right, then it is absolutely certain that he will perish. We would deserve to be dispersed through the earth like dust before the wind if we do not muster our powers at this late hour and finally find the courage which up to now we have lacked. Do not hide your cowardice behind a cloak of expediency, for with every new day that you hesitate, failing to oppose this offspring of Hell, your guilt, as in a parabolic curve, grows higher and higher.

Many, perhaps most, of the readers of these leaflets do not see clearly how they can practice an effective opposition. They do not see any avenues open to them. We want to try to show them that everyone is in a position to contribute to the overthrow of this system. It is not possible through solitary withdrawal, in the manner of embittered hermits, to prepare the ground for the overturn of this 'government' or bring about the revolution at the earliest possible moment. No, it can be done only by the cooperation of many convinced, energetic people—people who are agreed as to the means they must use to attain their goal. We have no great number of choices as to these means. The only one available is *passive resistance*. The meaning and the goal of passive resistance is to topple National Socialism, and in this struggle we must not recoil from any course, any action, whatever its nature. At all points we must oppose National Socialism, wherever it is open to attack. We must soon bring this monster of a state to an end. A victory of fascist Germany in this war would have immeasurable, frightful consequences. The military victory over Bolshevism dare not become the primary concern of the Germans. The defeat of the Nazis must *unconditionally* be the first order of business.[37] The greater necessity of this latter requirement will be discussed in one of our forthcoming leaflets.

And now every convinced opponent of National Socialism must ask himself how he can fight against the present 'state' in the most effective way, how he can strike it the most telling blows. Through passive resistance, without a doubt. We cannot provide each man with the blueprint for his acts, we can only suggest them in general terms, and he alone will find the way of achieving this end:

Sabotage in armament plants and war industries, sabotage at all gatherings, rallies, public ceremonies, and organizations of the National Socialist Party. Obstruction of the smooth functioning of the war machine (a machine for war that goes on solely to shore up and perpetuate the National Socialist Party and its dictatorship). *Sabotage* in all the areas of science and scholarship which further the continuation of the war—whether in universities, technical schools, laboratories, research institutions, or technical bureaus. *Sabotage* in all cultural institutions which could potentially enhance the 'prestige' of the fascists among the people. *Sabotage* in all branches of the arts which have even the slightest dependence on National Socialism or render it service. *Sabotage* in all publications, all newspapers, that are in the pay of the 'government' and that defend its ideology and aid in disseminating the brown lie. Do not give a penny to the public drives (even when they are conducted under the pretence of charity). For this is only a disguise. In reality the proceeds aid neither the Red Cross nor the needy. The government does not need this money; it is not financially interested in these money drives. After all, the presses run continuously to manufacture any desired amount of paper currency. But the populace must be kept constantly under tension, the pressure of the bit must not be allowed to slacken! Do not contribute to the collections of metal, textiles and the like. Try to convince all your acquaintances, including those in the lower social classes, of the senselessness of continuing, of the hopelessness of this war; of our spiritual and economic enslavement at the hands of the National Socialists; of the destruction of all moral and religious values; and urge them to *passive resistance*!

Aristotle, *Politics*: '... and further, it is part [of the nature of tyranny] to strive to see to it that nothing is kept hidden of that which any subject says or does, but that everywhere he will be spied upon, ... and further, to set man against man and friend against friend, and the common people against the privileged and the wealthy. Also it is part of these tyrannical measures, to keep the subjects poor, in order to pay the guards and the soldiers, and so that they will be occupied with earning their livelihood and will have neither leisure nor opportunity to engage in conspiratorial acts ... Further, [to levy] such taxes on income as were imposed in Syracuse, for under Dionysius the citizens gladly paid out their whole fortunes in taxes within five years. Also, the tyrant is inclined constantly to foment wars.'

Please duplicate and distribute!

As Jakob Knab has shown, the voice of Haecker was one among several contributing to the first three White Rose leaflets—and indeed was to become the dominant one in the fourth. At the time, Haecker was Hans' most important mentor and so was influential in shaping the style and content of the leaflets. Expressions used in the leaflets, such as 'maw of the insatiable demon' and 'atheistic war machine' in the first, 'constant lies' and the 'meaning of our history' in the second, and 'dictatorship of evil and 'offspring of Hell' in the third, were all phrases culled or adapted from Haecker's journal, and they indicate that Hans had adopted his mentor's prophetic opposition to the regime.[38] When the first leaflet suggested 'passive resistance' as a means to 'forestall the spread of this atheistic war machine before it is too late', it invoked the spirit of Haecker, which is conveyed so clearly in his journal:

> *To the Germans 1941.* Your fame is without lustre. It sheds no light. You are spoken of because you have—and are— the best machines. And in the world's astonishment there is not a spark of love. Without love, there is no lustre. You regard yourselves as chosen, because you build the best machines, the best machines of war, and serve them best. [...] From the Christian point of view there is only *one* way: to turn back; an active remorse.[39]

By the time the fourth leaflet was sent out (on 12 July) the German military forces had notched up several victories in the Soviet Union and North Africa. Despite these, the leaflet anticipated the eventual fall of the Third Reich and urged the German people to recognise their guilt. The first three leaflets read as earnest student exercises in rhetoric and political theory, embellished by apposite quotations, but the fourth leaflet struck a different tone. No longer is 'civil freedom' the predominant theme, rather that of war as a cosmic struggle between heaven and hell for the soul of man. In this battle, reason alone—Rousseau reinforced by Kant—was insufficient; recourse to 'freedom' was insufficient as man had lost his freedom through complicity in evil. So what explains this change of tack?

The fourth leaflet was written on 11 July. Crucially, the previous day was the first occasion on which Haecker read from his works to a circle of friends that Hans and Schurik had gathered. It was a long meeting and during the evening Haecker drew from Kierke-gaard and Newman in his attempt to discern the metaphysical background of the war. At the time, Haecker was completing

Kierkegaard the cripple. At the beginning of the story the young Kierkegaard speaks to his father about the 'master criminal' and defends this demoniacal figure. His father 'interrupted him gravely and said: "There are crimes which can only be combated with God's constant support." Sören was impressed, hurried to his room, and "gazed into the looking glass." '[40] This is precisely what Haecker urged the White Rose students to do; he wanted them to rely on a strength and wisdom that was not their own, rather than on reasoned arguments and appeals to common sense.

In his diary Willi Graf records that Haecker read from his theology of history, *Der Christ und die Geschichte* (1935, *The Christian and history*), in which he examines the role of divine providence in time.[41] From this Haecker developed his ideas of fallen angels and pure spirits, of good and evil, the driving forces of history, of Christ and the Antichrist, of God and the devil, of the liar's false image of the true nature of man, as well as of the appearance of the Antichrist in person in the last days of history.[42] Haecker also read from his journal. Many of the entries confirmed Hans in his understanding of events and the need for the White Rose leaflets to point the way for others: 'The prophetic [i.e. teaching] voice of the Church has fallen silent, as if her prophetic office were suspended', Haecker wrote. 'Does that too belong to the hour of the evil one? And every individual man is left to fumble his way through the night.'[43] To judge from their choice of language and strident tone, Hans and Schurik must have listened to some forcefully-expressed entries, such as the following: 'Virgil who was so often able to express his horror of war, would today be silenced in a concentration camp. That is one of the characteristics of this accursed *Reich*, which by its express apostasy from "the Faith", has fallen infinitely below an Adventist paganism.'[44] Evidently, they absorbed from Haecker his conviction that such an apostasy would pave the way for the Antichrist, or at least his shadow. The impulsive and spirited Hans took up this cluster of apocalyptic images and used it to draw up the fourth leaflet.

[Fourth] 'Leaflet of the White Rose'

There is an ancient maxim that we repeat to our children: 'Pay attention or pay the consequences'. But a wise child will not burn his fingers the second time on a hot stove. In the past weeks Hitler has chalked up successes in Africa and in Russia. In consequence, optimism on the one hand and distress and pessimism on the other have grown within the German people with rapidity quite inconsistent with traditional German apathy. On all sides one hears among Hitler's opponents—the better segments of the population—exclamations of despair, words of disappointment and discouragement, often ending with the question: 'Will Hitler now, after all...?'

Meanwhile the German offensive against Egypt has ground to a halt. Rommel has to bide his time in a dangerously exposed position. But the push into the East proceeds. This apparent success has been purchased at the most horrible expense of human life, and so it can no longer be counted an advantage. Therefore we must warn against *all* optimism.

Neither Hitler nor Goebbels can have counted the dead. In Russia thousands are lost daily. It is the time of the harvest, and the reaper cuts into the ripe grain with wide strokes. Mourning takes up her abode in the country cottages, and there is no one to dry the tears of the mothers. Yet Hitler feeds with lies those people whose most precious belongings he has stolen and whom he has driven to a meaningless death.

Every word that comes from Hitler's mouth is a lie. When he says peace, he means war, and when he blasphemously uses the name of the Almighty, he means the power of evil, the fallen angel, Satan. His mouth is the foul-smelling maw of Hell, and his might is at bottom accursed. True, we must conduct the struggle against the National Socialist terrorist state with rational means; but whoever today still doubts the reality, the existence of demonic powers, has failed by a wide margin to understand the metaphysical background of this war. Behind the concrete, the visible events, behind all objective, logical considerations, we find the irrational element: the struggle against the demon, against the servants of the Antichrist.[45] Everywhere and at all times demons have been lurking in the dark, waiting for the moment when man is weak; when of his own volition he leaves his place in the order of Creation as founded for him by God in Freedom;[46] when he yields to the force of evil, separates himself from the powers of a higher order; and, after voluntarily taking the first step, he is driven on to the next and the next at a furiously accelerating rate. Everywhere and at all times of greatest trial men have appeared, prophets and saints who cherished their freedom, who preached the One God and who with His help brought the people to a reversal of their downward course.[47] Man is free, to be sure, but without the true God he is defenceless against the principle of evil. He is like a rudderless ship, at the mercy of the storm, an infant without his mother, a cloud dissolving into thin air.

I ask you as a Christian wrestling for the preservation of your greatest treasure, whether you hesitate, whether you incline toward intrigue, calculation, or procrastination in the hope that someone else will raise his arm in your defence? Has God not given you the strength, the will to fight? We *must* attack evil where it is strongest, and it is strongest in the power of Hitler.[48]

So I returned, and considered all the oppressions that are done under the sun: and behold the tears of such as were oppressed, and they had no comforter; and on the side of their oppressors there was power; but they had no comforter. Wherefore I praised the dead which are already dead more than the living which are yet alive ...

Ecclesiastes 4[:1–2]

True anarchy is the generative element of religion. Out of the annihilation of every positive element she lifts her gloriously radiant countenance as the founder of a new world ... If Europe were about to awaken again, if a state

of states, a teaching of political science were at hand!
Should hierarchy then ... be the principle of the union of
states? Blood will stream over Europe until the nations
become aware of the frightful madness, which drives them
in circles. And then, struck by celestial music and made
gentle, they approach their former altars all together, hear
about the works of peace, and hold a great celebration
about the works of peace, and hold a great celebration of
peace with fervent tears before the smoking altars. Only
religion can reawaken Europe, establish the rights of the
peoples, and install Christianity in new splendour visibly
on earth in its office as guarantor of peace.

Novalis

We wish expressly to point that the White Rose is not in
the pay of any foreign power. Though we know that
National Socialist power must be broken by military
means, we are trying to achieve a renewal from within of
the severely wounded German spirit. This rebirth must be
preceded, however, by the clear recognition of all the guilt
with which the German people have burdened themselves,
and by an uncompromising battle against Hitler and his
all too many minions, Party members, quislings, and the
like. With total brutality the chasm that separates the
better portion of the nation from everything that is identified with National Socialism must be opened wide. For
Hitler and his followers there is no punishment on this
earth commensurate with their crimes. But out of love for
coming generations we must make an example after the
conclusion of the war, so that no one will ever again have
the slightest urge to try a similar action. And do not forget
the petty scoundrels in this regime; note their name, so
that none will go free! They should not find it possible,
having had their part in these abominable crimes, at the
last minute to rally to another flag and then act as if
nothing had happened!

> To set you at rest, we add that the addresses of the readers of the White Rose are not recorded in writing. They were picked at random from directories.

> We will not be silent. We are your bad conscience. The White Rose will not leave you in peace! Please read and distribute!

On reading the first leaflet, which she received in the post, Traute suspected it came from within her circle, and her unease increased with each new leaflet. Recognising the quote from Ecclesiastes as one which she had brought to the attention of Hans, she was convinced that he was responsible. On confronting him, she received the evasive reply that it would be better for her if she knew as little as possible.[49] To test the impact of the leaflets, Hans and Schurik asked their friends what they thought about them, without revealing their authorship. While the Gestapo were now convinced that they were dealing with a large organisation, possibly aided by the Allies, Hans considered abandoning the campaign as he thought the leaflets had had little effect. At the invitation of Hans and Schurik, Professor Huber attended one of the regular reading evenings for their reliable friends, but when he realised he was being drawn into politics and discussion about the leaflets, he became guarded and declared that active resistance was impossible—then made an early exit. He may have suspected that Hans and Schurik were behind the leaflets and that they wanted to involve him. Nevertheless, he re-joined the students at a hastily arranged farewell party on 22 July, the night before the medical students left for Russia. It is difficult to know exactly what took place: very little to judge from the Gestapo's interrogation reports; a great deal according to Inge—but it is likely that she conflates some of the conversations with those that took place in the autumn, after the soldier—medics returned from the east.

According to Inge, the students talked with Huber about the leaflets and decided that if they returned alive from Russia the activity of the White Rose should be developed further, so as to form a coordinated and disciplined resistance movement, with Hans at helm. Professor Huber said:

> We will have to let the truth ring out as clearly and audibly as possible in the German night. We must try to kindle the spark of resistance in the heart of millions of honest Germans, so that it burns bright and bold. The isolated individuals who have stood up one by one against Hitler must be made aware that a large body of like-minded people stands with them. This knowledge will give them the courage and the strength to persist. Beyond this, we must try to enlighten those Germans who are still unaware of the evil intentions of our government and awaken in them the will to resistance and forthright opposition.[50]

But what if they failed? one of them asked. Christl answered:

> Then it is our duty by our behaviour and by our dedication to demonstrate that man's freedom still exists. Sooner or later the cause of humanity must be upheld, and then one day it will again prevail. We must gamble our 'No' against this power which has arrogantly placed itself above the essential human values and which is determined to root out all protest. We must do it for the sake of life itself—no one can absolve us of this responsibility. National Socialism is the name of a malignant spiritual disease that has befallen our people. We dare not remain silent as we watch its course, as the German people suffer its ravages.[51]

The difficulty they all faced was how to come to terms with wanting defeat for their own people.

On 23 July there were emotional scenes at Munich's Ostbahnhof (East train station) as Sophie and Christl said goodbye to Hans, Schurik, Willi and all the other medical students she had made friends with, who were now setting off for the Russian front for a three-month stint of duty. 'I still preserve such a vivid recollection of every little farewell word and gesture', Sophie told Lisa a few days later. 'I'd never have believed I could become so attached to them all, especially Hans.'[52] But there was no time for day-dreaming; in order to qualify for another term at university she would have to spend the next two months undertaking war service in a munitions factory. Besides, Sophie was unsure whether she would be able to return to her studies at all, as her father was awaiting trial for criticising the Führer; if he was sentenced, she would have to take care of her mother.

At the time, Sophie's prayer drew heavily from the Psalms:

> My soul is like an arid wasteland when I try to pray to you, conscious of nothing but its own barrenness. My God, transform that ground into good soil so that your seed does not fall on it in vain. At least let it bring forth a yearning for you, its creator, whom it so often declines to see. I beseech you with all my heart. I call aloud to you, I call 'you', even though all I know about you is that my salvation resides in you alone. Do not turn away from me if I fail to hear you knock; open my deaf, deaf heart. Make me restless so that I may find my way to the repose that dwells within you. I am so powerless. Receive me and do with me as you will, I beseech you, I beseech you.

> Into your hand I give my thoughts of my friend, that little ray of solicitude and warmth, that modicum of strength. Do with me the best you can, for you wish us to call upon you and have also made us responsible in prayer for our fellow creatures. I likewise think of all others. Amen.[53]

Robert Scholl's trial took place on 3 August at the Special Court in Stuttgart and the presiding judge was none other than the one who had presided over Hans' trial. The judge ruled that, since Robert did not have a 'treasonous' attitude and was generally a law-abiding member of the national community, he should be sentenced to four months' imprisonment for 'treachery', the sentence starting in three weeks, so as to give him time to sort out his business affairs. This was bleak news for the family's finances and a distraught Magdalena Scholl wrote to Hans and Werner, both now serving on the eastern front, to write letters of clemency for a reduction in the sentence; she pointed out that a letter written from the front would carry more weight than one from her. Her sons initially declined to do so—Hans for the obvious reason of wishing to avoid implicating his father with his own seditious activity, as well as being indignant about the affair—but changed their minds. Fritz also wrote to the judge. Posted near to Werner on the Russian front, Hans told his younger brother, 'We must not take this blow as others would take it. It is a mark of distinction.'[54] Meanwhile, for the duration of the sentence, an accountant friend called Eugen Grimminger took over Robert's affairs and Inge saw to the office work.

Sophie stayed at home to lend a hand with her father's affairs before starting her war-service work, and on a number of summer evenings she stood outside the prison wall playing on her flute a tune her father loved, *Die Gedanken sind frei* ('Thoughts are free'). Her head was spinning from all that was going on in her life, and she continued to seek refuge in prayer.

> I am so weak-willed that I can't even fulfil and act on my own perceptions, nor can I ever renounce my own will, which I know to be imprudent and self-seeking, and surrender myself to His [will]. Yet I would like to, and I am happy to reflect that he is the ruler of all things. Being unable to relinquish my foolish hold on it voluntarily, I pray every night that he may wrest my will away and subject me to his—if only I did not stand in my own way. I pray for a compassionate heart, for how else could I love? I who am so shallow in everything must pray for every-thing. A child can be compassionate, but I too often forget the sufferings that ought to overwhelm me, the sufferings of mankind. I place my powerless love in your hands, that it may become powerful.[55]

Meanwhile, Fritz was serving on the southern sector of the eastern front and saw the corpses of Russian prisoners of war, who had collapsed from exhaustion and been shot by their German guards. He had heard, too, of mass executions of the

Jewish population. Writing to Sophie from east of the Donets Basin, he lamented:

> It's frightening, the cynical insensitivity with which my commanding officer describes the slaughter of all those Jews in occupied Russia, and the way he is totally convinced of the rightness of his course of action. I sat there, my heart pounding. How relieved I was to be back on my own, lying on my camp bed, where I could take refuge in prayer, and in thoughts of you.[56]

Fritz wrote about the source of his inner strength. Thanks to Sophie, he had gone to the front armed with two volumes of Newman's sermons, and, as he told Sophie, had absorbed every line like 'drops of precious wine'. Newman left a profound impression on him. After the appalling anti-Jewish diatribe of his superior officer, he told his Sophie: 'What a fallacy it is to take nature as a model for our actions and to describe its cruelty as "great".'[57] Evidently, he had entered into Sophie's thoughts about nature and begun to form his own opinions about them.

In another letter, written on 4 July 1942, there is more evidence of the fruit of his reading: 'But we know by whom we were created, and that we stand in a relationship of moral obligation to our Creator. Conscience gives us the capacity to distinguish between Good and Evil.'[58] A close examination of the text reveals that, in these crucial days, Fritz had read Newman's sermon 'The Testimony of Conscience' and made sense of it. Here Newman— he had delivered this sermon in 1838 at the University Church of St Mary the Virgin in Oxford when his influence in the Oxford Movement was at its height—develops the central theme of his doctrine about conscience, using a passage from the Second Letter of St Paul to the Corinthians as his starting point: 'We are by nature what we are: very sinful and corrupt [...] Man is capable of both good and evil [...] If what he does well be an evidence of faith, what he does ill will be to him a more convincing proof that he has not faith.'[59] Fritz finished his letter with this insight: 'We must submit our reason to these mysteries, and confess the faith'.

Here too he draws almost word for word from Newman, who spoke of faith as 'submission of the intellect to mystery' that is, of obediential faith. Fritz's conscience was deeply disturbed by what he saw in Nazi-occupied Russia, and he eventually found the strength and language to speak out against the mass execution of Jews, thanks to Newman who, as Fritz wrote, had disclosed many beautiful insights to him.[60]

On 9 August Sophie recorded in her diary that she had just torn out a page 'because it was about Schurik'. It would seem that she was becoming fond of him—too fond—after spending so much time in his presence. In her confusion she added, 'but why tear him out of my heart. I will pray to God to assign him his rightful place in it. He shall go back in the notebook with the rest, and I will include him in my prayers every night with Fritz and the others'. Her diary continued to function as a prayer journal, containing her intimate prayer thoughts.

> Many people believe that our age is the last. All the omens are terrible enough to make one think so, but isn't that belief of secondary importance? Must we not all, no matter what age we live in, be permanently prepared for God to call us to account from one moment to the next? How am I to know if I shall still be alive tomorrow? We could all be wiped out overnight by a bomb, and my guilt would be no less than if I perished in company with the earth and the stars. I know all that, but don't I heedlessly fritter away my life just the same? O God, I beseech you to take away my frivolity and self-will, which clings to the sweet, ephemeral things of life. I can't do so myself, I'm far too weak.[61]

Sophie found it incomprehensible that so-called devout folk could fear for God's existence, given that 'mankind is dogging his footsteps with the sword and vile atrocities'. As if God was not in control and did not have the power—'I feel that everything is in His hands'. Rather, 'All we should fear for is the existence of humanity, because it has turned away from him who is its very life.'[62]

Dreams or dream-experiences feature occasionally in Sophie's diary, and evidently she recorded them because they were so vivid and because of their prescient or near-prophetic nature. She describes a 'curious' dream on 9 August, which reveals the high regard in which she held Hans, if not a conviction that he might be commissioned to act as an agent of God. The dream may explain decisions she took six months later.

> I was out walking with Hans and Schurik, with them on either side of me and our arms linked. Half walking, half skipping along, I was lifted off the ground by the two of them and soared through the air for a little way. Then Hans began: 'I know quite a simple proof of God's existence and intervention in the world of today. Human beings need a certain amount of air to breathe, so the whole sky would eventually become polluted by their stale breath. To prevent them from running out of this nourishment for the blood, God periodically injects our world with a mouthful of his own breath, which permeates the stale air and renews it. That is how he does it.' And then Hans raised his face to the very, very gloomy sky. Drawing a deep breath, he expelled the whole of it from his lips. His breath streamed forth in a bright blue jet. It grew progressively bigger and rose into the sky, driving away the murky clouds until the sky ahead and above us was as flawlessly blue as blue could be. It was beautiful.[63]

Sophie's work on a production line at a munitions factory near Ulm left her physically tired and mentally bored. She told Fritz that she was working alongside a Russian woman who had a childishly naïve and touching faith; she smiled at everyone, even her bullying German overseers, and had a profound effect on the German women about her, who were surprised to find that Russians were, after all, human beings and unsophisticated ones, with no mistrust of others. In this letter Sophie enclosed a photograph of Muth.[64]

Sophie did not see Hans, Schurik or Willi until they returned at the end of October, by which time they were changed men. On the way to the front the medical corps stopped at a station in Poland and spotted a group of women and girls doing heavy work with pickaxes; evidently they were Jews because of the yellow Star of David they wore on their blouses. Hans jumped out and offered his 'iron ration'—chocolate, nuts and raisins—to a small emaciated girl, and then had to jump back onto a moving train; as it pulled out, he offered his tobacco pouch to the sad Jewish man he saw at the rear of the forced labourers. The three soldier–medics found Warsaw sickening. They spent two nights there and saw how hunger ravaged the city; daily rations were limited to 2000 calories for Germans, 699 for Poles and just 184 for Jews. Unbeknown to them, the daily deportations from the Warsaw ghetto to the death camp at Treblinka had just begun: 6000 Jews boarded the train each day. Deeply moved, Hans described what he saw to his parents, 'Half-starved children sprawl in the street and whimper for bread while provocative jazz rings out across the way, and the peasants kiss the flagstones in churches while bars seethe with unbridled, insensate revelry. The mood is doom-laden, but I nonetheless believe in the inexhaustible strength of the Polish people.'[65]

By chance Hans found himself assigned to same sector as his brother Werner and the two saw each regularly and wrote joint letters home. Remarking how vulnerable the German supply lines were, Hans' letters strike a detached note. He commented,

> It is amazing how quickly the Russians recover from extremes of terror. When evening comes and the sun goes down in all colours behind the fields, this country is overcome by a melancholy that weighs even heavier than the war. That is when wounds are forgotten and voices are raised in song.[66]

With little to do in his first few weeks, Hans wrote to Professor Huber on behalf of himself, Schurik, Willi and Hubert Furtwängler. After relating how Warsaw and its ghetto had made a profound impression on them, he went on to describe Russia, its vastness and the Russians' love of their land. 'War sweeps across the countryside like a rainstorm, but after the rain the sun shines once more. Suffering takes total possession of people, purifies them—but then they laugh once more.'[67] At night they mixed with Russians and drank schnapps and sang with them.

This sort of behaviour was completely at odds with official Nazi policy, which was supposed to penetrate all aspects of the *Wehrmacht*. Traditional notions of chivalry were meant to be dropped and every restraint removed in what was masked as a crusade against Communism. Hitler publicly demanded that this struggle be conducted with 'unprecedented, unmerciful, and unrelenting harshness'.[68] The elimination of Bolshevism and the establishment of a greater German Reich were seen in terms of the creation of a new world order led by the master race of the West, which had been chosen by destiny. Schurik found it highly repugnant to be dressed in the uniform of a foreign predator while he trod on his native soil, and by way of making amends he taught his fellow medics to speak Russian and introduced them to Russian workers. They soon caught Schurik's fervour for all things Russian and refused to tolerate the brutish behaviour they were supposed to mete out to the Slavs, whom official propaganda branded an inferior race, if not subhuman. In this way the common bond of human fellowship briefly triumphed over hatred for the enemy.

Hans marked the day his father began his imprisonment with a letter—almost a sermon—to his mother. Anticipating that his father would find prison tough, as he knew all too well from his own experience, when he was starved of contact with the outside world and cooped up alone in a cramped grey cell, Hans reassured his mother:

> He will survive, though. Being strong, he will emerge from captivity even stronger. I believe in the immeasurable strength of suffering. True suffering is like a bath from which a person emerges born anew. All greatness must be purified before it can exchange the narrow confines of the human breast for a wider world outside.

> We shall never escape suffering, not till the day we die.
> Isn't Christ being crucified a thousand times every hour,
> and aren't beggars and cripples still being turned away
> from every door, today as always? To think that human
> beings fail to see precisely what makes them human:
> helplessness, misery, poverty.[69]

With little to do and a great deal of time on his hands, Hans
befriended a local fisherman and formed a choir at camp from
prisoners of war and a few Russian girls; on one occasion they
danced half the night away, so much so that they were exhausted
the next day. He also had plenty of time to think. 'We all need that',
he wrote home. 'My last few weeks in Munich were grand and
worthwhile but hurried, so they prevented many of my ideas from
maturing.'[70] He did not say more about the momentous events
which had recently taken place, the 16-day leaflet campaign, so
only Sophie would have known what he referred to, not Inge, Lisl
or his mother. Nor did he write about these events in the diary he
kept, since he could not take the risk of exposing his family to
further danger, if the White Rose leaflets were traced to him.

Like Sophie's diary, Hans' records his intimate thoughts and
provides a fascinating window into the mind and soul of the
young man who had dared to confront Hitler and the Third Reich
with its outrageous crimes. After living on adrenalin for three
weeks, Hans now had to endure three months of enforced
inactivity, much of it spent 80 yards from the Russian line in a
crowded, gloomy bunker, thick with the smoke of tobacco.
Reading in such conditions was difficult, and despite all the time
on hand it was not easy to summon up the energy to write to
friends or relatives, despite his eagerness to share his inward
thoughts with others. He described to Rose what he could not
tell his loved ones in Ulm, due to censorship of the family mail,
that a month in Russia had enabled him to sever all his ties with
the 'old world'; his one desire was to 'roam ever eastward, free
from all constraints and far from the musty smell of European

civilisation', yet he knew that in reality that 'I am every inch a European, [...] a guardian of a sacred heritage'.[71]

Writing to his mother (and thus to his father, too) Hans thanked them for their letters and various gifts of food. Rather than dwell on the butchery and depravity around him, he described his newly acquired passion for riding and the thrill of galloping through the high steppe grass, soaking in the enchanting beauty of nature, which contrasted markedly with the darkness of the war, the other side of the coin of reality. The war accentuated the antithesis between the two sides 'to such an extent that a weak person sometimes cannot endure it'; overall, the static nature of the war was 'an immense test of endurance'. Schurik had gone down with diphtheria but recovered, and he himself had briefly succumbed to an illness. The two of them had donated so much blood that it lowered their bodies' natural resistance; this was risky, as their sector was teaming with infections of every type, which as doctors they had to deal with. He confessed that he thought a great deal about his father. In fact, all the factors playing on his mind meant, 'I often run the entire gamut of emotions within a few minutes, rising to a shrill pitch of fury and then, just as quickly, subsiding into an expectant, confident, equable frame of mind'.[72]

But there were observations, reflections and prayer-like considerations that he did not wish to include in any letter and only expressed in his diary, either because they could be construed as mutinous or because they were too personal. Some entries were critical of the war, others full of admiration for the Russians—supposedly the arch enemy of the German people; some dealt with suffering, despair and suicide, others viewed the war as a titanic battle between God and the fallen angels or else gave expression to the hunger of his soul.

30 July 1942

God is closest when home is furthest, hence the young person's desire to go forth, leaving everything behind, and

wander aimlessly until he has snapped the last thread that
held him captive—until he stands confronting God in the
broad plain, naked and alone. He will then rediscover his
native soul with eyes transfigured.[73]

31 July 1942

How splendidly the flowers are blooming on this railroad
embankment! As if all had assembled so that no colour
should be missing, they bloom here with gentle insist-
ence—everywhere alongside ruined buildings, gutted
freight cars, distraught human faces. Flowers are blooming
and children innocently playing among the ruins. O God
of love, help me to overcome my doubts. I see the Creation,
your handiwork, which is good. But I also see man's
handiwork, our handiwork, which is cruel, and called
destruction and despair, and which always afflicts the
innocent. Spare your children! How much longer must
they suffer? Why is suffering so unfairly meted out? When
will a tempest finally sweep away all these godless people
who disfigure your likeness, who sacrifice the blood of
countless innocents to a demon?[74]

7 August 1942

I am tired of doing nothing, and the dugout is shuddering
and groaning because the Russians are dumping one bomb
after another onto the runway. I am redundant here. I walk
alone in the midst of meaningful absurdity. War holds me
spellbound only between shot and impact. The Russians
are a remarkable people.[75]

9 August 1942

I managed a visit to the Russian church [in Vyaz'ma]. The
hearts of all believers vibrated in unison. One could sense
the stirring, the outpouring of souls unfolding after a long
and terrible silence, souls that had at last found their way
back to their true home. I could have wept for joy, because
my heart, too, was loosening its bonds one by one. I wanted
to love and laugh because I could see that hovering above

these defeated people was an angel stronger than the powers of nothingness. Spiritual nihilism was a major threat to European civilisation, but as soon as it underwent its ultimate development in the total war to which we have finally succumbed, and as soon as it veiled the mighty sky like a sea of grey, it was vanquished. Nothing comes after nothing, yet something *must* come because all values can never be destroyed among all men. There still exist custodians who will kindle the flame and pass it on from hand to hand until a new wave of rebirth inundates the land. The veil of cloud is rent asunder, as it were, by the sunlight of a new religious awakening.[76]

12 August 1942

The army is the most unimaginative thing in the world, and what makes this war so foul, and distinguishes it from previous ones, is its very unimaginativeness.[77]

16 August 1942

I see Dostoyevsky differently than in Central Europe. Almost all men experience the same thing, daily and hourly. [...] They trample purity with clumsy feet, and thousands unload their own guilt onto the shoulders of a frail, innocent child. Only one person opens his eyes and sees the world of men, sees that every creature seeks mercy and redemption, but he is Russia's greatest writer. I am ruining my eyesight in this gloom, but I understand Dostoyevsky here.[78]

17 August 1942

Sheer exuberance prompted me to get drunk on schnapps last night. I didn't drink because I'm melancholy, or, as many would assert with a mournful air, to banish dismal thoughts—I hold melancholy far too sacred to avoid it. I drink with cheerful abandonment, as an aid to singing and telling jokes. [...]

I sometimes feel badly in need of a priest, though I am mistrustful of most theologians, who might disappoint me if I found I knew all they said before it left their lips; ah, yes, if only Father Schwarz were here, or Muth, or Haecker, or preferably dear old [Josef] Furtmeier, or better still, I'd like a chat with an intelligent girl of fifteen and a half.

It isn't melancholy that drives a man to suicide. By the time he's ready to surrender by engaging in a last, monstrous act of self-destruction, melancholy has entirely deserted him, because melancholy was insufficient to restrain him. The melancholy man ceases to act altogether. He is chained to the immense and unfathomable depths of his own soul by a hundred anchors, so to speak, and every tempest rages over him unnoticed.[79]

Like Sophie, Hans had dreams which gave expression to unconscious thoughts playing on his mind which refused to be banished. One of his dreams was particularly graphic and eerily prophetic.

18 August 1942

My nights are filled with confused dreams. I wanted to get away from the others for a better look at some mountains. [...] I noticed an exceptionally high iron bridge spanning the valley. I made for it without hesitation. Although my head swam a little when I stole an apprehensive glance at the chasm beneath, I briskly strode on. All at once it dawned on me: I had to cross this bridge or die in the attempt. Then the ironwork beneath my feet began to slope, more and more steeply, until it was vertically suspended over the chasm. Calmly, holding on tight I descended step by step. I was an expert climber, so the procedure presented no difficulty whatsoever.

The only difficulty I could see was how to escape some men who were waiting to arrest me as soon as I reached the foot of this fantastic ladder. I debated what to do. There was nothing for it, I told myself, and when I reached the ground I voluntarily gave myself up.[80]

Another diary entry shows that Hans spent a good deal of time rebutting the theory of German superiority in literature, especially over Russian literature. These were no idle speculations but an attempt to integrate his passion for and knowledge of literature into a wider scheme of things, one which drew on the ruminations of Haecker, and it led him to scorn the official Nazi explanation that the Germans were defending civilisation against ignorant hordes. In fact, Hans turned his insights *against* German intellectuals, who he said were selling themselves.

> 22 August 1942
>
> We Germans do not have Dostoyevsky or Gogol. Nor Pushkin nor Turgenev. What about Goethe or Schiller? someone retorts. Who does? A scholar. When did you last read any Goethe? I don't recall—in school or somewhere. I ask a Russian, What writers do you have? Oh, says the Russian, we have them all, all of them. There aren't any under the sun we don't have. What Russian says this? A peasant, a washerwoman, a postman. [...]
>
> To think, my worthy academic: I reproach you with that word. You're surprised, eh, you representative of the spirit? The spirit you serve at this desperate hour is an evil spirit, but you're blind to despair. You're rich, but you're blind to poverty. Your soul is withering because you refused to hear its call. You ponder on the ultimate refinement of a machine gun, but you suppressed the most elementary question in your youth. The question why and whither?
>
> How small must a nation be that calls Frederick II 'the Great'? That nation fought for its freedom against Napoleon, only to choose Prussian slavery. I know how limited human freedom is, but man is essentially free, and it is his freedom that renders him human. Freedom and poverty are human, enslavement and arrogance Prussian.
>
> Did Goethe ever suffer extreme hardship? Did he sample destitution even once? That question, which intrudes discreetly at first, gains strength like a storm until it finally

becomes all embracing. When did he ever eat his bread with
tears, and why? Wasn't he careful to avoid every sickness,
everything ugly and evil under the sun, and didn't he himself
fear death like the plague? Oh yes, he sampled hardship, but
only sampled it. Snugly ensconced in his silk and velvet coat,
he strode through the depths of human misery like a horned
Siegfried. Never once did he bow his proud head, never once
did he lie naked and bleeding on the ground at night, and
never once did hunger torment him to the point of despair.
He knew neither the melancholy of a whore excluded from
human society nor the sorrow of a homeless child. His mind
was always focused on the stars.[81]

Towards the end of August, Hans penned an entry that conveys
his weary but excited state of mind, in which thoughts dart from
one subject to another in a bewildering stream of consciousness.
(At this time he was probably administering to himself a drug
called Pervetin, a methamphetamine prescribed by the German
military for soldiers at the front and nicknamed *Panzerschokolade*
('tank chocolate'); as a medic he would have had easy access to
this performance-enhancing stimulant.[82]) Hans was clearly in a
dreamlike state—and knew it—battling hard against pessimism,
though at least on this day his entry finished on a high note.

28 August 1942

My father is in prison. I am sure he is thinking of me at
this moment. I am sitting on a wooden crate. A candle is
burning fitfully. Strange shapes are flowing down it, waxen
formations that are either haphazard or, for all I know,
fashioned by fate. The candle will get smaller and smaller
and eventually go out. What is death? Why are people so
afraid of it? Why do your fingers tremble when you touch
the dead? Ah, and your thoughts turn with a trace of
pleasure to a mother's tears, or a beloved's anguished heart
that yearns to stop beating, and a thought sneaks into your
mind, just a thought with which you casually toy—strictly
in secret, of course—to the effect that you are still alive,
that your heart is still beating, and that death really matters

to you as little as your neighbour's corns. My father in prison. Detonations outside. Bombs. How long it is since I left prison! I was still quite young in those days. Wrote a girl's name [Lisa Remppis] in breadcrumbs on the table in my cramped, vaulted cell. The red notice hanging on the door said 'Juvenile'.

She got engaged to someone else because I treacherously abandoned her. She wanted to die at first, but she did the right thing. A person has to go on living, come what may. Yes, and shun death at all costs, even when the autumn arrives and the whole of Nature, in an extreme of grief, externalises melancholy and transforms it into beauty— yes, beauty. You, too, were once beautiful.

If there is one thing I'd still like to do, should I ever be able to breathe freely again, it would be to head for Asia as a beggar and roam from village to village across desolate plains and through mysterious forests. To sleep beneath overhanging fir trees or in ditches and roam further, even further afield. May God never grant me an earthly destination, so that I never come to rest till the end of my days. Will I have to leave you too, beloved, because you don't understand; because I don't even dare to sow such seeds in your heart; because you're still a delightful child, a cornflower, a wisp of a girl and a kiss? I mean to forsake all the gardens of delusion and coat my feet with dust, renounce the writers and talkers and seek wisdom among the stars. Perhaps I'll go to prison a second time, perhaps a third and fourth. There are things far worse than prison. It may even be among the best.

Father may undergo a religious awakening there. I found the love that death inevitably follows because love flows gratis and cannot be repaid.

Ten die here daily. That's not many, and nobody makes a fuss about it. How many flowers are heedlessly trampled? Isn't Christ crucified a hundred times every hour? Even so, don't children continue to spring up irresistibly, like young birch trees, tender and bright-eyed?

Recently Alex [i.e. Schurik] and I buried a Russian. He must have been lying there a long time. The head had come away from the trunk and the soft parts were already decomposed. Worms were crawling out of the rotting clothes. We'd almost finished filling in the grave when we found another arm. We ended by nailing a Russian cross together and sticking it in the ground at the head. Now his soul is at rest.

Art's function is to make the world a more cheerful place, Hubert said today. But, oh, I'm tired. At present I've lost sight of that kind of art.

Where is it now? Not in Dostoyevsky. Not here. Not in the dugout and not outside in the moon light. I don't have any music with me. All I hear day and night are the groans of men in pain and, when dreaming, the sighs of the forlorn, and when I think, my thoughts perish in agony.

If Christ hadn't lived and died, there really would be no escape. To weep at all would be utterly futile. I should have to run full tilt at the nearest wall and smash my skull in. But not as things are.[83]

In early September, Hans was badly shaken by the news that Ernst Reden had been killed on the Russian front; the news seems to have darkened his outlook, to judge from his diary:

11 September 1942

The Germans are incorrigible. Their duplicity is so deep-seated by now that it could not be excised without killing the entire body. A doomed nation.

My pessimism gets worse every day. Skepticism is poisoning my soul. I want to save it by running away, but where to? In desperation, I erect a wall around me. It consists of sarcasm and satire.[84]

Hans knew he should not have been surprised by Ernst's death, but Ernst was someone he knew well, one of the Ulm circle, and, furthermore, romantically attached to his sister Inge. Such was the shock that it took Hans over a month before he could summon up the energy to write to Inge, but when he did so he poured out his heart to her and apologised profusely for being such a lousy correspondent. 'I now feel an inner compunction to say what really goes without saying but must be said for all that', he wrote. 'I'm with you in spirit every hour of the day. When I awake in the mornings, and also in the evenings, when I review my innermost thoughts, my love speeds on its way to you. I know how little I am compared to what you've lost, but the little I am wants to be as much use to you as it can.'[85]

By early October, Hans had turned the corner. Work eased off as preparations were made for a return to Germany, then he heard the uplifting news that his father's sentence was reduced from four months to two and that he was due to be released on 25 October. Hans started reading again. He tackled Adalbert Stifter's *Nachsommer* (1857, *Indian summer*), a novel about educational development, as well as a history of the Church in which he found the chapter on the persecution of Christians especially interesting.[86] He was also cheered by two letters from Otl, which made him reflect on his own 'internal crisis' and the feeling that he had left boyhood behind. 'I'm grateful to God that I had to go to Russia. I have experienced a change of scene that has cut me off from all the flower gardens of the past and set me down in the great plain, where I have found a solitude for which I have been searching for years.' The purgative effect of his dark night of the soul was evident to him. 'It's only here that I've finally learned to stop taking myself so infinitely seriously, to turn my aimless contemplation inside out and direct my mind outward, at material things.' Half of himself wanted to 'cut loose right now and tramp east, alone and devoid of material possessions [...] if only I wasn't a European and unable to desert Europe at this eleventh hour. That is my reason for wanting to return to Germany: that the West and I shouldn't lose touch.'[87]

Hans, Schurik and Willi were changed young men when they returned from the eastern front to recommence their studies at the start of November 1942. Hans had seen at first-hand how the German forces had destroyed the lives of the Russian people; Schurik had witnessed his homeland violated by the Nazis; and Willi was outraged by the terrible treatment inflicted on the people of Eastern Europe. Their time in the east fortified them in their determination to offer resistance to Hitler and encouraged them to contemplate more daring deeds so as 'to make a breach in the wall of terror'.[88]

Notes

[1]   Sachs, *White Rose history* vol. ii, ch. 1, p. 4.

[2]   Fritz Hartnagel to Sophie, 10 May 1942, quoted in Sachs, *White Rose history* vol. ii (2007 update), ch. 1, p. 2.

[3]   Quoted in Hanser, *A noble treason*, p. 133.

[4]   Keller's political jeremiad was written in 1878 and addressed to the inhabitants of Zurich after the persecution in the press of the director of a hospital for mental patients.

[5]   Quoted in I. Scholl, *White Rose*, p. 30.

[6]   Hanser, *A noble treason*, pp. 137–9.

[7]   A. Dru in preface to *Journal in the night*, p. xii.

[8]   Fritz Hartnagel to Sophie, 30 May 1942, quoted in Sachs, *White Rose history* vol. ii (2007 update), ch. 3, p. 1.

[9]   Sophie to Lisa Remppis, 30 May 1942, *Heart of the White Rose*, p. 202.

[10]   Above all Hans prized *Wort und Wunder* (1940, *Word and wonder*), where von Radecki develops his *Weltanschauung* (world-view). See Knab, 'Die Newman–Rezeption der "Weißen Rose" ', p. 23.

[11]   Sophie to Lisa Remppis, 30 May 1942, *Heart of the White Rose*, p. 202.

[12]   See *Heart of the White Rose*, p. 316, n235.

[13]   Sophie to her parents, Inge and Lisl, 6 June 1942, *Heart of the White Rose*, p. 203.

[14]   Sophie to her parents, Inge and Lisl, 6 June 1942, *Heart of the White Rose*, p. 203.

[15]   Hanser, *A noble treason*, p. 157.

[16]   R. B. Melon, *Journey to the White Rose in Germany* (Indianapolis: Dog Ear, 2006), p. 38.

[17]   Dumbach & Newborn, *Sophie Scholl and the White Rose*, p. 54.

[18]   Quoted in Hanser, *A noble treason*, p. 116.

[19]   Quoted in Hanser, *A noble treason*, p. 144.

[20]   Quoted in Hanser, *A noble treason*, p. 146.

[21]   Comment under interrogation, quoted in Sachs, *White Rose history* vol. i, ch. 1, p. 2.

[22]   Quoted in Hanser, *A noble treason*, p. 151.

[23]   Sophie to Fritz Hartnagel(?), 24 June 1942 (extract), *Heart of the White Rose*, p. 204.

[24]   Sophie to Fritz Hartnagel(?), 24 June 1942 (extract), *Heart of the White Rose*, p. 204.

[25]   The name was decided on by Hans and may have come from the white rosebud he had kept in his breast pocket following his military conscription in 1938; at the time he told his sister Inge of this, but not Sophie (27 June 1938, *Heart of the White Rose*, p. 12). At this stage the 'White Rose' was merely a reminder of his emotional life, which he and his friends sustained through music, painting, poetry and drama, though, by chance, the symbol of the white rose conveniently contrasted with the 'brown dirt' of Nazi ideology.

[26]   Around this time Muth gave Hans 300 Marks to buy books, even though Hans had agreed to reorganise his library *gratis*.

[27]   C. Moll, 'Acts of resistance: the White Rose in light of new archival evidence', *Resistance against the Third Reich 1933–1990*, ed. M. Geyer & J.W. Boyer (Chicago: University of Chicago, 1994), pp. 178–9.

[28]   The Greek legend about Epimenides held that he fell asleep as a boy and remained isolated in a cave for fifty-seven years until the time of his awakening arrived. Then, filled with knowledge and wisdom, he proclaimed through poetry and prophesy themes about purification and sacrifice.

[29]   McDonough, *Sophie Scholl*, p. 98. This report was dated 18 February 1943.

[30]   J. Fest, *Plotting Hitler's death: the German resistance to Hitler* (New York: H. Holt, 1997), p. 198.

[31]   In a letter to his parents Hans had quoted the first of the two verses by Goethe, prefaced by the remark: 'A poem by Goethe from Parmenides, which the British might well bear in mind' (Hans to his parents, 17 January 1941, *Heart of White Rose*, p. 187).

[32]   I. Scholl, *The White Rose*, p. 34.

[33]   Sophie's diary, 29 June 1942, *Heart of White Rose*, pp. 207–8.

34   This last sentence was a saying used by dissidents towards the end of the
     First World War (Hanser, *A noble treason*, p. 161).

35   H. Siefken, introduction to *Die Weiße Rose und Ihre Flugblätter, Doku-
     mente, Texte, Lebensbilder, Erläuterungen* [*The White Rose and their
     leaflets: documents, texts, biographical sketches, explanations*] ed. H.
     Siefken (Manchester: Manchester University Press, 1994), p. 6.

36   Moll argues that, as with the paragraph in the second leaflet about the
     elimination of the Jews and Poles, much of the third leaflet was composed
     by Schurik, with its emphasis on the joint guilt of all Germans and its
     suggestions for 'passive resistance' ('Acts of resistance', p. 178).

37   The context of this remark, that the 'first concern for any German should
     not be the military victory over Bolshevism, but the defeat of National
     Socialism', was not generally accepted at the time because most Germans
     were persuaded by Nazi propaganda to fear the Bolshevik threat above all
     else, even those unsympathetic to Nazism (D. Sölle, introduction to I.
     Scholl, *White Rose*, p. xi).

38   '"Wir schweigen nicht, wir sind Euer böses Gewissen" Die Newman–Rezeption
     der "Weißen Rose" und ihre Wirkungsgeschichte', J. Knab, *Newman Studien*
     xx (2010), pp. 26–8.

39   January/February 1941, *Journal in the night*, no. 504, p. 150.

40   *Kierkegaard the cripple*, trans. C. Van O. Bruyn (London: Harvil Press,
     1950), p. 2.

41   The relevant passage from *The Christian and history* is reproduced in *Die
     Weiße Rose*, ed. Siefken, pp. 165–6.

42   W. *Graf, Briefe und Aufzeichnungen*, ed. A. Knoop-Graf & I. Jens (Frank-
     furt: Fischer, 1994), p. 41.

43   June 1940, *Journal in the night*, no. 289, p. 76.

44   19 May 1940, *Journal in the night*, no. 234, p. 59. Haecker uses the
     expression 'Adventist paganism' to refer to the way pagans like Virgil
     prepared the way for Christianity and anticipated some of its mysteries.

45   This sentence is 'pure Newman', says Dermot Fenlon ('From the White
     Star to the Red Rose', p. 60).

46   This, says Fenlon, is 'pure Haecker' ('From the White Star to the Red Rose',
     p. 60).

47   About this section, Fenlon writes: 'this is the Newman whose Christology
     of the Apocalypse pervades both his published and unpublished Anglican
     sermons' ('From the White Star to the Red Rose', p. 60).

48   This leaflet makes clear the futility of attempting to combat evil without
     being in union with God. Clearly, the argument is a religious one, but as
     the White Rose students sought to align themselves with the wider
     resistance movement, the leaflets they produced six months later were

more overtly political and less religious.

49   Hanser, *A noble treason*, p. 164.
50   I. Scholl, *White Rose*, p. 36.
51   I. Scholl, *White Rose*, pp. 36–7.
52   Sophie to Lisa Remppis, 27 July 1942, *Heart of White Rose*, p. 209.
53   Sophie's diary, 15 July 1942, *Heart of White Rose*, p. 208.
54   I. Scholl, *The White Rose*, p. 39.
55   Sophie's diary, 6 August 1942, *Heart of White Rose*, p. 209.
56   Fritz Hartnagel to Sophie, 26 June 1942, quoted in 'From the White Star to the Red Rose', p. 63.
57   Fritz Hartnagel to Sophie, 26 June 1942, quoted in 'From the White Star to the Red Rose', p. 63.
58   Fritz Hartnagel to Sophie, 4 July 1942, quoted in 'From the White Star to the Red Rose', p. 63.
59   'The testimony of conscience', *Parochial and plain sermons* vol. v, pp. 240, 250.
60   Fritz Hartnagel to Sophie, 25 June 1942, quoted in 'From the White Star to the Red Rose', p. 64.
61   Sophie's diary, 9 August 1942, *Heart of White Rose*, p. 210. This reference to the last age suggests that she had thought about the Scriptural prophecies concerning the end of the world.
62   Sophie's diary, 9 August 1942, *Heart of White Rose*, p. 210; I. Scholl, *The White Rose*, p. 48.
63   Sophie's diary, 9 August 1942, *Heart of White Rose*, pp. 210–11.
64   Sophie to Fritz Hartnagel, August 1942, *Heart of White Rose*, p. 211.
65   Hans to his parents, 27 July 1942, *Heart of White Rose*, p. 213.
66   Hans to his parents, 7 August 1942, *Heart of White Rose*, p. 214.
67   Hans to Kurt Huber, 17 August 1942, *Heart of White Rose*, p. 216.
68   Hanser, *A noble treason*, p. 177.
69   Hans to his mother, 24 August 1942, *Heart of White Rose*, pp. 217–18.
70   Hans to his mother, 2 September 1942, *Heart of White Rose*, p. 219.
71   Hans to Rose Nägele, 10 September 1942, *Heart of White Rose*, p. 220.
72   Hans to his parents, 18 September 1942, *Heart of White Rose*, p. 221.
73   Hans' diary, 30 July 1942, *Heart of White Rose*, pp. 222–3.
74   Hans' diary, 31 July 1942, *Heart of White Rose*, p. 223.
75   Hans' diary, 7 August 1942, *Heart of White Rose*, p. 223.
76   Hans' diary, 9 August 1942, *Heart of White Rose*, pp. 224–5.
77   Hans' diary, 12 August 1942, *Heart of White Rose*, p. 226.
78   Hans' diary, 16 August 1942, *Heart of White Rose*, p. 227.
79   Hans' diary, 17 August 1942, *Heart of White Rose*, p. 229.

[80]   Hans' diary, 18 August 1942, *Heart of White Rose*, pp. 230–1.

[81]   Hans' diary, 22 August 1942, *Heart of White Rose*, pp. 231–3.

[82]   Sachs, *White Rose history* vol. ii, ch. 13, p. 3.

[83]   Hans' diary, 28 August 1942, *Heart of White Rose*, pp. 234–6.

[84]   Hans' diary, 11 September 1942, *Heart of White Rose*, p. 238.

[85]   Hans to Inge, 15 October 1942, *Heart of White Rose*, pp. 241–2.

[86]   Hans' diary, 13 October 1942, *Heart of White Rose*, p. 241. The unnamed
       book might have been Haecker's *Der Christ und die Gerschichte* (1935,
       The Christian and history).

[87]   Hans to Otl Aicher, 9 October 1942, *Heart of White Rose*, pp. 239–40.

[88]   Hanser, *A noble treason*, p. 184.

6 STALINGRAD AND THE TURN OF THE TIDE: AUTUMN AND WINTER 1942

SOPHIE WAS PLAYING the piano at home in Ulm on 23 August when her mother told her the news of Ernst Reden's death. She stopped playing, went into Inge's room, and silently, after standing there for a moment, placed a picture of the Pietà d'Avignon in front of Inge, then left quietly. Later Lisl found Sophie standing beside a window with tears rolling down her cheeks; angrily and with a certain determination, Sophie said, 'That's it. Now I'm going to do something.'[1]

As far as Sophie was concerned, her father was in jail for his own good—'It is the best thing that could have happened'—and told him as much. He needed the solitude; and she needed to reflect on why he was in jail, though 'not from motives of hatred or revenge'.[2] She told her father that friends sent him their regards—the Scholl family were permitted to write once a fortnight and Robert once a month—and that 'they are all at work on the wall of thoughts surrounding you'. The phrase the 'wall of thoughts' would have meant nothing to the censors, but to Robert it was full of meaning. It was the title of a newspaper article by Ernst Wiechert thanking readers who had kept faith with him when the authorities tried to isolate him in retaliation for his speech at Munich University in April 1935; the speech was entitled 'The writer and his time' and the Scholl family possessed a copy. In 1937, a year before his two-month incarceration at Buchenwald, Wiechert had written about the thousands standing round his house, a faithful, steadfast wall of people, 'there purely so that I shall know they are there', so that 'my house shall not be hemmed in by alien territory, solitude, or bitter desolation [...] nor a wall of power or authority [...] but a wall of love'.[3] That was why Sophie ended her letter, 'You can sense that you are not alone, I am sure, because our thoughts can breach any gate or wall: thoughts!'[4]

During her war service at the munitions factory Sophie found work on the production line soulless and degrading, and could not but notice that most people were unhappy. She admired the Russians working around her as they were more straightforward, trustful, and ready to help others than the German women. 'What a pity it would be if they, too, became infected with the suspicion and commercialism of "superior" Europeans like us', she told her friend Lisa.[5] She was pointedly considerate to the Russian girls who formed part of the Nazi system of imported slave labour from the occupied zone—around seven million, mainly Slavs— and along with her friends pooled ration coupons for them, so as to treat them not as aliens but as sisters.

An opportunity arose to turn her mind towards more academic subjects when Otl became embroiled in a discussion with Hans and Muth about Goethe. In response to one of Otl's letters, she told him that she now considered that Goethe's conceit contrasted unfavorably with St Augustine's humility and prevented him from seeing that he, too, was part of God's creation. It was clear to her now that humility of heart paved the way for a hunger for things of the next world, and that self-regard and self-sufficiency were serious handicaps. Sophie had reached this conclusion because her heart had been changed as a result of meeting such a wide variety of people over her three years of National Labour or war service, and she no longer saw the 'herd' around her. In the sanatorium at Bad Dürrheim she had learned to see the demanding sick as people in their own right; at the kindergartens at Ulm and Blumberg she had learned to see the children as lovable; and in the munitions factory she had learned the meaning of simplicity from the Russian workers. She had experienced the poverty and neediness of others and this had helped her to appreciate her own.

She kept working on her article on music (originally intended for *Windlicht*), but found it difficult to finish because 'fresh perspectives keep opening up'. She had listened to Bach's Brandenburg Concertos during the summer and felt that they did not enrich the soul in the way that Beethoven's music did; Beethoven 'stirs and ploughs you up and leaves you feeling like a furrowed field'. Instead, Bach was more like seed because it contained 'an element of crystalline clarity, of indestructible order'.[6] She could play Beethoven when she was gloomy, but not Bach. At present she did not want to broadcast her views too widely as she was still not finished with the subject.

Once she had completed her factory work in mid-September, Sophie intended to travel to Munich to sort out her room with her sister Lisl, and then to head off to the mountains as a way of offsetting the madness she saw all around her. She had the impression that people had lost control over themselves and their actions and were 'impelled by some evil power'.[7] There was even a hint of this in the factory, where the machines seemed to be acquiring a demonic quality. Reading *Creator and creation* she was struck by Haecker's contention that all tragedy is resolved not only in heaven and eternal salvation, but in hell and eternal damnation. While generally assenting to the argument, she still had problems with hell: how can I be happy knowing that some of my fellow creatures are unhappy, she reasoned? She found it difficult to comprehend how Lazarus failed to hear the plea of the rich man in hell for a drop of water. But she recalled a passage in Bernanos' *Diary of a country priest* which ran, 'Eternal damnation is the inability to love anymore'. Perhaps it was also the fact of not being loved anymore? she wondered. These were terrible and unsolvable questions, and she could only take the answers on trust, 'for hell is as much a mystery as heaven'.[8] She reassured Otl that she did not doubt a truth simply because it was still hidden from her, and asked him to shed light on the matter for her, if he could.

Sophie's diary continued to record her difficulties in prayer and the manner in which she battled on, despite feeling that words just drained out of her when she tried; at times, all she could manage was the cry, 'Help me'. She felt unable to offer up any other prayer because she was far too miserable. 'So I pray to learn how to pray'. The cause of her sadness arose from her realisation that she had not kept a check on her affection for Schurik and had led herself into a state of self-deception over him: 'It was simply my vanity that wanted to possess a person who was worth something in the estimation of others', she admitted. Disgusted with herself, she saw 'how ludicrously I distort my own image'—but she longed for the chance to prove herself.[9] Even nature did not console her now, as it filled her with melancholy and reminded her of her guilt.

Yet the very same day Sophie wrote to Lisa to say she was delighting in the last autumnal rays of the sun and marvelling at the beauty that was not created by man.

> It is all so wonderfully beautiful here that I have no idea what kind of emotion my speechless heart should develop for it, because it is too immature to take pure pleasure in it. It merely marvels and contents itself with wonder and enchantment. Isn't it mysterious—and frightening, too, when one does not know the reason—that everything should be so beautiful in spite of the terrible things that are happening? My sheer delight in all things beautiful has been invaded by a great unknown, an inkling of the creator whom his creatures glorify with their beauty. That is why man alone can be ugly, because he has the free will to dissociate himself from this song of praise. Nowadays one is often tempted to believe that he will drown the song with gunfire and curses and blasphemy. But it dawned on me last spring that he can't, and I will try to take the winning side.[10]

Instead of going off to the Bohemian Forest with her sister Lisl, as planned, Sophie decided to remain in Munich to help Professor Muth as his house had recently been damaged during one of the first RAF bombing raids on Munich. To judge from a spate of letters to Fritz, whose unit had been posted to Stalingrad (now Volgograd), a large industrial city on the River Volga, it is clear that Sophie sought to make amends for becoming over-friendly with Schurik by investing her heart and mind more fully in Fritz's affairs. Giving heartfelt thanks for his last letter, she assured him that she wanted to back him up in the arguments he felt compelled to have with his fellow officers about the trampling of the weak by the strong; such behaviour was degenerate or else utterly insensitive. She realised there was no solution in this life, and quoted Romans 8:19–20: 'For the earnest expectation of the creature waiteth for the manifestation of the sons of God. For the creature was made subject to vanity, *not* willingly, but by reason of him who hath subjected the same in hope.'[11]

She urged Fritz to read the whole chapter, particularly those wonderful words, 'For the law of the Spirit of life in Christ Jesus hath made me free from the law of sin and death' (Romans 8:2). 'Aren't they terribly, terribly poor, the people who neither know nor believe that? Their poverty ought to make us eternally patient with them (that, and the knowledge of our own weaknesses, for what would we amount to by ourselves?), even if their stupid arrogance tends to infuriate us.' If his companions believed that might was right, did they believe that man and beast were on a par? Or did they believe that man shared in the world of the spirit, in which case, why should brute force prevail in the world of the spirit? Should a poet such as Hölderlin count for less than a world-champion boxer like Max Schmeling? What lazy thinkers his opponents were! No-one really believed that the strong should trample on the weak. That urge for self-preservation would only lead Fritz's fellow officers to self-destruction. 'They know nothing of a world of the spirit in which the law of sin and death has been overcome.'[12]

Sophie knew that Fritz had not used up all his annual quota of leave, so she urged him to join the Scholl family at Ulm over Christmas. She had made plenty of Advent crowns with Inge, including one for him which she put in the post. She told him, 'I have been giving a lot of thought lately to the kind of job you might take up after the war', and suggested he might think of farming.[13] That same day Fritz openly expressed his love for Sophie: 'I count my love, in which you are wrapped, as part of my portion. More and more I sense it is more blessed to love than be loved.'[14]

Hans' student company arrived back in Munich on 6 November. Writing to Fritz just hours before Hans was expected home the following night, Sophie ought to have been full of joy, as she was soon to begin sharing lodgings with her elder brother at 13 Franz Josef Strasse, but instead her letter was full of foreboding. Her words, 'I suppose I should be glad he's back with us', showed how heavily the leaflet campaign was preying on her mind; and her comment that, 'They may well turn out to be productive times, but I can't feel wholeheartedly happy', was consistent with her anticipation of menace and dread. Without disclosing any details, she summed up her fears, while displaying courage in facing up to them:

> I am never free for a moment, day or night, from the depressing and unremitting state of uncertainty in which we live these days, which precludes any carefree plans for the next day and casts a shadow over all the days to come. [...] Every word has to be examined from every angle before it is uttered, to see if it carries a hint of ambiguity. Faith in other people has been forcibly ousted by mistrust and caution. It is exhausting—disheartening too, sometimes. But, no, I won't let anything dishearten me. Trivialities like these can never master me while I am in possession of other, unassailable joys. Strength flows into me when I think of them, and I'd like to address a word of encouragement to all who are similarly affected.[15]

When writing these rousing words Sophie had no idea that the Battle of Stalingrad was beginning to swing in favour of the Russians, although Fritz's next letter now spoke of the need to dig in for the winter, despite the fact that the Stukas and artillery were pounding the Russian positions by the river Volga.[16] The battle had begun that August. Nazi propaganda had reported victory after victory as the German Sixth Army reached the outskirts of the city in early September, effectively surrounding the Russians, and by late September the swastika was raised over the city centre. The invaders had fought their way street by street against fierce resistance, and both sides suffered tremendous losses in the bitter urban fighting. On some days, what the Germans gained in day-light, the Russians regained by night. Soon the blasted ruins of houses and factories began to stink as winds carried the smell of decaying corpses into every nook and cranny. Despite pouring in men and occupying as much as ninety percent of the city, the Germans could not dislodge the Russians from the sprawling industrial quarters along the Volga. By early November positive media reports began to dry up, and winter approached. Fritz reported on 11 November that they had almost run out of food and that the ground was frozen and hard to dig, while he struggled to maintain the morale of his men.

On 19 November General Zhukov launched a counter offensive to the north and south of Stalingrad, and within five days the German Sixth Army was surrounded. The *Luftwaffe* was called in to drop supplies to the beleaguered Army, who were forbidden by Hitler to break out and retreat, but with limited success. The intention of the air bridge was to supply the Sixth Army until a new German offensive broke the encirclement, but the attempt was abandoned just before Christmas. Desperate close-quarter fighting continued during mid-winter, and many soldiers died through starvation, cold, wounds and infections. But all this was kept from the German public, who were not officially told of the disaster until 31 January 1943, the day after the tenth anniversary of the seizure of power, though unofficially it was impossible to prevent the news from seeping out. Nor was it possible to suppress news of the Allied amphibious landing in French North Africa on 8 November 1942, the biggest of its kind in history, and the Allied victory at El Alamein in Egypt three days later.

Sophie was relieved to receive a letter from Fritz on 17 November, as it meant he was alive. She was cheered to read that he was determined to overcome boredom in his work and isolation, for he declared he had been living in a 'wasteland' for five years or more. 'If I could', replied Sophie,

> I'd redouble my efforts to arm you against potential apathy, and I wish your thoughts of me were a permanent incentive to resist it.
>
> If only you could go to church sometime and take Communion. What a source of consolation and strength you might find it.
>
> The only remedy for a barren heart is prayer, however poor and inadequate.[17]

She reminded him of the time he had visited her the previous year at Blumberg, when they had prayed together. 'I'll keep on repeating it for us both: we must pray, and pray for each other, and if you were here, I'd fold hands with you, because we are poor, weak, sinful children.' She felt unable to write more because she was filled with fear, though she felt 'an undivided yearning for Him who can relieve me of it'. She confessed, 'I am still so remote from God and don't sense his presence when I pray', sometimes feeling as if her appeals to God were met with silence. 'But prayer is the only remedy for it, and however many devils scurry around inside me, I shall cling to the rope God has thrown me in Jesus Christ, even if my numb hands can no longer feel it. Please remember me in your prayers.'[18]

It was nearly four weeks before Fritz could write again. When he did so, he explained that they had abandoned the airport on 22 November and that his signals corps had been given six hours to re-train and take up defensive duties as an infantry corps.

Three days later they had been under constant fire from the Russian forces, who were just 300 yards away, but they had had to be careful in returning fire as their ammunition was limited. In this dire situation he saw how brutality against the enemy was viewed as 'an outstanding virtue', as men's consciences became dulled beyond all recognition. He assured Sophie that he continued to pray, as it was his 'only foothold in all the frenzy'.[19]

Russia had had a marked effect on Hans, as he and his medical friends had spent a great deal of time together on the eastern front discussing how to follow up the White Rose leaflets. Their carefree and reckless behaviour on the return journey signaled the change they had undergone and was a token of what was to follow. Hans and four of his friends had begun the journey home on 1 November, and their singing in a cattle truck encouraged other soldiers to join in. At one stop-over they caused a scene by offering cigarettes to Russian POWs. Later, at Warsaw, they asked a band in a restaurant to play a Russian tune for them to sing to, but were refused—until Hans took out a gun; when the band left, they sang the British national anthem. What had come over Hans and his friends? What was going through their minds? It seems that they were more determined than ever to do something, having seen how human life was risked and wasted on an unimaginable scale. They reasoned, Why not, then, risk it in opposing the regime? Rather than living in continuous fear of being under surveillance or informed upon, and overwhelmed by danger and risk, why not resist the regime actively rather than just passively?

Instead of heading straight home, where he was expected on 8 November, Hans delayed his return to Ulm so as to work on resistance matters. On arriving in Munich, he and Schurik paid a visit to Schurik's friend Lilo Ramdohr to see how they could meet her close friend Falk Harnack, the former director and producer of the National Theatre based in Weimar. As a student in Munich in the mid-1930s, Harnack had actively opposed the brown shirts with leaflets, and in 1938 he had helped to organize a strike at the University; his brother Arvid, a high-ranking civil servant, was a leader in the resistance movement in Berlin and currently under arrest. Hans and Schurik also met up with Christl and told him of the plans they had made while on the Russian front, and asked him to draft a leaflet which would help to open German eyes. Hans could not talk of anything but Russia those days, and spoke openly about what he had witnessed. After taking over his new apartment on 15 November, which had access to a phone, a hot bath and a kitchen, he finally returned to Ulm and took Schurik with him. Hans was dismayed to find that his family friend Hans Hirzel had nearly exposed them by his careless behaviour. Hans Hirzel was, it seems, mentally unstable and had vacillated about taking part in dissident activity—and, unbeknown to the others, had stolen cyanide with a view to taking his own life. Nevertheless, Hans Scholl showed him a poster which featured the Star of David and the caption, 'He who wears this sign is an enemy of our nation'; Hans suggested that he design another, replacing the Star with the swastika.

Willi, meanwhile, had returned to his home in Saarbrucken and discovered that the town had been heavily bombed. To judge from his diary entries, life was not easy there as his parents were ardent National Socialists. Furthermore, he discovered that friends of his had clearly enjoyed their military duties, rather than reacting against the war, which had so far taken the lives of two of his friends. Willi then travelled to Bonn, officially to arrange a fencing tournament between the students of Bonn and Munich, unofficially to sound out his *Grauer Orden* and *Neudeutschland* friends; he took with him a Russian icon of our Lady for a friend who was engaged to be married. He journeyed on to Cologne to see Marianne Thoeren, the girl he had fallen in love with in 1939 and corresponded with from various war zones; Willi asked her to marry him, only to discover she was already engaged to someone else! He was devastated—like the city—but the emotional blow had a liberating effect on him; now he made up his mind to get fully involved in the resistance against Hitler, and so did not let up on his round of visits.

On 19 November the Scholls heard that their father would no longer be able to practice his profession as a tax lawyer, because he was deemed politically unreliable, though he would be allowed to work as a bookkeeper. Thirty of his clients signed a petition for the ban to be lifted, but to no effect, and so the parents had to consider how they could continue to support their five children and large family apartment. Sophie told Fritz that his offer of financial help would now come in useful.[20] Once released from jail, Robert Scholl continued to display his usual indomitable attitude towards the regime, frequently muttering, *Allen Gewalten zum Trutz* (Stand firm against all the powers that be). News of the sufferings of close friends of the Scholls put their own problems into context: after an air raid on Stuttgart, Susanne Hirzel came through unscathed, but Jürgen Wittenstein's mother had lost her home.

Around 23 November, a week before lectures were due to start, Hans and Schurik left Ulm for Munich to begin the next phase of their resistance work, visiting Stuttgart, Bonn and Freiburg in search of supporters, investors and materials. In Stuttgart, Sophie had arranged for them to meet Eugen Grimminger, the account-ant friend of her father; to avoid being overheard, the conversa-tion took place outdoors, while the crucial part was confined to a noisy commercial site on the outskirts of town. Schurik and Hans explained that they needed financial backing to tour the Reich seeking out like-minded students who were willing to join them in their resistance work. Initially Grimminger was alarmed by their proposal and feared that the two had absorbed Bolshevik ideas from their time in Russia, but by the end of the meeting he was satisfied enough to give them 1000 Marks, with the promise of paper and envelopes to follow, and a commitment to find others who would give.

Willi continued to sound out old friends, speaking to them about the senseless deaths caused by the war, condemning its perpetrators, and explaining that there were others who felt as he did. Besides Gogol's *Reflections on the divine liturgy*, Willi was reading Michael Brink's latest book on *Don Quixote* which contained passages with an unambiguous call to resistance. Four years earlier he had listened to Brink read from his works at an illegal *Bündische* meeting in Bonn. Meetings like this had inspired students in Bonn to undertake activities against the regime and Willi was in touch with these Bonn friends, who fed him information about Brink's activities. Willi had also been in touch with the Munich priest Alfred Delp (who was among the 5000 people who would be executed in the aftermath of the 20 July 1944 attempt on Hitler's life)[21] and others linked to the non-violent resistance group called the Kreisau Circle.

By 27 November all the White Rose students were back in Munich, and Willi was now joined by his sister Anneliese. The following day Hans and Schurik visited Falk Harnack at Chemnitz, near the old Czech border. Schurik told him about the White Rose leaflets and showed him drafts for new ones. Harnack told them he preferred the tighter style and more down-to-earth emphasis of the drafts over the four leaflets already circulated. Once they had finished speaking about the leaflets, Hans talked about his plans for their distribution. How could they link up with the resistance movement in Berlin and spread their leaflets more widely? Was it possible to set up cells in every German university? Harnack believed in integrating the activities of the resistance groups, whatever their political persuasion, into a broader coalition rather than working independently, and he suggested they begin with left-wing groups, which had good structures in place, before working round to the more conservative groups. Before handing over the names of contacts, Harnack asked if Hans and Schurik were willing to help rescue his brother Arvid and his co-conspirators who were awaiting trial and almost certain execution; if so, he would put them in touch with his cousins Dietrich and Klaus Bonhoeffer. But Hans and Schurik declined. Harnack responded by saying that he was unable to involve himself in their plans while there was still a chance to save his brother. Nevertheless, he contacted his cousins and told them about the plans of the Munich students to unite student resistance movements across Germany.

On their return to Munich, Hans told Lilo about his response to Harnack's demand, admitting, 'It cannot ever go so far that we risk our lives'. She agreed and thought her friend impertinent in his request. But the meeting with Harnack had at least convinced Hans and Schurik of one thing: that it was simply not possible for a revolt to occur within Hitler's army. Some other means had to be sought to topple the regime.

When the Grafs, Scholls and Christl Probst met up one evening it was to say goodbye to Christl who was about to be transferred to Innsbruck. Whenever Anneliese was out of earshot, they spoke about their plans for more leaflets and a graffiti campaign, as Willi had ascertained that his sister was not fully on board. Willi might do shocking things, like conversing with Russian women in the street while wearing his army uniform, but he had a sixth sense when it came to identifying who might join them, and he made his sister promise not to look around his room. Willi's diary entry for 1 December reads, 'the business has started to get going a little'. Traute Lafrenz set off to test the waters at her former university in Hamburg, taking one of the White Rose leaflets with her; she explained that she needed to give strong stuff to her friends, who had at one time had intended to blow up railway bridges. Hans later asked Traute to acquire a duplicating machine in Hamburg, to supplement the one he and Schurik had recently purchased for 240 Marks.

Around fifty people were active in the loosely-connected Hamburg resistance group and they met up at two bookstores or selected coffee houses; their leader was Hans Leipelt, a decorated soldier who had been discharged from the army because his mother was a Jew, even though he was now a Christian. In Hamburg, Traute met up with Heinz Kucharski and Greta Rothe, who had previously helped to distribute the banned speeches of Thomas Mann; they liked the White Rose leaflet and asked for copies of the other three to be sent them, so that they could join the Munich students in distributing them. Meanwhile, Hans visited Muth and Huber, telling them tales from the Russian front, while Sophie contacted Susanne Hirzel with a view to visiting Stuttgart so that she could meet Eugen Grimminger herself.

Somehow the students managed to combine all this with their studies and a social life which centred on music; they also managed to operate in relative harmony, despite their political differences. Though Schurik was nervous about the way Hans and Willi went about contacting individuals, rather than relying on established resistance networks, he nevertheless trusted them entirely. Both he and Hans were thinking of leaving medicine once the war was over, Schurik to become an artist, Hans to enter politics, with hopes of fostering a democracy and of removing the enmity between Russia and Germany. Like Schurik and Hans, Willi was an avid reader and, as a practising Catholic, he imbibed literature with a Catholic outlook, especially if it was banned and circulated in typewritten or manuscript form.[22] Despite recommencing classes, he was keenly applying himself to Michael Schmaus' *Katholische Dogmatik* (3 vols, 1938–41, *Christian dogmatics*), which attracted him because he was weary of abstract theology and wanted something with a more practical, living approach. The vibrancy of his faith can be seen from a letter he wrote to a young, married friend who needed support:

> I am happy that your faith in God gives you a foundation and a way to be able to lead such a life. Isn't that absolutely the only possibility of surviving in this darkness? After all, is it really so unbearable to be alone when you have the love of God, even if there isn't a soul around you who is 'related' to you? Maybe it is good that you are forced to rely on yourself at this time, for once to be without the variety of a nice life and comfortable things that can also be a distraction.[23]

Not everything went the way of the young conspirators. Willi's *Grauer Orden* friends in Munich declined to join him, much to his disappointment and disbelief, and Hans returned to Ulm to sound out his sister Inge, but without success. The White Rose students usually met to discuss plans in the evening or at weekends, and often ended their meetings with songs. Some of them sang for the Bach Choir, most of them listened to the lectures of Professor Huber, and they all attended concerts. On 8 December, the feast of St Nicholas, the whole group attended a performance of Handel's Messiah, and then had lunch together. On Sundays, Hans and Sophie would often disappear to the countryside together.

Hans wrote few letters at this time, as he had 'temporarily lost [his] zest for writing'. Though tempted to indulge his social propensities in an expanding circle of friends, he deliberately limited his engagements, using the excuse that he had 'more urgent business in the offing'[24]—though when Sophie's friend Gisela Schertling began her course in Munich, Hans immediately took an interest in her. In a strained letter to Rose, he referred to his preoccupation in cryptic fashion: 'Once wild beasts have burst their bars and are roaming the streets, every able-bodied person must take up arms, irrespective of class and inner vocation.' He explained that he was disinclined to pick up a pen because he found that letters were not helpful for mutual understanding and were a poor substitute for the 'conversational give-and-take' which could resolve the hundred questions which attached to every written word. At present,

> I prefer to cultivate the company of older people, but those whose hinges have not yet been rusted by bourgeois thinking, and who can still provide access to the peaks and troughs of human thought. [...] I don't attach much importance to the views of people who are fundamentally alien to me.[25]

On the Third Sunday of Advent 1942 (13 December) a meeting took place at the house of the student Eugen Turnher which marked a spiritual turning point for Hans, Sophie and Christl. The gathering was addressed by Theodor Haecker, who unfolded to his young listeners Newman's typology of history, based on his

four sermons on the Antichrist, which Haecker was busy translating at the time.[26] Newman, he told them, saw Christianity as
a constant 'watching' for Christ amidst various precursors of the
Antichrist; these precursors were repeatedly resisted by saints
and prophets, and in that way they held back the advent of the
Antichrist. Newman pointed out the benefit of prophecies for
Christians in the world when he said, 'I must think that this vision
of Antichrist, as a supernatural power to come, is a great provi-
dential gain, as being a counterpoise to the evil tendencies of the
age.'[27] Speaking in Advent, a time to mark not just the First
Coming (i.e. Christmas) but the Second Coming too, Newman
hoped to create 'watchers' who marked the season in the spirit
of the Church. By this, Newman meant Christians with an
awakened conscience, not those using violence. Haecker wanted
his hearers to focus on the hidden presence and living power of
Christ, which alone could withstand evil and overwhelm it.

Hitler was not the Antichrist, asserted Haecker, he was just a
messenger or *ante*type; the advent of the real Antichrist would be
accompanied by extraordinary signs and wonders, and by widespread apostasy. He was yet to come. But Hans disagreed, and he
argued with Haecker: the Antichrist *had* come, and was none other
than Hitler, and he must be overthrown by the German resistance.
This was no mere quibble; it signalled a new phase of the White
Rose, for Hans was now thinking like a resistance fighter, even
though he was not ready to resort to violence. The tone of the
White Rose leaflets had already shifted in the direction of active
resistance when the third leaflet encouraged sabotage; now Haecker's voice in them was to be muted. Haecker followed Newman
when he placed emphasis on the warfare conducted *inside* the
human person, in that private space called conscience where
decisions turn on fidelity to the inner voice and reality of God.
Hans, it seems, no longer wanted to listen to this advice. The next
(and last) two leaflets he and Schurik oversaw no longer bore the
name 'White Rose' (though historians call them White Rose
leaflets), but simply spoke of resistance.

When Willi arrived at the Scholls' apartment on 17 December he found Professor Huber there, and spent the next two hours listening to him. After Huber's departure, Hans, Sophie and Willi discussed what needed to be done over Christmas and by whom. Two days later, Hans and Sophie took Gisela with them on a pre-Christmas visit to Muth and Haecker, and at some stage in the proceedings Hans had a private conversation with Haecker. We don't know what passed between them, but after their departure, Haecker wrote to Inge, 'In my youth, I did not forge on ahead to Peter's last question, "But where shall we go?" ... But today that is very different, at least for thinking young people.'[28]

On 19 December Arvid Harnack was one of the thirteen conspirators sentenced to death after a high-profile, four-day trial in Berlin overseen by Roland Freisler, the president of the People's Court. Denied a defence by the SS, Harnack was hung on meat hooks three days later and slowly strangled to death. His wife Mildred was given a six-year prison sentence, but Hitler refused to endorse it and ordered a new trial, which ended with a death sentence; she was beheaded on 16 February 1943. The Gestapo gave the name *Die Rote Kapelle* (Red Orchestra) not only to the Soviet spy rings operating in German-occupied Europe but to the resistance movement in Berlin, which had arisen from a merger of the activities of Arvid Harnack and the *Luftwaffe* staff officer Harro Schulze-Boysen. By labelling the movement as 'Red' the intention was to discredit the resistance group with the taint of Bolshevism. With his wife Mildred, Harnack had formed a discussion circle to debate the political future of Germany after the downfall of the National Socialists, and afterwards the group had been in contact with Soviet agents, attempting to thwart the German invasion of the Soviet Union in June 1941. That year Harnack began publishing the resistance magazine *Die innere Front* (*The Inner Front*).

At a social event after the Bach Choir Christmas concert on Sunday 20 December, the two Scholls, Schurik and Willi got down to business, once Gisela had departed, for she was the daughter of staunch National Socialists and a keen supporter herself. Hans told them all about his conversation with Huber—his views on Bolshevism, his hopes of uniting science and philosophy, and of seeing the separation of church and state come about (along the lines recommended by Muth)—and reported that he had told Huber that he and Schurik had been responsible for the White Rose leaflets. The students then decided who was to be responsible for what: Sophie, Traute and Willi for the recruitment of new students; Hans and Schurik for obtaining financial backing, with Sophie looking after the cash and keeping the account books; everyone for paper and envelopes; Traute and Willi for a second duplicating machine; Hans, Schurik and Christl for the text of the next leaflet; and Schurik for pursuing Sophie's idea about graffiti. During the meeting Sophie commented that 'It was horrible how many good Christians were risking their lives in this war for a doubtful if not outright senseless cause, and, yet in contrast, hardly a single person was willing to risk his life to fight evil. Someone must do so.'[29]

The leaflets left over from the previous campaign were stored in a broom cupboard at Lilo Ramdohr's house and it was there that Schurik worked on stencil letters for graffiti slogans such as 'Down with Hitler'. Hans, Schurik and Sophie travelled to Stuttgart, where Sophie told Susanne Hirzel about the leaflet campaign, invited her to Hans' soirées in Munich, and asked her to coordinate the work in Stuttgart. Susanne related later that Sophie spoke along the lines, 'I have decided to do something. If one simply expresses an opinion against this system and does nothing, he has made himself guilty. This entire catastrophe is possible only because no one is yelling about it'. Sophie's mind was fixed; 'she was living on a totally different plane', and 'felt herself called by her own conscience'.[30] Meanwhile Hans and Schurik paid another visit to Grimminger. He was more at ease with the students this time and gave them thousands of envelopes, which were in short supply; his secretary contributed 500 Marks. When they all met up in a café afterwards, Hans was delighted: 'It won't be long before the sparrows are singing from the rooftops that we are governed by criminals. If many, very many people agree [with us], a deed can follow, and the torch that we take up can light new torches.'[31]

Susanne recalls that this talk made her very nervous: she thought—so she claimed under interrogation—that they had overestimated their own strength and not listened enough to those who disagreed with them; they were courageous, and expected others to be just like them; they were convinced about the rightness of their views and, as they only associated with like-minded people, these views were ever being reinforced. How could one justify a likely disaster for their families? she wondered. Nevertheless, Susanne told the other three musicians in her string quartet about Sophie's plan, and their reaction was to offer support, so long as the plan was not doomed to failure. Susanne was not the only one to grow fearful. After meeting Schurik again, Lilo also became frightened with his casual talk about death.

Before returning to Ulm for Christmas, Sophie's last visit was to a military hospital near Linz (Upper Austria) to see Otl, who had bluffed his way back from the eastern front and taken huge risks by pretending to be much more severely affected by his wounds than he really was. Otl told her that, after the Russians had retaken the Caucasus and the mess in Stalingrad, he wished to escape back to the west. Sophie told him all about their plan, then they spent hours discussing politics and religion: why Catholic countries seemed more susceptible to fascist powers, why so few Catholic intellectuals other than the philosopher and political theorist Lamennais favoured republicanism—and about Muth. Sophie suggested that after the war Germans should be forced to wear their Party numbers on their back, perhaps for the same length of time as they had belonged to the Party. On parting, Sophie made her way to Ulm, while Otl set off for Munich to spend the Christmas vacation with Muth.

In his last letter before Christmas, Fritz described the desperate times he was living through and how the Russians were attacking with a ferocity that had reduced his own battalion to the size of a company. 'Perhaps all the terrible things that are happening around me will contribute to the celebration of Christmas within', he told Sophie. Oddly, the worse things were, the more detached he became; he did not dread death any longer. He recalled a passage from St Augustine which he had intended to send to Inge after Ernst Reden's death: 'My sorrow was so great because I poured out my heart into the sand in that I loved a mortal as though he would not die'.[32]

During the Christmas holidays the White Rose students combined family celebrations with their resistance tasks. Their letters and diaries make it clear that family life was marked by tension and reserve, especially when the conversation turned to current affairs and politics, but this was typical of many German homes at the time where political divisions operated. Hans spoke to Inge for the last time about what he hoped would happen after the downfall of the National Socialists; while he was deeply satisfied with caring for the sick, he told her he did not want the Communists to be the only ones who could hold their heads high after the war, because then they would occupy the moral high ground over Christians. Inge was so alarmed at this that she made him swear he would do nothing that would leave the family open to criticism. Traute spoke to an aunt in Vienna about the White Rose activities in the hope of gaining contacts with like-minded students, and to an uncle who owned a typewriting business in the hope of obtaining a duplicating machine, but without success.

In conversation with his father, Willi happened to mention the idea of resistance and the two got into an argument; in the presence of his sisters, Willi told him that someone had to give a visible sign against the Nazis, even if it cost him his head. Generally, Willi was ideally suited to the task of recruitment as he was capable of throwing himself into a cause and was passionate and articulate in argument, though without denigrating opposing views. After Mass one Sunday he met two brothers, friends from *Neudeutschland*, who turned out to be in complete agreement about the need for resistance, whether active or passive. Heinz Bollinger was lecturing in philosophy at Freiburg and had already tried to set up a resistance group there, claiming that they had been given a duplicating machine and money for paper and stamps. His brother offered to help the White Rose students acquire weapons, army rail tickets, passes and forged leave papers. Willi mentioned that the White Rose students had connections with high-profile figures such as the chief of police in Berlin, Wolf-Heinrich Graf von Helldorff, and the diplomat Ulrich von Hassel (both of whom were hanged after the 20 July 1944 attempt on Hitler). The brothers gave Willi a two percent chance of success.

Hans sent copies of the White Rose leaflets to the manager of the Trumpf chocolate factory in Bonn and followed up his letter with a phone call. The manager was cautious at first, though he promised financial aid; soon he became impressed on account of the positive reaction he had received from those to whom he passed the leaflets. One of these was a coat-attendant at a theatre in Bonn who made copies of the leaflets and inserted them in the coats of theatre-goers. Hans and Sophie shared this story with their Ulm friend and collaborator Hans Hirzel, but their friend continued to vacillate in his commitment to their cause. He had been given money by Sophie to buy a duplicating machine, but had dumped the machine in the Danube, a deed he was careful to hide from them. Nevertheless, he told them he was willing to distribute leaflets in Stuttgart and Ulm—and even to duplicate them—so Hans Scholl gave him 350 envelopes. Hans also told the Hirzel schoolboy about his hopes for the political system in Germany after the war.

Hans' mind was not completely given over to politics since he kept up his more literary reading. One of the Christmas presents he gave a friend was Johannes von Tepl's *The ploughman from Bohemia*, which he inscribed with the words, 'Life is nourished by suffering'. The book is a spirited medieval dialogue between a ploughman, whose wife has recently died, and Death, and deals with their opposing views on life, mankind and morality. Willi, meanwhile, was reading *On the Christian view of man* by the Thomist philosopher Josef Pieper. Sophie was concerned that she had not received news from Fritz and wrote urging him to read! 'We have received a brain so we can think' she told him; 'That is work, and no emotion will save us from it.' Little did she know that he was under continuous fire in Stalingrad, along with 280,000 German soldiers. By now Sophie was using the wrong address for Fritz, which meant that her letters would eventually be returned to her. Nevertheless she wrote, 'You know of course what I wish for you. I place it all in the hand that makes our powerless love powerful.'[33]

Notes

1   *Heart of the White Rose*, p. 317, n238.
2   Sophie to Lisa Remppis, 2 September 1942, *Heart of the White Rose*, p. 243.
3   *Heart of the White Rose*, pp. 317–18, n238.
4   Sophie to her father, 7 September 1942, *Heart of the White Rose*, p. 247.
5   Sophie to Lisa Remppis, 2 September 1942, *Heart of the White Rose*, p. 244.
6   Sophie to Otl Aicher, 5 September 1942, *Heart of the White Rose*, pp. 245–6.
7   Sophie to her father, 22 September 1942, *Heart of the White Rose*, p. 247.
8   Sophie to Otl Aicher, 9 October 1942, *Heart of the White Rose*, pp. 248–9.
9   Sophie's diary, 10 October 1942, *Heart of the White Rose*, p. 249.
10 Sophie to Lisa Remppis, 10 October 1942, *Heart of the White Rose*, p. 250.
11 Sophie to Fritz Hartnagel, 28 October 1942, *Heart of the White Rose*, p. 251.
12 Sophie to Fritz Hartnagel, 28 October 1942, *Heart of the White Rose*, pp. 251–2.
13 Sophie to Fritz Hartnagel, 4 November 1942, *Heart of the White Rose*, p. 253.
14 Fritz Hartnagel to Sophie, 4 November 1942, quoted in Sachs, *White Rose history* vol. ii (2007 update), ch. 20, p. 1.
15 Sophie to Fritz Hartnagel, 7 November 1942, *Heart of the White Rose*, p. 255.

16   Fritz Hartnagel to Sophie, 7 November 1942, Sachs, *White Rose history* vol. ii (2007 update), ch. 20, p. 2.

17   Sophie to Fritz Hartnagel, 18 November 1942, *Heart of the White Rose*, p. 256.

18   Sophie to Fritz Hartnagel, 18 November 1942, *Heart of the White Rose*, pp. 256–7.

19   Fritz Hartnagel to Sophie, 12 December 1942, quoted in Sachs, *White Rose history* vol. ii (2007 update), ch. 24, p. 2.

20   Sophie to Fritz Hartnagel, 19 November 1942, *Heart of the White Rose*, p. 257.

21   Brink had visited Huber and tried to introduce him to Delp. Brink ended up in a concentration camp, first in Ravensbrück then in Sachsenhausen, and died in 1947 from prison and war injuries.

22   Around this time he read Reinhold Schneider's *Macht und Gnade* (1940, *Power and grace*), Josef Pieper's *Über das christliche Menschenbild* (1936, *The Christian idea of man*) and Romano Guardini's *Die Offenbarung als Geschichte* (1940).

23   Willi Graf to Otto Vieth, 1 December 1942, quoted in Sachs, *White Rose history* vol. ii, ch. 23, p. 4.

24   Hans to Otl Aicher, 6 December 1942, *Heart of the White Rose*, p. 259.

25   Hans to Rose Nägele, 14 December 1942, *Heart of the White Rose*, pp. 260–1.

26   In late summer or autumn 1943 Haecker read passages of his translation to members of the Oratory of St Philip Neri in Leipzig.

27   'The religion of Antichrist', *Discussions and arguments*, p. 75.

28   Sachs, *White Rose history* vol. ii, ch. 25, pp. 5–6, quoting from a heavily censored letter.

29   Sachs, *White Rose history* vol. ii, ch. 25, pp. 5–6.

30   Sachs, *White Rose history* vol. ii, ch. 25, p. 10, quoting from S. Hirzel, *Vom Ja zum Nein*, pp. 147–9.

31   Sachs, *White Rose history* vol. ii, ch. 25, p. 10.

32   Fritz Hartnagel to Sophie, 23 December 1942, quoted in Sachs, *White Rose history* vol. ii (2007 update), ch. 26, p. 1.

33   Sophie to Fritz Hartnagel, 26 December 1942, quoted in Sachs, *White Rose history* vol. ii (2007 update), ch. 27, p. 1.

7 MORE LEAFLETS: JANUARY–FEBRUARY 1943

N New Year's Day 1943 Haecker's diary opens with the words:

> One can already hear the howls and the whines of the demons more clearly in their dread-filled phrases. It is the last breathless gasp of the crazed man who runs amok, just before the end. An official, public call to hate! The hate will certainly be found, all right, but it will not be the hate they intend, and want, today; it will be different. Hate is the last revealing phase of the fallen spirit, and the very logic of dissolution.[1]

Feeding off Haecker, Hans had written in the fourth White Rose leaflet of demons 'lurking in the darkness', convinced that those resisting Hitler were battling against the forces of evil. In his own copy of the New Testament, Hans had marked the passage, 'For we wrestle not against flesh and blood, but against principalities, against powers, against the rulers of the darkness of this world, against spiritual wickedness in high places' (Ephesians 6:12). But in the fifth leaflet, which appeared in late January 1943, Haecker's voice was muted and there was no reference to demons or the Antichrist. In fact, the name 'White Rose' was dropped for 'Leaflets of the Resistance Movement in Germany'. The fifth leaflet was shorter, less literary, and more political than the fourth, and pitched at a wider audience: the emphasis was on German resistance. Roland Freisler, the president of the People's Court, later described the leaflet as a declaration of war against the Nazi Party.

The White Rose students had begun operating at the height of Hitler's success, when his hold on the German people was greatest and when those resisting him thirsted in vain for signs that pointed to a reversal of his long run of luck. Now, in January 1943, there were dramatic signs of such a reversal, both in the east and in North Africa, not to mention the steady flow of armaments from across the Atlantic intended for the Allied forces. The conviction among the White Rose students that the times must not be accepted passively, but opposed, was now being steeled and strengthened. They had changed from an anonymous small group based in Munich run by idealist students to a more dedicated and organized anti-Nazi resistance organization which planned to expand its field of operations.

On 8 January, Hans, Schurik, Sophie and Willi were all back in Munich for lectures. After a concert that evening, they reconvened at Manfred Eickemeyer's studio and listened to him relate the horrors he had seen in Poland, such as the gassings and concentration camps. (Although Eickemeyer had contributed 200 Marks to the White Rose activities, Hans kept him in the dark as to the precise nature of them and of his plan to use the studio basement as the hub of activity.) In the discussions that arose, Sophie voiced her difficulties in reconciling these atrocities with belief in God. The following day Hans, Schurik and Willi met up to discuss strategy, then Hans and Willi paid a visit to Professor Huber to tell him about their plans for the distribution of the next leaflets, without divulging any of the details. After listening to their plans, Huber told them that change was more likely to occur in southern Germany and he advised them not to bother with the north; overall he thought another leaflet campaign would have no appreciable effect on the public, while being fraught with danger. That day Willi told more of his Munich friends about the leaflet campaign, only to find that they were terrified of getting involved.

Hans had returned to Munich in an ebullient mood. A letter of his to Otl is full of fighting talk and even mentions the 'circle of people I have brought here together'.

> Their faces would delight you if you could see them. All the energy one expends flows back, undiminished, into one's heart. Only weaklings stint their strength. Fools

remain silent because they can't speak, and the unimaginative act tough and inflexible. Making a virtue out of a shortcoming, that's what I call Prussianism. It's a virtue we disown.[2]

By contrast, Sophie was low in spirits.

As January 1943 marked the 470th anniversary of the founding of the University of Munich, the Nazi Party decided to infuse the occasion with a heavy dose of discipline and morale-stiffening, particularly for those students who showed less patriotic ardour than was expected in the capital of the movement. On 13 January students, university officials and lecturers in full academic costume were addressed in the largest auditorium in the city by *Gauleiter* Paul Giesler, Nazi leader of the region and group commander of the Storm Troops. An ardent defender of Nazi ideology, Giesler was eager to imbue the students with the Party spirit and, knowing that the White Rose leaflets had circulated among them, to shake the recalcitrant into line. The ground floor was packed with the military, while the students occupied the balcony. In typically blunt fashion, Giesler launched a tirade against students who were draught-dodgers and malingerers, and threatened to filter out the fit among them so that they could serve in the army or factories, rather than wasting their time over books. Addressing the female students, he told them that instead of reading books they should be using their healthy bodies to produce a child a year for the Fatherland, preferably a male one, and he told them that his adjutants could help them, if any of them could not find a man.

His crude, leering speech produced a negative reaction: feet shuffling and noise from the balcony grew steadily louder until whistling and boos rang out and students began to leave by the score. Scuffles broke out as the Storm Troopers tried to hold back the exodus, and random arrests were made. On the ground floor crippled army soldiers joined in the protest, some waving walking sticks and crutches, all of which left the Storm Troopers helpless. The demonstration continued in the street outside with students shouting and singing—one of the few open protests of its kind in Nazi Germany—until the riot police moved in and dispersed them. A state of emergency was declared in Munich, and radio broadcasts and telephone were suspended. Not realising that the protest was spontaneous, Heinrich Himmler, the chief of Security Services, ordered agents to find out who the perpetrators were. Not a word about the affair appeared in the press, but news about it spread quickly and set off small protests in Vienna, Frankfurt and the Ruhr. Hans, Schurik and Sophie were not present at Giesler's speech, since they boycotted all official Nazi events, but they soon heard reports about the reaction it caused and were delighted.

Huber's response to Giesler's speech was to canvass his academic colleagues about composing a statement of protest, but not one of them offered to join him. This was Huber's tipping point, and from now on he decided to disassociate himself from his colleagues. Instead, he aligned himself with like-minded students— around 250 attended his lectures—and told Hans that he was willing to advise him about the leaflets. Later, when he found himself in court on trial for his life, he explained: 'In a state where free expression of public opinion is stifled, a dissident must necessarily turn to illegal methods.'[3] Huber now began to visit Hans, and when Sophie was around she stayed out of the way so as to give the impression she was not involved. Shown two alternative drafts of the fifth leaflet, one composed by Hans, the other by Schurik, Huber flatly rejected Schurik's on account of what he perceived to be its Bolshevik tone. Hans' draft, however, was to his liking, though he set about correcting it as if he were a professor marking a student's essay. Hans, however, would not accept all the 'corrections', and insisted on ensuring that the overall tone was not overly academic and on dropping the White Rose designation for one which spoke of the 'Resistance Movement in Germany'.

On 24 January, the day after the capture of German and Italian troops in Tripoli, Christl listened to a BBC broadcast (in German) of President Roosevelt's speech at Casablanca in which the President declared that the United States was entering the war and asking for unconditional surrender. The speech had a marked effect on Christl and he decided he would draft a leaflet based on it—which, though never printed, would have been the seventh produced by the White Rose students. A separate reason for composing it was the dire situation in Stalingrad and the appalling news that Hitler intended to abandon the 280,000 troops left in the city to the Russians. Since 6 November the Sixth Army had only been receiving one third of its rations, and on 22 January it lost its airbase for drops. It was effectively abandoned, since it had turned down (on Hitler's order) a chance to surrender on 8 January, and as many were dying of starvation and cold as were being killed by the Red Army.

For months Hans had been scheming how to boost the impact of the leaflet campaign without jeopardising the lives of those involved. The base of the operation was to be Eickemeyer's studio, though most of the work would be carried out at the Scholls' apartment. Hans had acquired the use of the studio and arranged for an artist from Ulm called Wilhelm Geyer (whose works on religious themes were commissioned by the Church) to set up his studio there, though the father of six was not told what it would be used for at night. The studio was centrally located and housed an exhibition of art work, which furnished a reason for all the comings and goings, and thus a cover for the operation. Schurik had acquired a large duplicating machine and borrowed a typewriter, and Sophie and Traute had procured special mimeograph paper from different stationery shops all over Munich, purchasing small quantities at a time so as to avoid suspicion. Thousands of copies of the fifth leaflet were cranked out one by one on the duplicating machine over several nights, an operation which required a great deal of stamina and patience. Addresses were taken from address books kept at the Deutsches Museum in Munich. The method of distribution was more sophisticated than that used for the earlier leaflets because the aim was to disguise the fact that Munich was the centre of the operation; this was achieved by the students going out alone or in pairs to other cities to post the leaflets.

In the fourth year of the war there was no free movement, so unsanctioned travel was fraught with danger. To travel by train meant passing through controls and check-points which required identification documents, travel permits and sometimes even a certificate of Aryan ancestry; young men had to produce documents about their draft status if they were dressed as civilians, or else an army pay-book, leave papers and travel orders if dressed in uniform—all of which had to be properly signed, countersigned and stamped. Random patrols would conduct searches on trains and occasionally in the street, especially if someone was carrying a large bag, not with the aim of discovering subversive literature but of detecting such items as smuggled goods, black-market currency, or rationed food without ration points. If one of the students was discovered carrying highly-subversive leaflets they would all be at risk, so to reduce the chance of detection when travelling by train, they hoisted their bags onto the overhead baggage-rack in one carriage before moving into another carriage for the rest of the journey, collecting their luggage at the end. Nevertheless, their bags could always be searched at their destination. Running such huge risks while looking inconspicuous and hiding any nervousness added a considerable psychological burden to the undertaking.

The courier system was planned by Hans. Schurik took a suitcase containing around one thousand leaflets to occupied Austria, posting two hundred in Salzburg, another two hundred in Linz (where Hitler had spent his boyhood), several hundred in Vienna to locations in Austria and another four hundred to Frankfurt, and the rest on his return journey at Salzburg. Willi took fewer leaflets in his suitcase as he carried a small duplicating machine, which he used to run off copies at different stops in towns along the Rhine. Some of his contacts were unwilling to cooperate in the scheme, even though Willi had chosen them carefully, but no-one sought to betray him. Willi left the duplicating machine in Saarbrücken with Willi Bollinger, who installed it in his hospital office and there ran off further copies, which were posted to likely sympathisers in the locality.

Sophie, too, had her own system. She took two thousand copies to Ulm where, with the assistance of Hans Hirzel, she set up a distribution base at the Lutheran Church where the Rev. Ernst Hirzel was pastor. Along with two of Hans Hirzel's friends, the four conspirators met behind the church organ to type addresses on envelopes from phone directories, fold the leaflets, stuff them in envelopes and seal them. Hirzel junior took several hundred to Stuttgart where he posted them with the help of his sister Susanne; Sophie took bundles in a briefcase to both Stuttgart and Augsburg, and over several journeys posted around eight hundred.[4] Somehow the leaflet reached Norway, where it was again copied and circulated; other copies passed through Sweden to Britain. This was fully in accordance with Hans' plans to set up cells in the large cities and foment a spirit of rebellion everywhere.

[The fifth leaflet]

A call to all Germans!

The war is approaching its destined end. As in the year 1918, the German government is trying to focus attention exclusively on the growing threat of submarine warfare, while in the East the armies are constantly in retreat and invasion is imminent in the West. Mobilization in the United States has not yet reached its climax, but already it exceeds anything that the world has ever seen. It has become a mathematical certainty that Hitler is leading the German people into the abyss. *Hitler cannot win the war; he can only prolong it.* The guilt of Hitler and his minions goes beyond all measure. Retribution comes closer and closer.

But what are the German people doing? They will not see and will not listen. Blindly they follow their seducers into ruin. *Victory at any price!* is inscribed on their banner. 'I will fight to the last man,' says Hitler—but in the meantime the war has already been lost.

Germans! Do you and your children want to suffer the same fate that befell the Jews? Do you want to be judged by the same standards as your traducers? Are we to be forever a nation which is hated and rejected by all mankind? No. Dissociate yourselves from National Socialist gangsterism. Prove by your deeds that you think otherwise. A new war of liberation is about to begin. The better part of the nation will fight on our side. Cast off the cloak of indifference you have wrapped around you. Make the decision *before it is too late*! Do not believe the National Socialist propaganda which has driven the fear of Bolshevism into your bones. Do not believe that Germany's welfare is linked to the victory of National Socialism for good or ill. A criminal regime cannot achieve a German victory. Separate yourselves in time from everything connected with National Socialism. In the aftermath a terrible but just judgment will be meted out to those who stayed in hiding, who were cowardly and hesitant.

What can we learn from the outcome of this war—this war that never was a national war?

The imperialist ideology of force, from whatever side it comes, must be shattered for all time. A one-sided Prussian militarism must never again be allowed to assume power. Only in large-scale cooperation among the nations of Europe can the ground be prepared for reconstruction. Centralized hegemony, such as the Prussian state has tried to exercise in Germany and in Europe, must be cut down at its inception. The Germany of the future must be a federal state. At this juncture only a sound federal system can imbue a weakened Europe with a new life. The workers must be liberated from their condition of down-trodden slavery under National Socialism. The illusory structure of autonomous national industry must disappear. Every nation and each man have a right to the goods of the whole world!

Freedom of speech, freedom of religion, the protection of individual citizens from the arbitrary will of criminal regimes of violence—these will be the bases of the New Europe.

Support the resistance. Distribute the leaflets!

Having accomplished their mission, the students were all back in Munich by 28 January and that night attended a cello concert together. Afterwards Hans, Schurik, Sophie and Willi took to the streets carrying suitcases and knapsacks loaded with leaflets, each going their separate way to distribute their load; over two or three hours they distributed around 3500 leaflets in a 10-square-mile area centred on the main railway station: Hans approaching it from the north, Schurik from the north-east, and Willi from the south. (No evidence survives about the route that Sophie followed.) Around 1300 of these leaflets were collected by the Gestapo. Over the next few days the students continued to distribute leaflets wherever they went, leaving them in telephone booths, on cars, in entrances to blocks of flats, in cafes and in the Englischer Garten. By not posting them to people in Munich, they hoped to give the impression that the leaflet had only been reprinted in the city rather than originating there.

Within days of the leaflets being posted and distributed by hand, large numbers were handed over to the police, though the denunciation rate varied markedly. In Stuttgart 670 out of 800 leaflets were handed in, a denunciation rate of around 84%; in Frankfurt 146 out of 250 (58%); in Linz 46 out of 100 (46%); in Augsburg 86 out of 250 (34%), and in Salzburg 40 out of 140 (27%).[5] In Munich a senior agent on the Gestapo staff called Robert Mohr was summoned to the office of the chief of staff to be given a new assignment: to investigate the source of the latest leaflets which were appearing in their thousands all over the city. Mohr, a veteran at his trade, who had joined the Nazi Party in May 1933 in order to gain promotion, was told that the leaflet was causing dismay at the highest levels within the Party, and that officials expected—and demanded—that swift arrests should be made so as to squash any further act of rebellion and prevent a 'chain reaction'. Mohr was told that the place of origin of the subversive leaflets was unclear since they had been posted from seven different cities to other cities all over Germany and Austria.

The Gestapo began scouring over maps, marking the sites where the leaflets had appeared and tracking the postmarks of those posted, while crime laboratory experts studied watermarks in the paper and the texture, grade and design of the envelopes so as to identify the supplier, and others analysed the typeface of the message. Patrols of railway stations were increased and customer lists of retailers selling paper were seized. A report on the White Rose leaflets commissioned by the Gestapo had suggested that they were probably looking for a Lutheran pastor, because the leaflets quoted from the old Lutheran translation of the Bible. Alongside the dangerous allure of 'freedom', the authorities were alarmed that the latest leaflet's anti-Prussianism might appeal to Bavarians and act as a veiled attempt to recruit soldiers; it was regarded as a more serious threat than the four White Rose leaflets that had appeared the previous summer both because it was more outspoken and because it came at such a bad time for the German Reich. To counter the setbacks at the Russian front, Goebbels had recently proclaimed to the world that the German people stood right behind their Führer—yet these leaflets were a sign of ebbing morale and therefore undermined this claim, and they gave the impression that there was now a well-organised anti-Nazi underground resistance movement *within* Germany with considerable resources at its disposal. Little did the authorities suspect that the leaflets were the output of half a dozen students whose main resources were their idealism, courage and initiative.

On the evening of 31 January, Christl called at the Scholls' apartment, which was anything but calm and ordered. Lisl had just arrived for a ten-day stay and, finding the house in a mess, offered to help Sophie to tidy it up. While doing so, Sophie came across a military pass to Saarbrücken lying on the floor, which made her annoyed with Willi for his carelessness. Hans had started an affair with Sophie's friend Gisela, who now wanted to break with Hans because he was unwilling to honour his commitment to marry her—he had promised to marry her in order to get her into his bed; Hans crumbled at the prospect of Gisela leaving him and hinted at taking his life, whereupon Gisela changed her mind. By now Hans' behaviour was becoming erratic, largely on account of the psychological pressure he was under, though also because of the morphine and amphetamines he was taking. Christl himself was at rock bottom: his wife Herta had just given birth to their third child and was suffering from a post-natal illness; he himself was preoccupied with composing his own leaflet. To add to all these woes, official confirmation of the defeat at Stalingrad had just been announced on the wireless. The previous day, the tenth anniversary of his coming to power, Hitler had chosen not to speak to the nation.

Hans, Schurik and Christl met in Hans' bedroom to discuss the military situation at Stalingrad, where the southern pocket of the encircled German forces had surrendered earlier that day; at some point, Willi arrived and joined in. Their discussions led on to practical matters and the proposal to paint anti-Nazi slogans round the city of Munich. Schurik had experimented with stencils made out of cardboard, but now his plan was to make them out of tin, and to use them with a black tar-based paint or else a green oil-based paint, which together with brushes they could obtain from Eickemeyer's art studio. Unbeknown to the conspirators, senior agent Mohr was summoned by the head of Gestapo in Munich the following morning and given five top agents to help him.

On the evening of 31 January, inspired by the Roosevelt press conference, Christl presented Hans with a draft text for a new leaflet. Hans glanced through it and, without commenting, kept it. Though it never reached the duplicating machine it was to cost Christl his life.

[The seventh leaflet]

Stalingrad!

200,000 German brothers were sacrificed for the prestige of a militaristic imposter. The human conditions of surrender set down by the Russians were hidden from the soldiers who were sacrificed.

For this mass murder, General Paulus received the Oak Leaves [a military decoration]. High-ranking officers escaped from the slaughter in Stalingrad by airplane. Hitler refused to allow those who were entrapped and surrounded to retreat to the troops behind the line. Now the blood of 200,000 soldiers who were doomed to death accuses the murderer named Hitler.

Tripoli! They surrendered unconditionally to the 8th English Army. And what did the English do? They allowed the citizens to continue living their lives as usual. They even let police and bureaucrats remain in office.

Only one thing did they undertake to do thoroughly: they cleansed the great Italian colonial city of every false ringleader and subhuman.

The annihilating, overwhelming super-power is approaching on every side with dead certainty. Hitler is less likely than Paulus to capitulate. There would be no escape for him. And will you be deceived as were the 200,000 who defended Stalingrad in a losing cause, so that you will be massacred, sterilized, or robbed of your children?

Roosevelt, the most powerful man in the world, said in Casablanca on January 26, 1943: Our war of extermination is not against the people, but against the political systems. We will fight for an unconditional surrender. More contemplation may be needed before a decision can be made. This is about the lives of millions of people. Should Germany meet the same fate as Tripoli?

Today, all of Germany is encircled just as Stalingrad was. All Germans shall be sacrificed to the emissaries of hate and extermination. Sacrificed to him who tormented the Jews, eradicated half of the Poles, and who wishes to destroy Russia. Sacrificed to him who took from you freedom, peace, domestic happiness, hope, and gaiety, and gave you inflationary money.

That shall not, that may not come to pass! Hitler and his regime must fall so that Germany may live. Make up your minds: Stalingrad and destruction, or Tripoli and a future of hope. And when you have decided, act.[6]

Years later, Christl's brother-in-law recalled how strongly Christl spoke at the time about the need to do something.

We must risk this 'no' against a power that not only wishes to eradicate everyone who thinks differently, but that increasingly places itself above that which is at the core and the holiest of the individual. We must do this for the sake of life. No one can take this responsibility from us. National Socialism is the name of an evil, intellectual illness that has befallen our nation. We may not watch and keep silent as it is slowly subverted.[7]

Noticing that the train station was at the centre of the leaflet operation on 28 January, the Gestapo concluded that the perpetrator had travelled from Vienna, where leaflets had been posted the previous night. Their first suspect was a former librarian of Munich University who had been dismissed in 1934 for his anti-Nazi attitude; he had been in Vienna at the right time and was put under surveillance—but without results. On 1 February a search was conducted on all trains in cities in the south of Germany. Once the headquarters for criminal investigation ascertained that the first five leaflets had been written on same portable American-made Remington typewriter, they concluded that the perpetrator lived in or near Munich, and a manhunt was conducted in the city.

Fritz Hartnagel was evacuated from Stalingrad on 22 January 1943, leaving on one of the last planes out of the German pocket, but he did not return to Germany in time to see Sophie. Naturally she worried for the safety of Fritz and his men, but she did not allow thoughts of the debacle to paralyse her. On 2 February, Sophie received a phone-call from Ulm to say that Fritz had been evacuated and was in hospital, having had two fingers amputated after frostbite. That same day the Battle of Stalingrad came to an end, when the northern pocket surrendered. It was one of the bloodiest battles ever fought, and the heavy losses inflicted on the *Wehrmacht* make it arguably the most strategically decisive battle of World War II, if not the turning point. Though it was not the first major setback for the German war machine, Stalingrad marked the first time that the Nazi regime publicly acknowledged a failure in the war; it was a crushing defeat where German losses (about 300,000) and those of its allies (100,000) were unprecedented. Out of the nearly 110,000 German prisoners captured in Stalingrad, only about 6000 would return from the prisoner camps in Siberia. Germany's Sixth Army had been destroyed, and the armies of Germany's European allies had been shattered. Germany's defeat at Stalingrad blew apart its reputation for invincibility and dealt a devastating blow to German morale. Many people round the world now believed that Hitler's defeat was inevitable.

The announcement on the wireless on 3 February that the Sixth Army had been overcome stunned the German nation. It was the worst military defeat in its history, and it came after victory had been all but promised. The newspapers were bordered in black, flags were lowered, funeral marches were staged, and three days of mourning were proclaimed, during which concert halls and cinemas were closed. The back pages of newspapers looked like cemeteries with all the black Iron Crosses marking the notices of fallen soldiers; there were so many fatalities that a special clothing coupon was issued to allow relatives to buy clothes for mourning. As the captured survivors of Stalingrad began marching to camps in Siberia, Goebbels attempted to use the disaster for propaganda purposes by speaking of it as a heroic battle.

After the defeat at Stalingrad there was a tightening of restrictions in Germany and an intensification of terror. Heads rolled like never before as guillotines were employed more readily, even for trivial offences: a businessman heard commenting on the train about how badly the war was going; a waiter for ridiculing the Führer; a manager for not reporting receipt of foreign currency. The guillotine at Munich broke down from over-use and a replacement had to be sent for from Stuttgart. For each death verdict announced in the People's Court there were ten which went unreported. The streets of Munich were full of German refugees from the north and the Rhineland, where the mounting intensity of bombing had made life unbearable. Although the fear of denunciation kept people from sharing their disquiet, the *flüsterwitze* (whisper jokes) continued. One went, Did you know that in the future teeth will be extracted only through the nose? Because, went the reply, nobody dares open his mouth anymore.

Newspaper reports about death sentences issued by the People's Court became more frequent: one day it was a well-known pianist, another day an engineer, a student or a priest. One of the most notable was Ernst Udet, a famous ace from the First World War, who later held the rank of a general and worked at the air ministry; on account of criticisms of Hitler, his death was arranged and reported as suicide—the standard way of dealing with public figures. Newspapers reflected the lie being lived, but everyone knew stories which expressed the silent cry uttered through all Germany. Some of the stories were deeply poignant: the young wife who wandered through the streets of Dresden with her dead child in a suitcase looking for a cemetery in which to bury him; the mother seen by soldiers at the Russian front walking across no-man's land, pulling her dead child behind her; the prison chaplain (known to Robert Scholl) who had a nervous breakdown after escorting men to the gallows on a daily basis; prisoners who had completed their sentences only to find that were being shipped off to concentration camps.

Buildings wrecked after the Allied bombing, floods of German refugees, and defeat on the Volga were all omens of collapse and disintegration. Among the student rebels there was a sense that the tide had turned and that the end of the war might be in sight. The second White Rose leaflet had proclaimed that 'the end is at hand' and spoken of 'a wave of unrest' leading many to 'join the cause' in 'a great final effort' to shake off the system, but in June 1942 such words had seemed fanciful. Now, in early 1943, the situation was very different, and these words invited belief that Hitler's regime would soon be toppled. However tantalising the prospect was, the prediction that the war would be over in a matter of weeks proved to be false, as the system Hitler had imposed by means of fear and propaganda proved to be more robust than anticipated and the German people more disciplined and resourceful than imagined.

On the night of 3 February a new outrage was perpetrated in the centre of Munich when Hans, Schurik and Willi wandered around the city painting anti-regime slogans on public buildings and ordinary houses. Twenty-nine slogans reading 'Down with Hitler' or 'Hitler the mass murderer' were painted using stencils, and another four reading 'Freedom!' were painted free-hand. Next to some of them were swastikas with an 'X' crossing them out. The letters were three feet high and painted in black tar-based paint, which was very hard to remove. At each location Schurik held the stencils and Willi daubed the paint on the ground or wall, while Hans stood watch in the drizzle, armed with a pistol, or else Hans and Willi would swap roles. They worked fast until around 3 am, when the moon came out; then they decided to pack up, for safety's sake.

Sophie was unaware of the operation and had prepared a small feast in Hans' room with food brought from Ulm. While waiting for her brother, she looked through the manuscript on his desk, which reminded her of a fairytale they had written together as children and which she had planned to illustrate as a children's book—but she fell asleep before they returned.[8] It was nearly morning when the three conspirators arrived with a bottle of wine, highly excited and flushed after their daring exploit. When they calmed down, they told Sophie their tale. The next day—or, rather, later that morning—as the city stirred, crowds gathered to stare at the political graffiti, and had to be moved on by the police, while cleaners were deployed to erase the shocking slogans which had been daubed on pavements and walls. As Sophie approached the University that morning, she encountered two Russian women on their knees attempting to erase the letters of 'Down with Hitler' and 'Freedom!'

This was not the first time that Munich students had daubed anti-Hitler slogans around the city, for something similar had happened just before the war had broken out, not long after Hans had arrived at the University. In July 1939 a Party speaker had been hissed at during a meeting at the University and at another meeting he had been pelted with eggs; overnight slogans had appeared on walls around the University, some of which read 'Down with Hitler', while others had compared him with Napoleon. In the aftermath of that affair ten students had been sent to Dachau.[9] It is almost certain that, four years later, Hans, Schurik and Willi were acquainted with the earlier graffiti affair—and with its outcome.

Coming just hours after the announcement about the defeat at 'Stalin's city', the overnight graffiti campaign caused fresh embarrassment for the authorities, especially as it was the first day of national mourning. The students who turned up to Huber's lecture that morning greeted him with rapturous applause and hung on his every word. In the afternoon, around thirty-five students and friends assembled in Eickemeyer's studio to listen to Theodor Haecker. Being a private meeting controlled by the White Rose students, it was a more intimate affair than Huber's lecture and the speaker used the occasion—the aftermath of Stalingrad—to maximum effect. Haecker spoke for about two hours, and read from *Creator and creation* and his journal. Several of those present left testimonies of this memorable meeting.

Sophie told Fritz,

> Haecker was with us on your birthday. It was a memorable occasion. He lets his words fall slowly, like drops you can see gathering beforehand, and expectancy lends their descent a special kind of momentum. He has a very serene face and an introspective look. I have never seen a face that carries more conviction.[10]

A friend of Sophie's called Gerhard Feuerle regarded that afternoon as a major part of his 'confrontation with life'. He listened spellbound to Haecker's words, though he could barely absorb them because they set his mind racing, as he records in his diary.

> I've got to chase down every single answer. This constant mad rush. It is terrible to be hunted, crushed, pursued everywhere I go. When I look at faces in the street car, in the market place, in pictures and sculptures, yes even my own face in the mirror, I'm confronted by a mask. Heads shorn, eyes empty, movements limp. Nothing points more clearly to a victory over the private citizen. The watchword is: save yourself if you can.
>
> The war has marked me as it has everyone. This assembly-line tailor has decked us all out in hopelessness. The substance of an entire people has been wasted in a tasteless and despicable manner. And for what?[11]

Haecker read from the section of *Creator and creation* entitled 'Theodicy: in defence of God', which seemed to start where Huber had left off.

> That appears to me to be the correct light in which a theodicy alone can be undertaken: the mercy of God, which in an instant turns a wild plaintiff into a defence attorney by means of illumination, and which transforms the legal relationship into a silent adoration of love. For therein rests everything that is almost brought to an end

in the book of Job. Every theodicy misses its mark if it does not partake of such a blessing, that namely at the end, God Himself grants justice and that he grants it in the existence and in the language of love.[12]

Willi recorded in his diary that it was 'a memorable occasion', and his sister Anneliese wrote in hers that for the first time she understood Willi.[13] Haecker's words helped her to see her wretchedness and guilt, the things that she had bottled up inside her, and they enabled her to free herself from them. She assumed that the others present had already assuaged their doubts and were therefore at peace with God, whereas she felt riddled with self-torment. Can I ever make it that far? she asked herself. But Haecker had said, 'The wheel that has started rolling cannot be stopped', and that gave her hope. She made a note of his words:

So it is better and more true to say that it is not theology and metaphysics that prevents us from falling into this world's pit of tragedy and suffering and doubt. Much more real is supernatural faith and the things that go along with it: hope and love, unchangeable love that presumes right-eousness.[14]

While some of those present left immediately after Haecker finished speaking, others stayed on to chat. Wilhelm Geyer, the artist who used the studio, opened several bottles of wine. To the amusement of all, Hans fell asleep at the party, exhausted after having been up most of the night. From the tone of the conversation, all the young people were in awe of Haecker.

The following day Willi left Munich to stay with friends in the mountains so as to calm down. Christl, who admitted to being fired up after the Haecker talk, wrote to his Jewish stepmother, 'It's an apocalyptic time. We all have yet to be shaken to the core so that peace can finally take hold in this half-destroyed world.'[15] Timid Gerhard was also roused, and he shocked his pro-Hitler mother by saying he would rather be hanged than make a pact with the devil. Sophie, meanwhile, went on a stamp-buying expedition and noticed that copycat graffiti had sprung up all round Munich. (One of the post offices she visited informed the Gestapo that a short, dark-haired girl had bought 100 stamps.) Sophie scolded Hans for not allowing her to join him on the graffiti campaign, though she was to miss the next outing (on 8 February) as she was called home to look after her mother and Inge, both of whom were ill. In Ulm she met up with Otl, but on this occasion they did not engage in one of their long philosophical discussions, no doubt because Sophie's mind was now on the resistance work.

Outwardly there were no signs of despondency in Sophie's demeanour, for she appeared buoyant and continued to display her radiant smile, but inwardly she was suffering, to judge from her diary and letters. Thoughts of all that Fritz was going through, while she had such an easy life, contributed to her anxiety. 'It often makes me unhappy that I am not a vehicle for universal suffering', she told him. 'That way I could at least remove part of my guilt from those who are undeservedly having to suffer so much more than I.'[16] When on her own, she was subject to attacks of melancholy and felt that there was only one remedy for 'this awful state of mind. Extreme pain, even if only physical, would be infinitely preferable to this vacuous inactivity.'[17] Her emotional paralysis sometimes deprived her of the will to function. 'My thoughts flit to and fro without my being able to control them properly',[18] she told Otl, yet she did not allow spells of depression to overwhelm her or to undermine her determination to counter the evil around her. She confessed to her friend Lisa that she was 'in a bad way', but was learning to be patient with herself.

> I occasionally used to wish I was just a tree, or better still, just a fragment of bark from a tree. I entertained such whims very early on, but nowadays I take care to stifle them and resist the kind of fatigue that seeks fulfillment in non-existence. [...] I am often, almost constantly, overwhelmed by a melancholy I am becoming fond of. [...] It is dangerous and even sinful to cherish one's own agony of mind. It was a female mystic, I think, who said: When I

praise God, I feel no joy whatever. I praise him because I *want* to praise him. How well I understand those words.[19]

On 5 February an advertisement was placed in several Bavarian newspapers appealing to the public for help in tracking down the illicit graffiti-writers, offering a reward of 1000 Marks. But this did not deter Hans and Schurik, who reckoned that, after Stalingrad, the time was ripe for a manifesto which would give fresh impetus to their activities and provide a rallying call for resistance. They consulted Professor Huber and found that he was willing to collaborate by writing the next leaflet. He was seething after the defeat at Stalingrad, which he regarded almost as a personal misfortune, and furious that the press were exploiting the tragedy for Nazi purposes, attempting to convince Germans that the battle was a heroic defeat. Hans and Schurik asked the professor to direct the leaflet to the Munich students by appealing to ideas that were currently under discussion among them. As Huber said afterwards, 'My purpose was to arouse the student community to a moral evaluation of the existing evils in our political life, not through an organization or any kind of violent action but through the unadorned word alone.'[20] On the night of 8 February, Huber's wife saw what he was up to, but was told not to meddle. Meanwhile, Hans, Schurik and Willi undertook their second graffiti operation, this time using green oil-based paint. The following day, the entrance of the University was put under constant surveillance.

On the evening of 9 February, Hans, Schurik and Willi hosted a meeting with the aim of introducing two of their supporters to each other, Falk Harnack and Kurt Huber, but the meeting turned sour. The two intellectuals had incompatible mind-sets, and, as they argued and slogged it out between themselves, their differences of opinion in history, politics and economics threatened to open up divisions among the students. Harnack wanted the resistance movement to woo both east and west, but this line of thinking was anathema to Huber, who regarded Harnack as dangerously left-wing. Huber deplored the tendency of the

National Socialists to ape the Communists in their unrelenting assault on religion and in trampling on all manifestations of opinion in the interests of doctrinaire materialism; he saw right and left merging into one brutal, inhuman system. Matters did not improve when Harnack left, for when Huber produced his draft for the sixth leaflet a fresh argument broke out. The students were delighted that Huber had used the leaflet as a response to the *Gauleiter*'s speech on 13 January, but Hans and Schurik took exception to a section which urged the German youth to give its support to the *Wehrmacht*.[21] A staunchly conservative national-ist, Huber wanted to realign the Party; the only way this could be achieved was for the armed forces to overthrow the Führer. But the three students, who had served in the military, viewed the *Wehrmacht* as the instrument of Prussian imperialism and wanted to strike out the passage. As Huber was adamant it should remain, an argument ensued and it ended with Huber leaving hurt and angry, telling them to do what they wanted with his draft. Huber and Hans never saw each other again, not even at Huber's lectures, as Hans now declined to attend them. Never-theless, Hans and Schurik decided that Huber's text, less the section on the *Wehrmacht*, should form the sixth leaflet.

Buoyed by Harnack's promise to link them with resistance groups in Berlin, Hans and Schurik worked long into the night typing up the stencils on their Remington typewriter and running off 2500 copies of the new leaflet. During the next week Hans supervised the production of the sixth leaflet and its distribution, going about the task in a way which shows he was becoming ever more daring and determined. He bought all the stamps for this mailing in one go and the clerk reported the purchase to the Gestapo—but Hans could not be identified, as he had paid in cash. He asked Gisela to purchase envelopes, without letting her know what they were to be used for, but on her return she saw what was in his bedroom and realised what he was up to. On 12 February, Hans threw caution to the wind when he asked one of the army administrators at the barracks to pass on all the circular mail he was about to receive. (Afterwards the official was severely reprimanded for doing this, but did not reveal that Hans had urged him to do so.) The following morning Hans and Schurik posted 1200 copies to student soldiers at four different locations in the city. When Otl and Inge visited Munich, however, Hans and Schurik took the precaution of clearing out everything from the Scholls' apartment for the duration of their visit and depositing it in the basement of the studio, even though Otl and Inge were staying with Muth.

Sophie's return to Munich on 14 February was a bonus for the leaflet operation as she was by far the quickest at typing addresses on envelopes; when they ran out of envelopes, they folded the leaflets and addressed them on the outside. Many of the addresses were taken from a registry of students attending Munich University during 1941/42, which Huber had given Hans; the students were bold enough to send a leaflet to the head of the Munich police, too. Leaflet production continued in the studio for a whole day, until Otl left town, and then it returned to the Scholls' apartment, where they had the run of the whole house, as the landlady had moved to the countryside after the first Allied bombing raids on Munich. On the night of 15 February, Hans, Schurik and Willi embarked on their final joint adventure, loaded with a cargo of around 1200 leaflets, as well as black paint, brushes and stencils. After posting the leaflets at various post offices, they began their third graffiti operation, writing 'Down with Hitler' on the walls of the Bavarian Ministry and the same slogan or 'Hitler the mass murderer' on three other buildings.

The sixth leaflet was a neatly-typed block of text without any illustration or typographical flourish. Despite making no concession to the reader, its contents were captivating, as it communicated a passion that only conviction could inspire.

[The sixth leaflet]

Fellow Fighters in the Resistance![22]

Shaken and broken, our people behold the loss of the men of Stalingrad. Three hundred and thirty thousand German men have been senselessly and irresponsibly driven to death and destruction by the inspired strategy of our World War I Private First Class. Führer, we thank you![23]

The German people are in ferment. Will we continue to entrust the fate of our armies to a dilettante? Do we want to sacrifice the rest of German youth to the base ambitions of a Party clique? No, never! The day of reckoning has come—the reckoning of German youth with the most abominable tyrant our people have ever been forced to endure. In the name of German youth we demand restitution by Adolf Hitler's state of our personal freedom, the most precious treasure we have, out of which he has swindled us in the most miserable way.

We grew up in a state in which all free expression of opinion is unscrupulously suppressed. The Hitler Youth, the SA, the SS have tried to drug us, to revolutionize us, to regiment us in the most promising young years of our lives. 'Philosophical training' is the name given to the despicable method by which our budding intellectual development is muffled in a fog of empty phrases. A system of selection of leaders at once unimaginably devilish and narrow-minded trains up its future Party bigwigs in the 'Castles of the Knightly Order' to become Godless, impudent, and conscienceless exploiters and executioners— blind, stupid hangers-on of the Führer. We 'Intellectual Workers' are the ones who should put obstacles in the path of this caste of overlords. Soldiers at the front are regimented like schoolboys by student leaders and trainees for the post of Gauleiter, and the lewd jokes of the Gauleiters insult the honour of the women students. German women students at the university in Munich have given a dignified reply to the besmirching of their honour, and German students have defended the women in the universities and have stood firm .... That is a beginning of the struggle for our free self-determination—without which intellectual and spiritual values cannot be created. We thank the brave comrades, both men and women, who have set us brilliant examples.

For us there is but one slogan: fight against the Party! Get out of the Party organizations, which are used to keep our mouths sealed and hold us in political bondage! Get out of the lecture rooms of the SS corporals and sergeants and the Party bootlickers! We want genuine learning and real freedom of opinion. No threat can terrorize us, not even the shutting down of the institutions of higher learning. This is the struggle of each and every one of us for our future, our freedom, and our honour under a regime conscious of its moral responsibility.

Freedom and honor! For ten long years Hitler and his coadjutor have manhandled, squeezed, twisted, and debased these two splendid German words to the point of nausea, as only dilettantes can, casting the highest values of a nation before swine. They have sufficiently demonstrated in the ten years of destruction of all material and intellectual freedom, of all moral substance among the German people, what they understand by freedom and honour. The frightful bloodbath has opened the eyes of even the stupidest German—it is a slaughter which they arranged in the name of 'freedom and honor of the German nation' throughout Europe, and which they daily start anew. The name of Germany is dishonoured for all time if German youth does not finally rise, take revenge, and atone, smash its tormentors, and set up a new Europe of the spirit. Students! The German people look to us. As in 1813 the people expected us to shake off the Napoleonic yoke, so in 1943 they look to us to break the National Socialist terror through the power of the spirit. Beresina and Stalingrad are burning in the East. The dead of Stalingrad implore us to take action.

'Up, up, my people, let smoke and flame be our sign!'[24]

> Our people stand ready to rebel against the Nationals
> Socialist enslavement of Europe in a fervent new break-
> through of freedom and honour.

Like the fifth leaflet, this one dispensed with philosophical
argument and instead issued a call to rebellion to German
students. The students behind the leaflet were conscious that
they had committed what would be construed by the authorities
as a treasonous act, and that they were now living in mortal
danger. A sense of achievement and exhilaration, mixed with
relief, followed the printing and distribution of the leaflets, since
the utmost risk had been taken. In putting conscience before
conformity, they were setting themselves apart from the bulk of
the population. Those who knew Hans well might have detected
a change in his behaviour, something strained about him instead
of his usual easy-going, self-assured manner. As with the previous
leaflets, Hans had sent a copy of the sixth leaflet to himself to
check that the system still worked, but this time received nothing
back. Equally worrying were the warnings from friends that the
Gestapo had him under surveillance and were likely to arrest him
within a day or two. The unnerving and menacing thought of
being followed must have preyed on his mind, but what could he
do? He had a job to undertake and would not flee, he told Gisela;
if he escaped to Switzerland, his family would be rounded up and
sent to the People's Court. No, he must take the blame on himself
and reduce the circle of risk to a minimum.

Besides mailing leaflets, Hans now became preoccupied with
his most daring plan to date: spreading the leaflets from within
his university. On 12 February, Hans outlined to Christl his
intention to carry this out on 18 February and asked him to help,
but Christl pulled back because of his wife and young family.
Though he was still in agreement with the White Rose aims,
Christl was dubious of its methods and thought that it was both
dangerous and silly to undertake the graffiti campaign. When
Schurik would not commit himself to the plan either, Hans'
reaction was to say, 'Sophie will do it', though she did not yet

know about the plan. Schurik then offered to watch for them outside the University, while they dropped the leaflets from a single point and exited via the rear. That evening Schurik burned his German military uniform and pay-book with a view to escaping to Russia.[25]

When Hans told the bookseller Josef Söhngen that he intended to carry out a spectacular gesture at the University, more open and defiant than before, Söhngen tried to dissuade him. Hans explained that, since he expected to be arrested at any moment, he wished to be 'active' one more time; the war had turned, he argued, the Allied invasion was imminent, so now was the time to sound the alarm and galvanize dissident elements into action. A torch was to be lit, a beacon set ablaze, alarm fires ignited—all phrases he had used in conversation or in his diary, and which echoed the words in the last leaflet: 'Up, up, my people, let smoke and flame be our sign!' That day he wrote to Rose Nägele explaining, ominously, that,

> life has become an ever-present danger—the danger is all of my choosing. I must head for my chosen destination freely and without any ties. I have gone astray many times, I know. Chasms yawn and darkest night envelops my questing heart, but I press on regardless. As Claudel so splendidly puts it: *La vie, c'est une grande aventure vers la lumière.*[26]

On her return to Munich, Hans asked Sophie to accompany him on the mission and she accepted. While Geyer drew a sketch of her at the studio, she explained that the Gestapo were on their trail and that they had considered fleeing, but feared for their family and friends if they did so. 'So many are dying for this regime', she said, 'it is high time that someone died in opposition to it.'[27] If they were arrested, she hoped it would be in public so that the whole world would find out about it. Otherwise, she was hardly able to think about life after the war. During the sitting and the breakfasts he had with the Scholls, Geyer sensed her reined-in rage at the injustice and cruelty around them, as well as her absolute fearlessness in combating them. All this she felt obliged to withhold from Fritz in the letters she wrote him. 'I so much look forward to being able to speak with you once more', she told him, 'because anything I write is just a drop from a big reservoir that has built up by slow degrees. Shall I pay you a visit?'[28] She described the security she had felt while at home in Ulm as being in the 'presence of selfless love', and though unsure what emotions she was 'allowed to show' in writing, told him to rest assured that 'they are never anything but love and gratitude'.[29] Her last surviving words to him are: 'Perhaps we can soon begin somewhere together'.[30]

On the days leading up to the fateful 18 February more leaflets were run off, folded and stuffed into envelopes, then stamped and addressed before being taken out in suitcases to post. On the evening of 17 February, Hans and Sophie carried the duplicating machine and typewriter from their apartment to the studio, then returned to relax by listening to Schubert—as described by Sophie:

> I have just been playing the Trout Quintet on the gramophone. Listening to the andantino makes me want to be a trout myself. You can't help rejoicing and laughing, however moved or sad at heart you feel, when you see springtime clouds in the sky and the budding branches sway, stirred by the wind, in the bright young sunlight. I am so looking forward to the spring again. In that piece of Schubert's you can positively feel and smell the breezes and scents and hear the birds and the whole of creation cry out for joy. And when the piano repeats the theme of cool, clear, sparkling water—oh, it is sheer enchantment.[31]

Thursday 18 February 1943 was the day that the Minister of Propaganda Joseph Goebbels, in his Sportpalast speech in Berlin, called on the German people to embrace 'total war', and thereby demanded all the resources and efforts of the entire population. It was also the day that Hans and Sophie Scholl were caught distributing leaflets at Munich University. Brother and sister rose around 8.30 am for a leisurely breakfast, then Sophie checked the post-box. She skipped her physics lecture at 9 am and both of them missed

Professor Huber's class at 10 am, which was attended by Gisela, Traute and Willi. Around 10.30 am Hans and Sophie set off for the university carrying a suitcase and briefcase between them, both filled with leaflets. Just after they had set off, Otl called at 13 Franz Joseph Strasse to deliver a message from Hans Hirzel to his namesake; the message—that a book *Machtstaat und Utopie* (*Dictatorship and Utopia*) was out of print—meant nothing to the bearer, but was a coded warning that the Gestapo had discovered White Rose activity in Ulm. (The previous afternoon Hans Hirzel had been interrogated by the Gestapo, as a result of a tip-off that he had bragged about involvement in resistance activities, but it turned out that the Gestapo knew nothing about the White Rose, and so released him.)

It was a mild and very sunny day, with a taste of spring in the air. Their short walk took them along the wide Leopold Strasse, lined on both sides with poplar trees, and by the Victory Arch marking the liberation of the region from Napoleon, then across the square that would one day bear their name. On arriving at the University, they passed through one of the arches at the entrance and into the main hall. They had timed their arrival to coincide with lectures and therefore empty corridors, but in the main hall they came across Traute and Willi, who had left one lecture early in order to arrive in time for another at a nerve clinic some distance away. A hurried exchange of greetings took place.

Brother and sister, who between them carried around 1700 leaflets headed 'Fellow Students', went coolly and methodically along the corridors leaving piles of leaflets outside the doors of each lecture hall, then placed others on window sills and on stairways and the statues adorning them. Despite encountering a group of soldiers, they stuck to their task. If they had left it at that, they would probably have escaped undetected, but instead Sophie went a step further. In a final gesture, she went to the top floor of the main stairway and, from the gallery overlooking the entrance hall (known as the *Lichtof*), threw the remaining leaflets into the air and watched them come fluttering down into the empty hall below. Just at that moment the University porter entered. Jakob Schmid was a Party member and part-time Storm Trooper, a *blockwart* (an informer) who had been briefed to look out for the perpetrators of the graffiti and leaflets. Schmid spotted them and immediately raised the alarm. Sophie had the presence of mind to dart into a room and hide the key to Eickemeyer's studio, but Hans failed to dispose of the contents of his pockets; in them were Christl's handwritten draft of the seventh leaflet and cigarette ration coupons that could be traced to the Geyer family.

Notes

1 Diary entry, 1 January 1943, *Journal in the night*, p. 187.
2 Hans to Otl Aicher, 12 January 1943, *Heart of the White Rose*, p. 271.
3 Hanser, *A noble treason*, p. 204.
4 Jürgen Wittenstein claimed he took a copy of the leaflet to Berlin, where a dissident student group already existed, headed by Hellmut Hartert who had once studied medicine in Munich and shared a room with Hans – but this is possibly a post-war fabrication (Sachs, *White Rose history* vol. ii, ch. 23, p. 2, n6).
5 Sachs, *White Rose history* vol. ii, ch. 36, p. 8.
6 *Gestapo interrogation transcript: ZC 13267 vols 1–16*, trans. R. H. Sachs, (Los Angeles: Exclamation, 2002–3), p. 204.
7 Sachs, *White Rose history* vol. ii (2007 update), ch. 37, p. 1.
8 I. Scholl, *The White Rose*, p. 47. Inge does not give a date for her account, though it seems to match with events on the night of 3 February.
9 Diary entry, 4 July 1939, Ulrich von Hassell, *The von Hassell Diaries 1938–1944: the story of the forces against Hitler inside Germany* (London: Hamish Hamilton, 1948), p. 50.
10 Sophie to Fritz Hartnagel, 7 February 1943, *Heart of the White Rose*, p. 275.
11 Quoted in Sachs, *White Rose history* vol. ii, ch. 39, p. 13.
12 The relevant passage from *Creator and creation* is quoted in *Die Weiße Rose*, ed. H. Siefken, p. 164.
13 Willi had written to her on 6 June 1942 about their responsibilities as Christians; see comments about this letter in H. Siefken, *Die Wiesse Rose*, p. 3; *Die Weisse Rose: student resistance to National Socialism*, p. 5.
14 Diary entries, 4 & 7 February 1943, quoted in Sachs, *White Rose history* vol. ii, ch. 39, p. 14.

15 Christl to Elisabeth Probst (née Rosenthal), 5 February 1943, quoted in Sachs, *White Rose history* vol. ii, ch. 40, p. 2.

16 Sophie to Fritz Hartnagel, 3 January 1943, *Heart of the White Rose*, p. 265.

17 Diary entry, 13 January 1943, *Heart of the White Rose*, p. 267.

18 Sophie to Otl Aicher, 19 January 1943, *Heart of the White Rose*, p. 267.

19 Sophie to Lisa Remppis, 2 February 1943, *Heart of the White Rose*, pp. 273–4.

20 Hanser, *A noble treason*, p. 221.

21 According to a statement made by Huber on 1 March 1943, the deleted passage read: 'Students, you willingly joined the German *Wehrmacht* in front-line actions and at the bases; you faced the enemy and helped the wounded, worked at your desks and in laboratories. There can be no other goal for us all than to destroy Russian Bolshevism in every respect. Join forces with our wonderful *Wehrmacht*' (Moll, 'Acts of resistance', p. 186).

22 When the stencil ripped, they typed a new one with the more familiar title 'Fellow Students!'

23 The expression '*Führer, wir danken Dir!*' was an expression the Minister of Propaganda had popularized to hail Hitler's achievements.

24 These words come from a military song, which draws from a poem by the nationalist (Prussian Protestant) poet Theodor Körner. He wrote the poem '*Aufruf*' ('Call') during the Wars of Liberation against Napoleon: 'The crops are ripe; reapers, do not tremble! Ultimate redemption lies in the sword! Press the spear into your loyal heart!'

25 A few days earlier he had told his girlfriend that only his 'obligations give me the moral right to stay' in Germany, and not return to Russia (Alex Schmorell to Nelly, 9 December 1942, quoted in Moll, 'Acts of resistance', p. 196).

26 Hans to Rose Nägele, 16 February 1943, *Heart of the White Rose*, p. 279.

27 Sachs, *White Rose history* vol. ii, ch. 44, p. 7.

28 Sophie to Fritz Hartnagel, 13 February 1943, *Heart of the White Rose*, p. 277.

29 Sophie to Fritz Hartnagel, 16 February 1943, *Heart of the White Rose*, p. 278.

30 Sophie to Fritz Hartnagel, 16 February 1943 (second letter), quoted in Sachs, *White Rose history* vol. ii (2007 update), ch. 44, p. 1.

31 Sophie to Lisa *Remppis*, 17 February 1943, *Heart of the White Rose*, p. 280.

8 ARREST, TRIAL AND EXECUTION: 18–22 FEBRUARY 1943

WHILE THE STUDENTS were coming out of the lecture halls, Jakob Schmid locked the main entrance to the University and alerted the building superintendent. He identified Hans and Sophie and told them that they were under arrest (for which he received a reward of 3000 Marks). Offering no resistance, the Scholls were taken to the SS colonel who acted as Chancellor of the University and remained with him until the Gestapo arrived. Meanwhile all activity in the University was suspended and no one was allowed to leave the building. When the senior Gestapo agent Robert Mohr arrived, brother and sister were asked to show their identification papers. At that moment Hans realised he still had in his pocket Christl's text for the seventh leaflet, and he tried to tear it up and dispose of it, but was prevented by a Gestapo agent, who collected up all the pieces. The Scholls were handcuffed, led out through the crowd of students who had been rounded up, and taken to Wittelsbach Palace, the Munich headquarters of the Gestapo. The students they left behind were ordered to hand in any leaflets they had and were then searched.

The interrogators at the Palace were unsure, at first, what to make of the two suspects. They seemed to be ordinary German students, good looking, polite and intelligent, the girl well-spoken and winsome, the boy a clean-cut soldier. Both appeared to be examples of good breeding and background. It was puzzling that students with such impeccable Aryan credentials should be accused of spreading rebellion—yet within five days the two of them would stand accused of the worst possible crime of high treason: urging the overthrow of the regime, the destruction of the Party, the defeat of their own army, and the removal of their leader as a mass-murderer and international outlaw. Initially the senior agent Mohr was reluctant to believe they were guilty and came close to releasing them, because their explanation for their empty suitcase—they were using it, they said, to pick up fresh laundry—sounded so plausible. But the Gestapo changed its mind once the Scholls' rooms were searched and new evidence came to light: stamps in large numbers, envelopes matching the ones used for mailing the leaflets, an account book which listed names and amounts of money in Sophie's hand, and then the shreds in Hans' pocket, which when pieced together revealed the draft text of another leaflet. As the evidence mounted and a narrative began to emerge, it became clear to the professionals, who had been searching for a sophisticated and well-organised underground resistance movement, that they had been outwitted for so long by a bunch of student amateurs.

Once on the scent, the Gestapo chased its prey ruthlessly. The incriminating evidence accumulated rapidly after they raided Eickemeyer's studio and discovered two typewriters, stencils, ink and duplicating paper used to make the leaflets, and the paint, brushes, gloves and outlines used in the graffiti campaign, as well as a pistol and 200 cartridges. When confronted with this evidence, first Hans and then Sophie changed their story from innocent denial to admitting full responsibility. By holding back information or else manipulating the evidence they sought to implicate as few others as possible. They were subjected to hours of intense interrogation and forced to reveal all their acquaintances, each one of whom opened up a new avenue of investigation. Gisela Schertling was named and under interrogation she gave away the names of everyone she had ever met in the White Rose circle, including those on the fringe who merely lent moral support to its activities. Clearly, Gisela believed that if she behaved as a good Nazi, she would receive a lighter sentence. The Gestapo in Munich were ordered to accumulate as much evidence as they could and as quickly as possible, as the highest authorities wanted an immediate trial. Heinrich Himmler himself was following proceedings closely. At Wittelsbach Palace everyone worked feverishly; the only calm ones, it seemed, were Hans and Sophie.

Brother and sister were kept apart and interrogated simultaneously in different rooms. They were treated well and not subjected to any form of physical torture, but they had no access to a lawyer, were allowed no visitors, and were given no information about their likely fate, factors which were designed to put pressure on them and make them break down. Mohr had never before encountered a suspect like Sophie, who seemed so self-composed and unflappable. At one moment, however, she did get agitated, and when asked why, she confessed she was afraid that they might be torturing Hans. Mohr at once took her to see her brother, who was being interrogated by his colleague Anton Mahler and showed no signs of having suffered brutality. Mahler, another old hand in the Gestapo, was highly impressed with his prisoner and his clarity and elegance of mind; he told a colleague that orders alone forced him to do his best and send such a fine German to his death. Despite his admiration, Mahler acted with cold professionalism as he seized on every hesitation or momentary lapse of his prisoner, and pressed him when cracks began to appear in his story.

At one moment, Hans said that he had come to the conclusion 'that I had to act out of my earnest conviction and I believed that this inner conviction was more binding than the oath of loyalty which I had given as a soldier'.[1] While cool under interrogation, Hans returned to his cell exhausted and shaken. As with Sophie, the lights in his cell were kept on day and night, an indication that he was on death row, and any implement that he might have used to take his own life had been removed. The cellmate appointed to watch over him was Helmut Fietz, a Bavarian farm boy arrested for insulting the Führer. Since Helmut did not appear to be in the employ of the Gestapo, Hans confided in him how close Mahler had come to the truth on a number of occasions, and also when Mahler was getting nowhere. Helmut was intrigued by his fellow prisoner, who loved to stand on a chair to see the sky outside and murmur lines of poetry.

Sophie's cellmate was a political prisoner called Else Gebel. Else was convinced that Sophie's arrest was a mistake because she was so composed and sweet, and a bond soon formed between them. Sophie was assigned one of the 'honour' cells usually reserved for Party officials who got into trouble, and given proper bed linen and other comforts. After her first two interrogations, which together lasted 17 hours, Sophie returned to her cell at 8 am on Friday 19 February exhausted but calm. She had been served real coffee—a luxury at the time—during the night, and was allowed some sleep before the next round of interrogation. Though gentle in tone, the interrogations were a torment for she knew that the lives of so many she loved hung on her every answer. After each session she was relieved to return to her cell where she met the warmth of Else and slept soundly. Her composure broke just once, not under interrogation but when Else told her that someone else connected with the White Rose had been arrested—not Willi, because she knew he had been taken in and was in a cell on the floor above. (Sophie managed to smuggle him a cigarette with 'Freedom!' written on it.) She feared it was Schurik, but was dismayed when she discovered it was the gentle, mild-mannered family man, whom she had last seen in the Bavarian mountains. She also felt deeply for his wife Herta, who had just given birth to their third child; her two brothers had had to flee from the Gestapo some years earlier and had never been heard of since.

Christl was identified as the author of the seventh leaflet by comparing the scraps in Hans' pocket with the innocent letters he had written to Hans. On the morning of Saturday 20 February, when he went to collect his pay at the *Luftwaffe* unit in Innsbruck, before rushing off to see Herta, who was confined to hospital, he was arrested by the Gestapo and ordered to change into civilian clothes; this was so that he could be tried by the People's Court, as Nazi law disallowed civil courts from trying members of the armed forces. Thinking that the end of the war was perhaps as few as eight weeks away and that Christl's sentence would be imprisonment, Sophie consoled herself that all would turn out well. Instead, the end of the war was two years off, and Christl would receive the death sentence.

When Sophie's own fate became clear, Mohr claimed he could save her life and offered her a way out so long as she agreed to testify that she disagreed with her brother's ideology. It was the most tenuous of chances, but in his 26 years of police work Mohr had seen that it was the kind of lifeline that people in peril of their lives always grasped without hesitation. Barely had he finished making his offer than Sophie dismissed it out of hand: she declared that she was fully aware of her actions, that she had not been misled, that she had done the right thing and did not regret her conduct, and that if Hans deserved the death sentence then she did too. On another occasion Mohr sought to persuade her that she had a mistaken view of National Socialism, not being mature enough to grasp its underlying philosophy, and hence did not appreciate the great gains made for Germany by the Party. 'Not at all', she replied. 'It is not I but you, Herr Mohr, who have the wrong *Weltanschauung*. I would do the same again.'[2] On this occasion Mohr gave up and sent her back to her cell, where Sophie found Else brewing tea and preparing a feast of sausages, bread rolls and biscuits, as well as cigarettes, to which the warders and other prisoners had contributed—the story of her arrest having filtered through the prison and caused a stir. Sophie sent some of the feast to Hans on the floor above.

On the afternoon of Sunday 21 February, a formal indictment was issued from the office of the chief prosecutor of the People's Court in Berlin charging three individuals: Hans Scholl, Sophie Scholl and Christoph Probst, all with 'no previous conviction'. They stood accused of acts of high treason with intent: to alter the constitution of the Reich by force; to render the *Wehrmacht* incapable of protecting the Reich against its enemies; to influence the masses through the production and dissemination of subversive literature; to aid and abet foreign powers in a time of war, damaging the fighting potential of the Reich; to paralyse the will of the German people in their determination to maintain their national integrity by military means. The indictment summarised the history of the White Rose activities and implied that Christl was as much to blame as the other two.[3] No mention was made of Willi or Schurik—or indeed anyone else. From the text it was unclear which of the Scholls was ultimately responsible for the leaflet campaign, an indication of how successful Sophie had been in misleading her interrogators and assuming as much of the blame as she could. Later prosecution documents declared Hans and Sophie were 'the soul of the truly treasonous organization that gave aid and comfort to the enemy and sought to undermine our ability to make war'.[4]

In her written account of the three days she spent with Sophie, Else describes how Sophie returned to the cell with the indictment and read it through with trembling hands.[5] She remained in silence for a long time gazing out of her window at people outside strolling about in their Sunday best, while the sun streamed into her cell, then she sighed and muttered, 'What a glorious, sunny day, and I have to go. But so many men are dying every day on the battlefields, so many promising lives are being lost. What does my death amount to as long as what we did served to stir up people and make them think? There will surely be a revolt among the students.' She continued her meditation, 'Or I could die of some sickness. Millions do. That way of dying would be perfectly senseless, without any point, wouldn't it?' Then her thoughts turned to her mother, who would be losing two of her children at once. 'It will be terribly hard on her—harder than on either of us. Father will be able to understand better why we did it'.[6] Suddenly Sophie snapped out of her reverie, stopped trembling and seemed to steel herself to face the outcome. By way of softening the blow, Else suggested that the court might simply impose a prison sentence, though she knew from her sources that the trial was set for the following day and that Roland Freisler, Hitler's hanging judge, would preside: the outcome was therefore decided upon.

The defence lawyer assigned by the court to Sophie came to visit her that evening, but she treated him with coolness. She did not bother to disguise her involvement in the White Rose activities and declined to furnish any material for her defence, insisting that she and Hans had done what was right. The only question Sophie wanted to ask was whether Hans, as a soldier of the *Wehrmacht* who had served at the Russian front, would have the privilege of facing the firing squad. The lawyer had no idea. He was used to grown men breaking down at such meetings, and was not prepared for the detachment and self-control of this young woman sitting in front of him, who did not flinch from asking whether she would be hanged or guillotined. In his confusion, he mumbled an evasive answer.

Unlike Else, Sophie slept soundly that night. She woke at 7 am and seeing Else awake told her about the dream she had been having. It was a sunny day and she was carrying a baby in a long white dress as she walked up a steep mountainside to a church for its baptism. All of a sudden a crevasse opened up before her which grew ever wider. She slipped, but managed to place the baby on the other side before plunging into abyss. Else was unable to make sense of the dream, so Sophie gave Else her interpretation. 'The baby in the white is our idea. It will survive us and succeed despite all the pitfalls and obstacles. We have been privileged to be forerunners of the idea, but we have to die so that it comes to fruition.'[7]

When Sophie next saw Hans he was pale and emaciated, but held himself erect. Mohr came to see them and suggested they write their farewell letters, since there would not be time after the trial, an ominous reminder that the verdict had already been decided upon and that the trial was a mere charade. In writing to their parents they expressed their love and gratitude for them, and asked for forgiveness for the pain and distress their actions had caused them; they said that they could not have acted otherwise and were sure their parents would understand their actions, which they hoped would be vindicated in the future. Sophie wrote to Inge (who had also been arrested) and asked her to send her love to Carl Muth, then she composed a farewell letter to Fritz. None of the letters reached their destination. Instead, they were sent to Reich security headquarters in Berlin and filed away, that way ensuring they could not be used as propaganda against the regime. None of these letters has survived; we only know about them by word of mouth.

Christl wrote too, but in his case his mother and sister Angelika were allowed to read the letters in the presence of a Gestapo agent, though not to keep them. They memorised the final words, which they committed to paper afterwards. To his mother Christl wrote, 'I thank you for the gift of life. If I consider matters properly now, it was nothing other than the road to God. I am preceding you by a little, to prepare you a splendid reception. I have only one hour left. Now I will receive Holy Baptism and Holy Communion'.[8] To Angelika he wrote, 'I go to my death free of all hate. [...] Never forget that life is nothing if it is not a continual growing through love and a preparation for eternity. [...] Your Christl, always.' Due to an administrative error, Christl's letter to his mother on the day of his arrest, two days earlier, *did* reach her; he told her that he had been arrested but was being treated well and was happy; 'I feel above all the indestructability of love [...] I know only that nothing is so difficult it cannot be borne.'[9]

At 9 am on Monday 22 February, Sophie was escorted to an unmarked car and driven to the Palace of Justice, followed by Hans and Christl in a separate car. Arranging the cell for the next occupant, Else noticed that Sophie had left her bed tidy and on it the indictment turned upside down with one word written on the reverse: *'Freiheit!'* (Freedom!) In his cell Hans had scribbled with a pencil on the whitewashed wall some of his father's favourite words by Goethe, *'Allen Gewalten zum Trutz sich erhalten!*' (Stand firm against all the powers that be!) No wonder that their actions caused a stir among the fellow prisoners, guards and even Gestapo officials—and sent ripples of consternation to the very top of the Party.

On arrival at the Palace of Justice, the prisoners were made to wait while spectators found their seats. Christl bore a look of brooding melancholy, Hans seemed impatient, and Sophie frowned slightly as she did when deep in thought. Room 216 of the Assize Court in Munich was packed. The better informed among them knew the reason for the hastily arranged trial: tension in the wake of Stalingrad and the revelation that subversion had spread from the capital of the movement throughout the Reich. The proceedings were aimed at stamping out swiftly and emphatically any budding signs of resistance. At 10 am President Freisler swept into the court with his billowing red robes and called it to order. Along with subsidiary judges, Roland Freisler was flanked by top military officials, whose presence, along with the specially-invited uniformed audience, sought to emphasise that power rather than justice was going to prevail. Behind the judge's bench hung a portrait of Adolf Hitler.

The three defendants sat to the left of the judge, with a policeman on either side of them. They looked pale and drawn after the strain of lengthy interrogations. The Chief Justice of the People's Court conducted the trial with a passion bordering on fury. He roared denunciations as if he were prosecutor rather than judge, and gesticulated, ranted and raved like a ham actor, to such an extent that even some of the select audience cringed. He snarled and spat out words such as 'treason', 'subversion' and 'sabotage'. On the upper left of his robe was an eagle with outstretched wings and talons that clasped a wreath enclosing the swastika. He berated the three students for having betrayed the National Socialist system that had nurtured them and entrusted them with responsibility in the Hitler Youth. Evidence was produced in the form of leaflets, a duplicating machine, stencils, brushes and paint, but no witnesses were called as the defendants admitted everything. Proceedings were almost entirely taken up with Freisler's rantings, as he goaded on the prosecution and only occasionally allowed feeble offerings from the defence lawyers to interrupt him.

The audience—'audience' is surely the appropriate term for a show-trial—expected the accused to wince, to recant, or to beg for mercy, but they appeared to be unmoved, Christl with almost an air of abstraction, and gained a grudging admiration from the sea of soldiers around them: the field-grey uniforms of the *Wehrmacht*, the brown of the SA, the Storm Troopers of the National Socialist Party, and the black of the SS, the elite Security Corps. As the lone female in the room, the young lady made the greatest impact. She had an aura of mingled girlishness and gravity, and occasionally frowned as she mused over what she heard. There was a subdued defiance about Sophie's demeanour which suddenly came alive when Freisler demanded to know how any German could possibly carry out what the indictment specified. Clearly and coolly she responded, 'Somebody, after all, had to make a start. What we wrote and said is believed by many others. They just don't dare express themselves as we did.' The courtroom stirred at this and the judge was momentarily taken aback, while Hans cast a sideways glance of approval at her, showing the sibling warmth between them. He must have reflected that, at the beginning, he had done his utmost to keep her from knowing about the White Rose activities, but here she was defying Hitler's top judge. Later in the proceedings she shocked the bench by adding, 'You know the war is lost. Why don't you have the courage to face it?'[10]

Towards the end, each of the accused was called upon to make a statement. Sophie chose to remain silent. Christl tried to explain that he wanted to save the Germans from further disasters like Stalingrad, but was shouted down and unable to continue; he then pleaded for mercy on account of his wife and three children. Hans backed up his plea by stating that Christl had contributed very little to the leaflet operation, but he was cut short by Freisler, who snapped, 'If you have nothing to say on your own behalf, please be quiet'. Like his sister, Hans declined to plead for himself. None of them retracted anything.

Just as the sentence was about to be read out, there was a commotion at the door which drew everyone's attention. Proceedings came to a halt as Magdalena and Robert Scholl forced their way into the courtroom, after a scuffle and protests from the guards. The parents of Hans and Sophie had been informed of the arrests the previous Friday and had tried to visit them, but were told that no visits were allowed at the weekend. After an anxious weekend they had travelled to Munich early that morning with their younger son Werner, who had unexpectedly returned on leave from Russia. They were met on the station platform and told that the trial was already under way and that they needed to hurry to get there before it was over. Once inside the courtroom, they had to stand, because there were no seats available; they were wild with anxiety.

Frau Scholl asked the attendant if the accused were going to die and he nodded, whereupon she collapsed and had to be carried out. On recovering she tried to re-enter but was prevented. She told the guard, 'But I am the mother of two of the accused', and was met with the response, 'You should have brought them up better'. Pulling herself together, she began to draw up a petition for mercy and for the chance to meet her children. Meanwhile, in court Herr Scholl managed to reach the table of the defence lawyer and told him, 'Tell the president of the court that I am here to defend my children', and, surprisingly, the lawyer did just this. Freisler was incensed and ordered Robert to be removed from court. As he was bundled out, Robert exclaimed, 'There is a higher court before which we all must stand', and just as the doors closed behind him, he added, 'They will go down in history'.[11]

Once order was restored, the judge proceeded to pronounce the words he had travelled four hundred miles to utter: 'For the protection of the German people, and of the Reich, in this time of mortal struggle, the Court has only one just verdict open to it on the basis of the evidence: the death penalty. With this sentence the People's Court demands its solidarity with the fighting troops'. Freisler explained the reasons for the verdicts and berated each of the accused individually, then swept out of the court with his entourage, while the prisoners were handcuffed and led away to their fate. As the grey, brown and black uniforms drained away, a soldier in grey pushed his way through to the condemned prisoners in order to press the hands of each of them. It was Werner. Tears were welling in his eyes as Hans said to his younger brother, 'Stay strong. Make no concessions!'[12]

Paul Giesler, the *Gauleiter*, wanted the conspirators hanged in public, either in the central square or at the University, and had commissioned a carpenter to make a start on the scaffold, but the decision was taken out of his hands by Himmler. He did not want to expose the regime to the charge of Nazi barbarism and feared making martyrs out of them, so instead the three condemned prisoners were transferred to Munich's Stadelheim jail. It had once housed Hitler for four weeks, after he was sentenced for his first act of public terrorism, breaking up a rival's political meeting, but was now an execution jail for hundreds of his opponents. Sophie asked to see her interrogator again as she wanted to make a supplementary statement, which she thought might exonerate the other two. At around 2 pm Magdalena and Robert Scholl hurried to the prison to see Hans and Sophie, insisting on their rights of visitation, and to their surprise had their request granted.

Hans was brought out first. Wearing prison uniform, he walked briskly and looked at them clearly and without despair or dejection. He bent over the barrier and took his parents' hands, saying, 'I have no hatred. I have put everything, everything behind me.'[13] His father embraced him and said, 'You will go down in history—there is such a thing as justice in spite of all this'.[14] At one moment Hans turned away from his parents, as he struggled to hold back his tears, then he asked them to pass on greetings to all his friends. He parted without the slightest sign of fear, his face beaming with affection for them as he was taken away.

Sophie was brought out in her regular clothes by a woman warden, walking slowly and looking relaxed and smiling. She accepted the sweet that Hans had declined, saying, 'Oh yes, of course, I did not have any lunch.' She looked thinner but rosier than usual, thought her mother. 'So you will never again set foot in our house', she said. 'Oh, what do these short years matter, mother?' Sophie replied. Then she repeated what Hans had said: 'We took all the blame, for everything. That is bound to have its effect in time to come.' Magdalena stammered, 'Sophie, remember Jesus.' Almost imperiously Sophie replied, 'Yes, but you too.'[15] Then she left, fearless, calm and smiling. Though composed while being led away, she broke down in tears in her cell a few moments later. When her interrogator Mohr saw her, she explained, 'I have just said goodbye to my parents. You understand.'[16] Magdalena and Robert, however, departed, hoping that they might be able to reverse the verdict or at least get it postponed.

None of Christl's family were informed about his arrest and they only learned about it after his execution. Though he had never committed himself to any creed, Christl had for the previous two years considered becoming a Catholic Christian, so he asked to see the Catholic chaplain. Christl was baptised by Fr Heinrich Sperr and received his First—and last—Communion from him, then exclaimed, 'Now my death will be easy and joyful.'[17] His youngest child was only four weeks old and he never set eyes on her. An hour before they were due to be executed, Sophie and Hans asked to be received into the Catholic Church but were dissuaded by the Lutheran pastor, who argued that such a decision would further upset their mother, who was a dedicated Evangelical Christian.[18] Unsure what to expect when he entered Hans' cell, the Rev. Karl Alt was relieved when Hans asked if they could pray Psalm 90 together. The only psalm attributed to Moses, it ponders the brevity of life set against the eternity of God, and asks for wisdom of heart:

Lord, thou hast been our dwelling place in all generations,
Before the mountains were brought forth,
Or ever thou hast formed the earth and the world,
Even from everlasting to everlasting, thou art God. [...]

They then read together the verses on charity from the thirteenth chapter of St Paul's Letter to the Corinthians, which Germans call the 'High song of Christian love'. Afterwards he celebrated Communion with Hans and offered him spiritual advice, quoting the Gospel passage where Jesus speaks about laying down one's life for others. He then left Hans to do the same with Sophie.

Though in Stadelheim for less than three hours, the White Rose prisoners exerted an influence on the prison guards and officials there—all civil servants, not soldiers—who marveled at their strength of soul and spiritual poise, and risked breaking their own rules by allowing them to come together for a cigarette and to exchange a few last words.[19] 'I didn't know that dying can be so easy', Christl said; 'In a few minutes we will meet in eternity.' Sophie was taken off first—'without a flicker of an eyelash', said one of the guards.[20] Handcuffed and with assistant executioners on either side, she walked with unwavering dignity the 40 yards to the unmarked building which housed the guillotine. A few moments later, at around 5 pm, a muffled thud was heard. The executioner Johann Reichhart had never seen anyone meet death with such serenity as she had. Next came Hans, then Christl. Before placing his head on the block, Hans shouted out, '*Es lebe die Freiheit!*' (Long live freedom!)[21]

The following day, posters in flaming red were displayed all round Munich, which read:

Sentenced to death for high treason:

Christoph Probst, age 24

Hans Scholl, age 25

Sophie Scholl, age 22

The sentences have already been carried out.

Newspapers explained that irresponsible lone wolves and adventurers had excluded themselves from the *Volk*, and that the president of the People's Court had been flown in from Berlin to deal with the matter and to execute swift judgment. Nazi policy was to play down the whole affair and one of the few articles to appear, in the Party's daily paper the *Völkischer Beobachter*, was entitled 'Just punishment for traitors to the nation'. Nevertheless, the news spread like wildfire through non-official channels and by word of mouth, so that many ordinary people became aware of the leaflet campaign. The general public may have linked the news to the picture and description of Schurik, which had appeared in newspapers and posters, advertising the 1000-Mark reward on his head.

Willi remained behind bars at Wittelsbach Palace, and he was joined on the night of 24 February by Schurik, who had been on the run for several days. Lilo Ramdohr had helped Schurik to forge the identification papers of a Russian worker and he had set off for Innsbruck hoping to gain entry to a camp for foreign workers, but his contact at Innsbruck missed her train and failed to meet him. Schurik then made for the mountains and was taken in by a Russian, but had to leave when his presence was reported to the police. Armed with a blanket and supplies, he set off into the mountains, but snowstorms forced him to turn back. Desperate by now, and realising that nearly all his friends were connected with the White Rose and so under observation or else arrest, he returned to Munich to locate a friend with no White Rose connection, Marie Luise Upplegger. On the night of 24 February he found her in a shelter during an air-raid– but he was recognised by nearly everyone else there, and one of the terrified civilians called the Gestapo, who came to arrest him.

Up to one hundred others were arrested, so many that prison space became a problem for the authorities. A number of those arrested were taken into 'kinship custody' on account of the ruling that 'kin must be held responsible for the traitor'. All the remaining Scholls were detained, and so were Huber's wife and sister. As there had been a swift and decisive response to the distribution of the White Rose leaflets, the Gestapo were not in a hurry to stage a follow-up trial and instead cast the net wide in their efforts to eliminate all pockets of resistance. Besides those at the centre of the White Rose resistance, the Gestapo seized those who had bought stamps or helped address envelopes, and even those who knew or suspected something was afoot but failed to report the matter. Some were arrested in the usual fashion, but others were arrested by post and locked up after being ordered to report to Wittelsbach Palace.

Two months later, with just a few days' notice, it was announced that fourteen prisoners were to appear before the People's Court. Three of them were accused of high treason: Professor Kurt Huber, Alex Schmorell and Willi Graf. It is difficult to know precisely how they were treated while being held, as there is little evidence to go on, but it is clear that, in accordance with a pact they had made with Hans and Sophie, Schurik and Willi took as much blame as they could so as to protect the others, not knowing, at first, that Christl, Hans and Sophie had already been executed. Schurik was probably given the hardest time, as he was half-Russian, but the treatment he received stopped short of physical torture. Huber, who was shuttled from one jail to another, spent his time working on academic articles on folk music and on his book on Leibniz, when not under interrogation, and seems to have been treated well. The night before the second White Rose trial, he wrote to his wife Clara: 'If I should have to suffer death in this fight for freedom, then I ask all of you to be happy and rejoice for one who has found his way home to the final freedom of spirit. Then the sacrifice of life will have made me totally free.'[22]

On the morning of Monday, 19 April 1943 a green police van took fourteen men and women to the Palace of Justice for the trial. On this occasion Roland Freisler was joined by a field marshal and other top dignitaries so as to make it even more impressive than the previous trial. The list of the accused was topped by the names of Schurik, Willi and Professor Huber, and they were called in that order. But before doing so, the tone of proceedings was set when, on hearing the contents of the sixth leaflet read out, Huber's defence lawyer rose to give the Nazi salute, resigned, and walked out, to great applause. In his place, the President assigned another lawyer, who knew nothing about the case. Throughout proceedings one family name was referred to again and again: that of the Scholls.

When called to speak, Schurik described how his attachment to Russia, through his mother, made him incapable of shooting at either a German or a Russian, which was why he had served in the medical corps. He reminded the court that as a recruit he had declined to take the oath of unquestioning loyalty to the Führer, but this only invited an outburst from Freisler: 'Look at this traitor. He stabs the Fatherland in the back in a time of great danger. And he is supposed to be a sergeant in the German army.'[23] With this, Schurik was dismissed.

Freisler fared less well with Willi, as his quiet manner and steady look had the effect of mollifying everyone. Although heavily implicated in trips to the Rhineland for the purposes of recruitment, Willi had proved difficult for the Gestapo to pin down. Although Freisler was finally able to say (with a forced smile), 'in the end we were too smart for you, weren't we?', even he could not turn the court against this young German who had all the makings of a war hero, with his service medal (second class with swords) for his exemplary work in the medical corps. In one of his last letters, to his sister Anneliese, Willi had written, 'You know I did not act frivolously but out of deep concern and in awareness of how serious the situation was.'[24] This conscious conviction was precisely what he articulated calmly and coherently to the crowded courtroom, and there was a stir of sympathy as he sat down.

Though Huber was disappointed to discover that a friend, who was supposed to act as a character witness, had not turned up in court, he recovered from the upset and steadied himself for own defence, which he had prepared with scholarly care—and which survives. It was intended as a vindication of his actions in opposing National Socialism, as well as a defence of the others, and he threw himself into it, overcoming his trembling and speech defect and refusing to be cowed by the antagonistic setting and the fierce interruptions of Freisler. Like the other two—and the three at the previous trail—his stance was conveyed by his assertion, 'I retract nothing.' He traced his involvement with the White Rose students up to the final leaflet, in which he had appealed to university students to rise up against Nazi tyranny. In his wide-ranging statement he spoke passionately about the corruption of German education, before moving on to jurisprudential considerations of the system that was trying him.

'What I intended to accomplish', he explained,

> was to rouse the student body, not by means of an organization, but solely by my simple words, to urge them, not to violence, but to moral insight into the existing serious deficiencies of our political system. To urge the return to clear moral principles, to the constitutional state, to mutual trust between men. That is not illegal; rather, it the restitution of legality.[25]

He went on to refer to 'the threatening rule of raw force over justice', 'mere arbitrariness over the will to the moral good', and the denial of 'free self-determination of even the smallest national minority'.[26] The basic rights of people had been abrogated by the systematic undermining of trust among men. There was ultimately a limit to formal or external legality beyond which it became invalid and immoral; this occurred when it was used as a cloak for a cowardice which dare not stand up against open injustice. He demanded the return of freedom for Germans, for the restoration of legality, the rule of law, and mutual trust of one person for another.

Rather than a revolutionary, Huber claimed he was a German patriot upholding traditional proprieties, pleading for those who were motivated by ideals of true justice, decency, and truthfulness. Amidst all this, he put in a person plea for a stipend for his wife and two children, who had no means of support now that he had been stripped of his professorship. He finished by telling the court:

> My actions and my intentions will be justified by the inevitable course of history; such is my firm faith. I hope to God that the inner strength that will vindicate my deeds will in good time spring forth from my own people. I have done as I had to do on the prompting of an inner voice.[27]

When he limped back to his place to re-join his young comrades in the dock, there was a sober silence in the courtroom.

All fourteen of the accused were examined in turn and allowed to offer a defence, so it was nearly 10 pm before the four judges retired to consider their verdict. When pronounced, the words of judgement for the first three names on the indictment came as no surprise. Schurik, Willi and Professor Huber were condemned to death for having 'produced leaflets urging sabotage of the armaments industry and the overthrow of the National Socialist way of life'; for the spread of defeatist ideas and having 'vilified the Führer in the grossest manner'; and for having thereby 'aided and abetted the enemies of the Reich'.[28] Their honour and rights as citizens were forfeited in perpetuity. Huber was singled out with a furious denunciation for having betrayed his mission to imbue students with an absolute faith in the Führer and for not moulding them into iron-hearted warriors of the Third Reich. Of the remaining eleven defendants, all received prison sentences of varying lengths, except for Falk Harnack who was set free. Harnack's brother and sister-in-law had recently been hanged, on account of their involvement with the Red Orchestra affair, so he realised that his release was just a tactic of the Gestapo who were eager to pin more on him.

As the convicted prisoners were driven away by van to Stadelheim, there was an upbeat atmosphere inside: 'it was like a party', said Traute. Despite the three death sentences, there was a spontaneous release of tension after weeks spent in detention cells and being interrogated, and they chatted loudly and animatedly. They reassured each other that condemned prisoners were usually granted months for appeals, that the war might soon be over, and that there was hope for all of them. Even the three on death row shared this optimism: Huber passed round photos of his two children as well as cigarettes; Schurik expressed his wish that the young lady who had betrayed him at the air-raid shelter would not suffer reprisals; and Willi was seen smiling. But on arrival at Stadelheim the mood changed. They were quickly sorted out according to sentence, so quickly that Willi had no time to say farewell; Harnack was able to tell Huber, 'Remember, it was not in vain'; Schurik called out, 'Give my very best to Lilo. Tell her to think of me often.'[29]

Unlike Hans, Sophie and Christl, the three sent to their death cells on 19 April had to endure the protracted terror of waiting helplessly for news about their execution. Each in his own way faced up to the ordeal by drawing on inner reserves. Huber had the academic distraction of trying to finish his book on Leibniz. As the weeks became months he kept up the intensity of his labours, greatly impressing the Catholic chaplain Fr Ferdinand Brinkmann, who regarded the scene of Huber working frantically in his cell as 'a picture of the spiritual situation of Germany—the human spirit imprisoned and sentenced to death'.[30] As the date for his execution approached, Huber was two chapters away from finishing, so he petitioned the People's Court to grant him a delay! Despite their refusal, he kept hard at it until the end, but was unable to finish.

The defence lawyer who had been allocated to Schurik at the start of the trial did not forget his client and visited him several times after the trial. He noticed that even in his final weeks Schurik did not lose his composure or the conviction that what he had done was right; though the lawyer was shaken, Schurik was serene and light-hearted. In one of his final letters to his family, Schurik wrote,

Inwardly I become more tranquil from day to day—yes, my mood is usually happier than it was before, when I was free! How could such a thing come about? I will tell you: this 'misfortune' was necessary to put me on the right path, and so it was not a misfortune at all. [...] what did I know of faith, of true faith, of the last and single truth, of God? Very little! But now I have reached a state where, even in my present situation, I feel calm and happy, come what may.[31]

To his Russian girlfriend Nelly he wrote a terse, sober farewell letter: 'It was my fate to leave the earthly existence earlier than we all thought. We worked with Wanja [Hans Scholl] against the German government, we were discovered and condemned to death.'[32]

Due to appeals against the court's verdict, the executions were delayed three months. The appeals for the two non-commissioned officers percolated up the military legal system until they reached Hitler, who personally rejected them; the appeal for Huber went through civilian channels, and it failed, too. When the order for execution arrived, the date given was 13 July 1943, but Willi's name was missing. Why? Undoubtedly, it was because the Gestapo felt they could get more out of him by prolonging the agony.

Before his execution, Huber was allowed a bottle of wine in his cell and he toasted his wife, his children and 'our beloved Fatherland'. He wrote farewell poems for his daughter Birgit and son Wolfi, and in his last letter thanked his wife for enriching his life as no one else could have done; he also thanked her for the alpine roses she had sent him. He had been reading Schmaus' *Christian dogmatics*, the work that Willi Graf had enjoyed the previous summer. Shortly before his execution, Huber lamented that he would have been a happier man if only he had followed the Catholic faith of his childhood more closely. In his final hours, he received the sacraments.[33] On the afternoon of 13 July, Schurik was visited by his lawyer—now a friend—to offer him comfort. Schurik was tranquil and convinced that even though his life had been short, he had fulfilled his mission in the world, to the extent that he was unsure that anything remained for him to do if he were to be released.

The executions were set for 5 pm but they were delayed when three SS officers arrived asking if they could witness the execution; they wanted to ascertain how long it took for a man to strangle to death through hanging, and were disappointed to learn that only beheadings were taking place that afternoon. The delay over, Schurik went first. Making his way across the court-yard to the guillotine, Huber lost one of his slippers and Fr Brinkmann, watching from a room above, thought he saw a smile: Huber's last words to him were: 'On the other side!'[34]

Willi's execution was delayed a further three months as the Gestapo tried to squeeze more names out of him, submitting him to psychological torture that was both brutal and subtle. They offered to commute his death sentence if he revealed more names, then threatened him with violent torture and reprisals against his family if he failed to provide answers. His sister Anneliese spent four months in prison, at one time sharing a cell with Christl's sister Angelika, and his parents were imprisoned for four weeks; the fear that they might all be deported to a concentration camp came close to breaking Willi. It was solace to him that over the weeks and months of solitary confinement, the Gestapo were not able to make one new arrest. During his ordeal he read the poems of Hölderlin that his sister had sent him and contemplated the ultimate questions of life. Above all he drew strength from the Scriptures. In one of his last letters, he wrote: 'In every destiny, no matter how hard it may be, there lies a distinct meaning, even though it may not be disclosed to us in this world. The more difficult the time we pass through, the closer we come to God.'[35]

Fr Brinkmann spent many hours with Willi towards the end and left on record his impressions: 'He was like a candle. So straight. So upright. Consuming himself in a holy idealism.'[36] He was beheaded on 12 October 1943. In his last letters to friends and family he wrote, 'Keep a good memory of me'. To his parents he wrote, 'I could never say to you while I was alive how much I loved you, but now in these last hours I want to tell you that I love you with all my heart and that I have respected you. [...] The love of God encircles us completely and we trust his grace. May he be a gracious judge unto us.'[37] His family were not informed of his execution and only learned of it when a letter was returned to them marked 'Deceased'.

Notes

[1]   Moll, 'Acts of resistance', p. 192.

[2]   Else Gebel to the Scholl family, November 1946, quoted in Hanser, *A noble treason*, p. 242.

[3]   Indictment drawn up by the Reich Attorney General, 21 February 1943, I. Scholl, *The White Rose*, pp. 105–13.

[4]   'Sentence of the resistance of the White Rose', 19 April 1943, Hanser, *A noble treason*, p. 244.

[5]   Else Gebel to the Scholl family, November 1946, I. Scholl, *The White Rose*, pp. 138–47.

[6]   Else Gebel to the Scholl family, November 1946, quoted in Hanser, *A noble treason*, p. 244.

[7]   Else Gebel to the Scholl family, November 1946, Hanser, *A noble treason*, pp. 245–6.

[8]   I. Scholl, *The White Rose*, pp. 60–1; Knab, 'Die innere Vollendung der Person', *Die Stärkeren im Geiste*, Bald & Knab (eds), p. 146.

[9]   Quoted in Hanser, *A noble treason*, p. 247; Donohoe, *Hitler's conservative opponents in Bavaria*, p. 195.

[10]   Hanser, *A noble treason*, p. 251.

[11]   I. Scholl, *The White Rose*, p. 59; Hanser, *A noble treason*, p. 252.

[12]   Hanser, *A noble treason*, p. 253.

[13]   Hanser, *A noble treason*, p. 255.

[14]   I. Scholl, *The White Rose*, p. 61.

[15]   I. Scholl, *The White Rose*, pp. 61–2.

[16]   Hanser, *A noble treason*, p. 256.

[17]   Hanser, *A noble treason*, p. 257.

[18]   This is the testimony of Susan Hirzel, who met Rev. Dr Karl Alt a few days after the execution (S. Hirzel, *Vom Ja zum Nein*, p. 214). James Donohoe offers a different explanation: they did not become Catholics because a change of religious allegiance required notice, according to German ecclesiastical law. His two sources are a letter from Georg Smolka, dated

2 November 1948, and a conversation with Clara Huber in 1951 (*Hitler's conservative opponents in Bavaria*, pp. 193–4).

[19] Vinke, *The short life of Sophie Scholl*, p. 188. Vinke relies on a report by a prison warder, but historians such as McDonough regard this detail as fiction (*Sophie Scholl*, p. 182, n14).

[20] I. Scholl, *The White Rose*, p. 62.

[21] Hanser, *A noble treason*, p. 260.

[22] Hanser, *A noble treason*, p. 265.

[23] Hanser, *A noble treason*, p. 267.

[24] Hanser, *A noble treason*, p. 268.

[25] 'Final statement of the accused', quoted in I. Scholl, *The White Rose*, p. 63.

[26] 'Final statement of the accused', quoted in I. Scholl, *The White Rose*, p. 64.

[27] 'Final statement of the accused', quoted in I. Scholl, *The White Rose*, p. 65.

[28] Hanser, *A noble treason*, pp. 270–1. The full transcript of the sentence is reproduced in I. Scholl, *The White Rose*, pp. 119–37.

[29] Hanser, *A noble treason*, p. 273.

[30] Hanser, *A noble treason*, p. 274.

[31] Hanser, *A noble treason*, p. 274.

[32] Alex Schmorell to Nelly, 18 June 1943, quoted in Moll, 'Acts of resistance', p. 173.

[33] Fenlon, 'From the White Star to the Red Rose', p. 67.

[34] Hanser, *A noble treason*, p. 276.

[35] Hanser, *A noble treason*, p. 278.

[36] Hanser, *A noble treason*, p. 279.

[37] Willi to his parents, 12 October 193, quoted in Sachs, *White Rose history* vol. ii, ch. 64, p. 20.

9 AFTERMATH IN MUNICH AND ELSEWHERE

THE PERSECUTION OF those linked with White Rose activities did not stop with the execution of Willi Graf, but continued until the final days of the war. There were further arrests, prison sentences, arranged suicides and executions as the Gestapo continued to seek out and eliminate all signs of rebellion. Rounding off the White Rose story requires at least a brief account of these developments, even if the brevity employed might seem to reduce the drama of so many heroic lives to a lifeless list of facts. Most of the people mentioned in this overview have already been cited earlier in the story, and further details can be found in the large and growing literature about the White Rose and its participants. It goes without saying that all those mentioned are worthy of further study and reading.

Ten prison sentences were given at the second White Rose trial on 19 April 1943. Three female students, Traute Lafrenz, Gisela Schertling and Katharina Schüddekopf, were each given a one-year prison sentence. Susanne Hirzel received a six-month sentence, while her brother Hans received five years. Two of his fellow school-pupils, Heinrich Guter and Franz Müller, received eighteen months and five years respectively. Longer sentences were given to Eugen Grimminger, Helmut Bauer and Heinrich Bollinger. Grimminger, Robert Scholl's close friend, had engaged in passive resistance by helping the oppressed and persecuted, and had supported the White Rose activities with financial aid and materials. He would have been given the death sentence but for his secretary, who told the court that Grimminger was under the impression he was donating to needy soldiers, and instead he was given a ten-year sentence. Later that year, on 2 December, his (Jewish) wife Jenny was killed in Auschwitz.[1] Bauer and Bollinger, friends of Willi Graf from *Neudeutschland*, had been stockpiling weapons for active opposition; they both received seven-year sentences. The only one set free, for 'unique and special circumstances', was Falk Harnack. Little did the prosecutors know that on 25 February, Harnack had waited for Hans Scholl outside the Kaiser Wilhelm Memorial Church in Berlin, in order to introduce him to other members of the resistance, including Dietrich Bonhoeffer, unaware that Hans had been executed three days earlier. Harnack was enlisted in a penal battalion in August 1943 and sent to Greece; later he was sent to a concentration camp, but escaped, and for the rest of the war he helped the Greek partisans fight the Nazis.

On 13 July 1943, the day Huber and Schurik were executed, a third White Rose trial took place in Munich at which four older friends of the group appeared: the bookseller Josef Söhngen, who had played a part in editing the leaflets and who had offered his cellar to store the leaflets and duplicating machine; Harald Dohrn, the father-in-law of Christl Probst; the architect-painter Manfred Eickemeyer, who had allowed Hans to use his studio; and the artist Wilhelm Geyer who had worked in the studio. Josef Söhngen received a six-month prison sentence and the others three months, due to a lack of conclusive evidence against them. Harald Dohrn was shot dead by the SS in the final days of the war for taking part in the *Freiheitsaktion Bayern* (Bavarian Freedom Initiative) during which the main radio station in Munich was occupied.

Other than a single trial in Saarbrücken on 3 April 1944, at which Willi Bollinger was given a three-month sentence, all the remaining trials sought to eliminate activity operating out of Hamburg. The Hamburg branch of the White Rose movement had been established in the autumn of 1942 and came to comprise around fifty students and intellectuals; according to the records of the Gestapo and the People's Court, thirty-two of them were sent to prison or concentration camps, and some were executed.

Many of them did not know each other and met for the first time in prison or concentration camps, as they had not attended the regular meetings at the two Hamburg bookstores, organized by Albert Suhr and Heinz Kucharski. Some of those involved were just seventeen and had joined after falling out with their teachers or Hitler Youth leaders. Communication between the Hamburg and Munich groups operated through Traute Lafrenz, who had delivered one of the White Rose leaflets to her Hamburg friends in the autumn of 1942.

After the Munich group was suppressed, by the three trials of 1943, and the imprisonment of Traute, a student of chemistry called Hans Leipelt ensured that the sixth leaflet continued to be produced and distributed. Additionally, he organized support for the widow of Kurt Huber and her two children; besides living expenses, Clara Huber needed to pay off the 3000-Mark bill she had been presented with for wear and tear on the guillotine that had killed her husband. Hans Leipelt had transferred to Munich in the winter of 1941/42 to work in the Chemical Institute of Munich University under the direction of Professor Heinrich Wieland, a Nobel Prize winner whose department had become a sanctuary for scientists who were opponents or victims of the regime. Hans had won the Iron Cross second class during the campaign in France in 1940, but had been dishonourably discharged because of his mixed (i.e. partly Jewish) blood.

In February 1943, Hans Leipelt and his girlfriend Marie-Luise Jahn made copies of the sixth White Rose leaflet with a new title, *'Und ihr Geist lebt trotzdem weiter'* (Despite everything, their spirits live on), and distributed it around Hamburg. It was the collecting of money for Huber's widow that led to the arrest of Hans on 8 October 1943 and Marie-Luise on 18 October, both in Munich, and the arrest of another forty in Hamburg. In the fifth White Rose trial, which took place at Donauwörth on 13 October 1944, a year after his arrest, Hans was sentenced to death, and executed at Stadelheim on 29 January 1945; his efforts to attribute all the blame to himself ensured that his girlfriend only received a twelve-year sentence. Hans' mother Katharina and his sister Maria were among those arrested in Hamburg. His mother was forced to take her own life in prison on 9 January 1945; his sister spent a year in solitary confinement, before appearing at the last White Rose trial on 20 April 1945, and was rescued by the Allies three hours before she was scheduled to be put to death.

Four White Rose trials took place in Hamburg in 1945, on 17, 19 (two) and 20 April. Just two of the accused were set free. The paediatrician Dr Rudolf Degkwitz was sentenced for seven years; and the bookseller Felix Jud for four years (and was freed by the British in May). Others, who had either been freed by the Allies or gone missing, were given prison sentences *in absentia*: Dr Ursula de Boor, Bruno Himpkamp, Thorsten Müller, Karl Ludwig Schneider, Gerd Spitzbart, Wilhelm Stoldt, Albert Suhr, Hannelore Wilbrandt, Dorothea Zill, and Emmy Zill. Heinz Kucharski was sentenced to death, but escaped from his executioners during an Allied air raid on the way to the guillotine at Bützow-Dreibergen.

There were several fatalities from the Hamburg circle in 1944 and 1945: Elisabeth Lange was forced to take her life on 28 January 1944; Reinhold Meyer, a student of philosophy, died under mysterious circumstances in prison on 12 November 1944; Friedrich Geussenhainer, a medical student who had once distributed the sermons of von Galen, died of starvation in Mauthausen concentration camp in April 1945; Greta Rothe, a medical student, died of tuberculosis in prison on 15 April; Gretl Mrosek was hanged on 21 April; and Dr Curt Ledien, a lecturer in law, was hanged on 23 April. These gruesome facts show that, despite the imminent downfall of the Nazi regime, they were brutal in extinguishing all resistance to the very end.

Although she was the link between the Hamburg and Munich branches of those distributing the White Rose leaflets, Traute had been able to conceal this from her accusers at the second White Rose trial and escaped with just a one-year sentence. A fortnight after she had completed her sentence, she was rearrested and spent the last year of the war in prison awaiting trial for treason, with the expectation that she would be sentenced to death; the town where she was held prisoner was liberated by the Allies on 12 April 1945, three days before her trial was scheduled to start.

In one of the first instances of what came to be known as *Sippenhaft* (the principle that families share the responsibility for a crime committed by one of its members—a new word coined for the purpose), the entire Scholl family were arrested, except for Werner who had returned to the Russian front (and went missing). According to the policy that kinship formed a basis for prosecution and punishment, all the Scholls served time in prison and were questioned endlessly, while kept in solitary confinement. Inge, Lisl and Magdalena were released early because of ill health, then were acquitted at the Scholl family trial in August 1943. Robert served a two-year sentence, and was released just before the end of the war. Otl Aicher deserted the *Wehrmacht* in 1945 and went into hiding at the Scholl's house in Wutach Gorge.

Fritz's last letter to Sophie lamented the loss of the two volumes of Newman sermons she had given him and of Haecker's *Creator and creation*; Sophie was dead when he wrote it.[2] When Fritz visited her parents the present he gave them was the collection of Newman sermons, translated by Haecker, called *The Church and the world*. Haecker also visited the Scholls, and he signed the visitor's book with Newman's cardinalate motto, *Cor ad cor loquitur* (Heart speaks to heart). Both Fritz and Haecker, it seems, considered Newman's words appropriate for the grief of the Scholls. Referring to his disagreement with Hans about whether Hitler was the Antichrist, Haecker told Frau Scholl that Hans was *homo politicus*, not *homo religious*.

As for Theodor Haecker, not long after the arrest and execution of Hans and Sophie, he was taken in and interrogated. It seems that Hans had noted down a conversation with Haecker in which he had said that, above all things, Germans lacked humility. When asked to explain to his interrogators what he meant, Haecker replied, 'Literally what I said', and was dismissed with the remark, '*Ach so, das ist in Ordnung*' (Ah really, it's OK).[3] The *Journal* he kept, like everything else he had written, was worked on by night. As much as possible of the manuscript was kept hidden in a leather briefcase—after the executions in February 1943 Otl Aicher buried them in an orchard—for Haecker had every reason to fear a visit of the Gestapo. When it occurred, and the police entered his flat, the current pages of the *Journal* lay in a music case on the sofa in his sitting room. Only the presence of mind of his daughter, who caught her father's whispered word *mappe* (case), saved it from discovery; she ran into the room, called out that she was late for her music lesson, and ran off with the case. In the nearby parsonage she exchanged her father's notes for sheet music; when she returned, her bag was searched.

On 9 June 1944 Haecker's house in Munich was completely destroyed during a bombing raid. A cryptic entry in his diary records the event and includes the only mention of the Scholls; at this moment of crisis was he perhaps crying out for Hans and Sophie?

> Friday morning towards ten o'clock. In the cellar. High-explosive bomb. The house and my flat destroyed. Unbelievable destruction. Some good people, helpers, people who console me by being what they are and by helping! Scholl. And also some *crapule* [scoundrels]. Upright souls. And miserable souls. God is merciful! God is great! God is precise, but magnanimous. What has happened to me is no injustice.[4]

After spending seven weeks with the Scholls, Haecker went to live on his own in Ustersbach, a village outside Augsburg, where his daughter visited him occasionally from Munich. His eldest son was a prisoner in England and his youngest son had been reported missing, shortly after being sent to the Russian front early in 1945.[5] Haecker's health had already begun to suffer and his sight began to fail; on 9 April 1945 he died of diabetes, coincidentally the same day as Bonhoeffer was hanged.

Carl Muth's house in Munich-Solln was one of many that were searched by the Gestapo after the arrest of Hans and Sophie.

Muth had good reason to fear a search as he kept hidden a copy of his letter to Pope Pius XII, a prophetic outcry about the extermination of the Jews. While the Gestapo were searching his house, Muth prayed fervently to St Thomas More (who had been canonised in 1935), and his prayers were answered.

In the immediate aftermath of the first White Rose executions, in the evening of 22 February 1943, several thousand students gathered in Munich to show their support for the regime and their outrage at the White Rose activities. They applauded Schmid, the porter who had spotted and arrested Hans and Sophie; and in a speech the student leader regretted that their execution had not taken place at the University. Nevertheless, not long after Hans, Sophie and Christl were buried (in the Perlacher Friedhof, next to the Stadelheim prison), the new version of the sixth leaflet, with the extra line 'Despite everything, their spirits live on', was circulated. This slogan was also daubed on walls and pavements around Munich.

A copy of the sixth leaflet was smuggled out of Germany by the jurist Helmuth von Moltke through Scandinavia to Britain, where it was used by the Allied Forces, when in mid-1943, they dropped millions of propaganda copies over Germany; it was retitled 'The Manifesto of the Students of Munich', and had an introduction. The leaflets by the White Rose were also spread secretly in occupied countries and even made their way into concentration camps. The White Rose students were hailed as heroes in Russia; and in the United States the exiled Thomas Mann, the voice of German culture, spoke of them on the programme on the wireless 'The Voice of America' as 'gallant, glorious people'.

After the war, Robert Scholl became mayor of Ulm (1945–48), and in 1952 was one of the founders of the All German People's Party. Magdalena never fully recovered from the trauma of losing three children during the war and she died in 1958. After Sophie's execution, Fritz began to support the Scholls financially and got to know Sophie's younger sister Lisl and later helped her to find a job. He was captured by the US forces in April 1945, released in

September, and in October he married Lisl. They had four sons and he became active in the peace movement, giving advice to young conscientious objectors. Initially barred from studying law at Munich University, because of his military background, Fritz was able to prove by means of testimonies and his relationship with Sophie that he had begun to oppose the Nazi regime—and had contributed 1000 Marks to resistance activities. Fritz eventually became Chief Judge of the Regional Court of Stuttgart. Inge Scholl, who had been spared being sent to a concentration camp because of her diphtheria, became a Catholic in February 1945 and was married (by the philosopher-theologian Romano Guardini) to Olt Aicher in 1952. With Otl, she helped to found the Ulm School of Design in 1953; she also wrote several books about the White Rose activities, including *Die Weisse Rose* (1952, *The White Rose*), which became a best-seller and went through many editions. She was also heavily involved in the peace movement. As a graphic designer, Otl is best known for his pictograms used in the 1972 Munich Olympics. After being released from her second prison sentence in 1945, Traute Lafrenz emigrated to the United States.

As a loyal Nazi supporter, Gisela Schertling incriminated many members of the White Rose circle during her interrogations, but she atoned for her actions after the war by devoting her life to educational projects that warned of the dangers of Nazism.

Judge Roland Freisler continued ordering executions—2566 in total—until 3 February 1945, when he was killed in a bombing raid while sheltering in the cellar of the People's Court in Berlin. *Gauleiter* Giesler committed suicide with his whole family on 8 May 1945, the day the Nazi authorities capitulated to the Allies. Robert Mohr was arrested in 1947 but released the following year, without being charged with any crime relating to his time as a Gestapo officer, and he even managed to retain his pension. Johann Reichhart, the executioner in Munich, continued his job and later found himself executing Nazi war criminals at Nuremberg.

Astonishingly, the wartime legislation banning any activities connected with the White Rose remained in force until it was rescinded in 1983 in order that the film *The White Rose* (1982) could be distributed outside West Germany.

Notes

1   When Grimminger was approached by Hans and Schurik, his wife had implored him not to take part in the conspiracy, because as a Jew she was only protected by her marriage to him. Grimminger explained, 'I did, nevertheless. I did it because I couldn't do otherwise. I could not continue to face all the atrocities and crimes which were taking place' (quoted in M. Kissener, 'Eugene Grimminger and the "White Rose" ', http://weisse-rose-crailsheim.de/eugen-grimminger/eugen-grimminger-and-the-white-rose).

2   He wrote from the military hospital in the city of Lviv in western Ukraine on 26 February 1943, telling her how much he missed his precious books which he had left behind in Stalingrad, books on or by St Augustine, St Thomas Aquinas, Bl. John Henry Newman and Theodor Haecker.

3   Dru in preface to Haecker, *Journal in the night*, p. xv.

4   *Journal in the night*, no. 704, p. 218.

5   Dru in preface to Haecker, *Journal in the night*, p. xv.

10 LEGACY

AFTER THE SECOND World War, Winston Churchill wrote:

> The political history of all nations has hardly ever produced anything greater and nobler than the opposition which existed in Germany. These people fought without any help, whether from within or from without, driven only by the uneasiness of their consciences. As long as they were alive, they were invisible to us, because they had to put on masks. But their deaths brought their resistance to light.[1]

This tribute to the resistance within Germany from Britain's wartime leader is recognition of countless, unrecorded deeds, and a corrective to the commonly-held conviction that the German people were collectively guilty for the sins of the Third Reich, on account of failing to oppose the regime. Only a few isolated deeds of resistance have come to the attention of the non-German public, most notably the attempts to assassinate Hitler, such as von Stauffenberg's failed coup of 20 July 1944. Few non-Germans know that, according to court files which survived the war, around 800,000 Germans were imprisoned for active resistance,[2] and that around 15,000 Germans were executed, some for merely spontaneous and minor criticism of the regime.[3]

The story of the White Rose illustrates how difficult and dangerous it was to show any form of resistance, and how successful the Nazi tactics were in desensitising consciences and gradually eliminating everything that stood in their way. Even the effort to maintain some form of inner or passive resistance required considerable determination. Yet the White Rose story reveals that there were perfectly normal individuals who chose to struggle for what they knew to be right, even if few others showed any willingness to assist them—Ian Kershaw describes

the White Rose activities as 'resistance without the people'[4]—
even if it meant forfeiting their lives. What was it that made them
act in this way? What lessons can we learn from them? What can
Hans and Sophie teach people with ideals, in particular others
who are also motivated by Christian faith, at the start of the
twenty-first century? Before answering the deeper questions
about the young Scholls and their friends, it is worth looking at
their legacy to see how their heroism has been commemorated.

Hundreds of schools, streets and squares have been named
after most of those involved in the White Rose activities, above
all Hans and Sophie Scholl. The square in front of Munich
University's main building has been re-named Geschwister-
Scholl-Platz (Scholl Sibling Square), and opposite the University
is Professor-Huber-Platz. Stamps have been issued and anniver-
saries marked with a growing frequency. Though Hans and
Schurik were the principle leaders, the iconic figure of the White
Rose is Sophie. Indeed, there is a bust of her in Valhalla, the hall
of fame of great Germans. Two films have been made about the
White Rose: Michael Verhoeven's *Die Weisse Rose* (*The White
Rose*), released in 1982; and *Sophie Scholl: Die letzten Tage* (*Sophie
Scholl: the final days*), released in 2005 (based on transcriptions
from the interrogations and trial), which was nominated for an
Oscar in the category Best Foreign Language Film. In *Sophie
Scholl*, Julia Jentsch played the title role and won the best actress
award at the Berlin Film Festival; commenting on her role, she
said, 'I tried to portray Sophie as a person, with a great sense of
compassion and strong religious beliefs.'[5] An opera called *Die
Weisse Rose* was premiered in 1967, and a revised version opened
in 1986 and became an international success. A lyric opera called
Kommilitonen! (Fellow students!)—the title of the second version
of the sixth pamphlet—was composed by Peter Maxwell Davies
and David Pountney in 1991.

Christian denominations have also given the White Rose
students due recognition. The Lutheran Church regards Hans
and Sophie, unofficially, as martyrs; within the Catholic Church,

petitions have been submitted to the authorities requesting the start of the processes for the canonisation of Willi Graf and Christoph Probst as martyrs. Because his mother was Russian and because his actions were informed by his Christian faith, Alex Schmorell was 'glorified' as a 'passion bearer' (i.e. canonized as a martyr) by the Russian Orthodox Church outside Russia in 2012, and during the ceremony in the Russian Orthodox Cathedral in Munich an icon of Schurik was unveiled in his honour. Archpriest Nikolai Artemoff, who had worked toward Schurik's canonisation since 1993, told the German media that the new Orthodox saint 'took a very important stance, rejecting both Bolshevism as well as National Socialism'.

The first publication to document the White Rose activities was Inge Scholl's *Die Weisse Rose* (1952). Since then, there have been dozens of studies published, some inspired by the discovery of new sources, others to mark anniversaries. Efforts to research and disseminate information about White Rose activities have become a collective endeavour, as can be seen by the number of societies and foundations that conduct research and perpetuate the memory of the Scholls and their friends. The first of these, the White Rose Foundation in Munich, began its work in 1987 at the instigation of the surviving members and close relatives of the White Rose circle, and this led to the opening of the White Rose Museum. Inevitably, the historiography of the White Rose has not been immune from ideological wars and interpretations have become increasingly contentious.

Despite the many tributes to the courage and idealism of those who took part in White Rose activities, some critics have argued that Hans and Sophie were impractical idealists who changed little and that lives were needlessly risked because of their reckless behaviour. These are three separate questions here that need to be answered separately: whether Hans and Sophie took unnecessary risks with their own lives, whether they were responsible for the arrest of their friends and collaborators, and what the overall effect was of their involvement in the White Rose movement. To answer these, it is necessary to analyse their actions and assess their motives—a task that can only be attempted with the utmost delicacy and caution, knowing that ultimately we can never be certain.

The evidence available to us suggests that reflecting on the potential consequences of their acts of resistance was only part of what motivated Hans and Sophie. At various times it seems that they anticipated that their actions would *not* result in a popular uprising or Hitler's overthrow, though that was the intention of the leaflets; and this appears to have been their prevailing belief. Towards the end, when they became more aware of left-wing resistance groups (which were generally accepting of or friendly toward Bolshevism), they saw the opportunity for collaboration that could lead to real effects; but at the same time they saw the dangers, both practical and ideological, of collaborating with them. Both Hans and Sophie seem to have been motivated by some fundamental urge that the right thing to do was to speak out, regardless of whether this would produce any popular reaction at all. When they saw that the first leaflets had little effect, they felt compelled to speak out more strongly still, and were reconciled to the idea that this would mean sacrifice, perhaps of their lives; but, at the same time, they may have been aware, or hoped, that this sacrifice would have practical effects in the long run: that their struggle—seen not just in their leaflets but in how they lived their lives—and their sacrifice would ultimately bear more fruit than if they had led a revolt.

Why did Sophie agree to help Hans on the final, fateful mission, especially when Schurik and Willi had declined to take part? What made Sophie put aside other considerations and pledge her loyalty to her moody elder brother? The vivid dream she recorded in her diary the previous 9 August offers a possible explanation. It suggests that she regarded Hans as having received a divine commission to play a part in the redemption of the Reich; and that, for this reason, she put to one side Hans' failings for the sake of the larger drama, in which she envisioned herself as having an important role. This would be one way to interpret her defiant tone when interrogated: 'I am, now as before, of the opinion that I did the best that I could do for my nation. I therefore do not regret my conduct and will bear the consequences that result from my conduct.'[6] Sophie's other dream, during her final night, about losing her own life but saving the baby in white, 'our idea' which 'will survive us and succeed despite all the pitfalls and obstacles', expresses the same conviction; as does her remark that, 'So many are dying for this regime, it is high time that someone died in opposition to it.'[7]

With regard to the effect of the White Rose movement, and the role of Hans and Sophie in particular, there are some who would judge on the basis of contemporaneous consequences, pointing to the absence of a popular uprising or claiming that their actions had no effect on how the war ended. This viewpoint, however, benefits from hindsight; had the Allied advance on Berlin been less rapid, then those influenced by the White Rose (or other resistance efforts) might have been moved to effectual resistance. More importantly, focussing only on tangible effects overlooks the importance of self-sacrifice for a noble cause, how it encourages both present and future generations and calls to mind the fundamental value of freedom and other basic goods. The Christian form of the ultimate self-sacrifice is called martyrdom, and it points to something greater still. Besides the inherent value of such witness, there is a spiritual, mysterious aspect of martyrdom that reminds us of the gift of life and its purpose.

The human longing for such inspiration can be grasped in the reaction to the White Rose executions of Ilse Aichinger, a half-Jewish poet in Vienna who lived by the day, unsure whether the next knock at the door would mean she would be taken off to a concentration camp. She describes the effect of seeing a poster proclaiming the execution of the Scholl siblings and Christoph Probst.

> I read the names of the White Rose. I had never heard of
> any of them. But as I read those names, an expressible hope

leaped up in me. [...] I was not the only one who felt that way. [...] This hope—which made it possible for us to go on living—was not just the hope of our survival. [...] It helped so many that still had to die: even they could die with hope. [...] It was like a secret light that spread over the land: it was joy. I remember I went out on the street to meet a friend and he said, 'Don't look so radiant—they'll arrest you!'

We did not have much of a chance to survive, but that was not what it was about. It wasn't survival. It was life itself that was speaking to us through the death of the Scholls and their friends. [...] You can live without owning anything. But you can't live without something ahead of you, ahead of you in the sense of something inside of you. You can't live without hope.[8]

Equally significant is the reaction of the Nazi regime. A month after the first arrests and executions, Munich was still greatly agitated by these events, according to the German diplomat Ulrich von Hassell (who was executed after the failed 20 July coup), and the Party was doing its level best to persuade the public that the students involved were Communists. Von Hassell recorded in his secret diary his regard for their deeds as a 'single, splendid, deeply ethical national appeal'.[9]

The difficult question to answer is why Sophie threw caution to the wind and endangered the lives of her family and friends in such reckless fashion when she threw the leaflets from the balcony. Why did she and Hans not destroy the evidence incriminating others before they set out for the University, knowing they were embarking on a high-risk operation? Considered in the context of other events of that month, the plan to distribute the sixth leaflet from within the University does not appear to be significantly more daring than, say, the third graffiti campaign, and on that occasion the White Rose students took no measures to hide their tracks. The fact is that, on 18 February, they nearly escaped being caught; they might have done so if they had made a quick exit. Sophie's final gesture in the *Lichtof* seems spontaneous, possibly the result of her euphoria on finishing their task, or perhaps caused by her mental and physical exhaustion. We should bear in mind that Hans sensed that the Nazi authorities had been converging on the White Rose circle and that he was in danger of being apprehended. As Sophie may have shared Hans' fears, it may be that they were taking more risks because they thought it was better to be caught in a public act of defiance, rather than by a tip-off and a knock at the door from the Gestapo. We will never know all that went through their minds with regard to the risks they took and why, but the evidence of their character is abundant. They acted with serenity, as well as courage and single-mindedness, with faith and lightness of heart, and without a trace of harsh fanaticism. This was no suicidal despair: their last act—in prison—was to try to save their friends, by assuming full responsibility themselves.

Apart from questioning their strategy, one thing we should be asking ourselves is what enabled Sophie to display such courage, both before and after her arrest. From where did she draw her strength? At the human level, her letters and diaries indicate that she was someone who worked at her shortcomings and fought for many years against personal flaws, laziness and pride. By dint of self-examination, daily effort to change, and determination not to give in to despair, she developed remarkable self-control. At the supernatural level, at the order of grace, she saw this project as one guided by her Creator and nourished through personal prayer and the reading of Holy Scripture. Sophie was able to be heroic in big things because she was heroic in little things, that is, as a result of her daily struggle as a Christian. Her defiant spirit, anchored in a search for truth, enabled her to swim against the current of mediocrity.

It remains to ask, What did the White Rose students stand for? What was the 'freedom' they died for? Not the 'freedom' to do anything they chose, but freedom to do what is true, good and beautiful, to act according to the dictates of a conscience informed by the laws of God imprinted on the heart, that is, according to laws not of *their* making but issuing from a higher source—none other than their Creator. Sophie, in particular, was sensitive to her informed conscience, having developed a rich 'theology of conscience' through reading Newman and discussing his writings in depth with Fritz and Haecker. It is this understanding of conscience which emerges in the interrogations as her primary defence for transgressing unjust laws. Haecker provided the White Rose students with arguments that strengthened their resolve to withstand the evil around them, but steered them away from active resistance and violence. His metaphysical analysis of wartime conditions against the backdrop of sacred history, including the prophecies of the Antichrist, enabled him to see divine providence at work and to conclude that Hitler was no Antichrist, only one of his many precursors and *ante*-types.

Theodor Haecker died from diabetes a month before the end of the war, just as Newman was beginning to captivate a generation of German Catholics. Among them was Joseph Ratzinger, the future Pope Benedict, who entered the seminary at Freising in January 1946, and was assigned to a group under an older student, Alfred Läpple, who was working on a doctoral thesis on Newman and conscience.[10] Their common interest in the great problems of theology and philosophy ensured that Läpple and Ratzinger became close friends. In his opening address to a symposium on Newman in Rome, Cardinal Ratzinger explained:

> For us at that time, Newman's teaching on conscience became an important foundation for theological personalism, which was drawing us all in its sway. Our image of the human being as well as our image of the Church was permeated by this point of departure.[11]

> We had experienced the claim of a totalitarian party, which understood itself as the fulfilment of history and which negated the conscience of the individual. One of its leaders [Hermann Göring] had said: 'I have no conscience. My conscience is Adolf Hitler'.[12] The appalling devastation of humanity that followed was before our eyes.

So it was liberating and essential for us to know that the 'we' of the Church does not rest on a cancellation of conscience, but that, exactly the opposite, it can only develop from conscience. Precisely because Newman interpreted the existence of the human being from conscience, that is, from the relationship between God and the soul, was it clear that this personalism is not individualism, and that being bound by conscience does not mean being free to make random choices—the exact opposite is the case.

[...] Freedom of conscience, Newman told us, is not identical with the right 'to dispense with conscience, to ignore a Lawgiver and Judge, to be independent of unseen obligations'.[13]

Ratzinger clarified that, 'this way of conscience is everything other than a way of self-sufficient subjectivity; it is a way of obedience to objective truth'. It seemed to Ratzinger that the 'characteristic of the great Doctor of the Church' was 'that he [Newman] teaches not only through his thought and speech but also by his life, because within him, thought and life are interpenetrated and defined'. On account of this, Newman 'belongs to the great teachers of the Church, because he both touches our hearts and enlightens our thinking'.[14]

During his lifetime Newman came to recognise the failure of Christians to influence public life and to understand the need to educate Christians to be responsible in an age of increasing antipathy to Christian truth. The state was no longer the outward and social expression of the Established Church; it could only act as a breakwater against a process of de-Christianisation which was driven by utilitarian consensus. It was up to the Christian laity to get involved in social and political life so as to provide Christian witness, and for this they needed to be educated so as to act according to an informed conscience. By the time he came to write his *Letter to the Duke of Norfolk* (1875)[15] he saw that the very concept of conscience was corrupting into self-interest.

Hans and Sophie Scholl were brought up in a Germany that was in the process of becoming post-Christian, where many young people were merely nominal or cultural Christians. Emerging from the Great War without any definite Christian bearings, the nation was ripe for the propagation of Nazi ideas of the eugenic state, which had been piloted and widely promoted in Britain, France and the United States.[16] Having drifted from Christianity, Germany succumbed to the *Herrgott* religion of the Fatherland that was aggressive, destructive and totalitarian. Aldous Huxley's *Brave new world* (1932) was written as a warning; George Orwell's *Nineteen eighty-four* (1949) as a post-war commentary. During the war itself, in the very week Hans and Sophie were executed, C. S. Lewis delivered the lectures that were published as *The abolition of man* (1943).[17] Possessing a philosophical literacy not unlike Haecker's, Lewis argued the case for objective (or absolute) values and the natural law, and warned against the slip into moral subjectivism. Like Haecker, Lewis realised that the only agency capable of conquering in the apocalyptic battle was that of God acting in the conscience of the participants—the theme of his later novel *That hideous strength* (1945).

The political history of nations has hardly ever produced anything more criminal and malevolent than Hitler's Third Reich, but at the same time there has hardly been anything nobler than the opposition which existed in Germany. Many of those who opposed evil drew on the rich Christian heritage of nineteen centuries. Indeed, these texts continue to inspire Christians today, in particular those who sense that the age of Sophie and Hans Scholl, Alex Schmorell, Christoph Probst, Willi Graf, Kurt Huber, Carl Muth, Theodor Haecker and Bishop von Galen is very much our own.

One other name should be added, that of Fritz Hartnagel, as he makes a compelling instance of the reception of Newman in Germany. Referring to Sophie, he later said,

> We often debated, and at first did not agree on anything.
> We argued vehemently. Only after much hesitation and

reluctance did I find myself ready to follow her ideas. Step by step I came to admit that her attitude was correct. What a tremendous plunge for me to take—to say in mid-war, 'I am against this war' or 'Germany has to lose the war'.[18]

The sermon by Newman which touched him so deeply in Stalingrad, 'The testimony of conscience', was based on the text: 'Our rejoicing is this, the testimony of our conscience, that in simplicity and godly sincerity, not with fleshly wisdom, but by the grace of God, we have had our conversation in the world, and more abundantly towards you.' (2 Corinthians 1:12) There, amidst the carnage, Fritz soaked in those 'drops of precious wine':

> Let us endeavour to become friends of God and fellow-citizens with the saints; not by sinless purity, for we have it not; not in our deeds of price, for we have none to show; not in our privileges, for they are God's acts, not ours; not in our Baptism, for it is outward; but in that which is the fruit of Baptism within us, not a word but a power, not a name but a reality, which, though it can claim nothing, can beg everything; an honest purpose, an unreserved, entire submission of ourselves to our Maker, Redeemer, and Judge. Let us beg Him to aid us in our endeavour, and, as He has begun a good work in us, to perform it until the day of the Lord Jesus.[19]

Notes

[1]   McDonough, *Sophie Scholl: the real story*, p. 6.

[2]   'Sophie Scholl: a woman of all seasons', inaugural lecture by F. McDonough, Liverpool Moore University, January 2012.

[3]   Kershaw, 'Resistance without the people?', *Die Weisse Rose*, p. 61.

[4]   Kershaw, 'Resistance without the people?', *Die Weisse Rose*, p. 62.

[5]   McDonough, *Sophie Scholl: the real story*, p. 153.

[6]   This was Sophie's response to the closing question as to why she had not 'come to the conclusion that your conduct and the action along with your brother and other persons in the present phase of the war should be seen

as a crime against the community, in particular against our troops fighting arduously in the east, that merits the severest sentence?', official examination transcripts, 21 February 1943, Bundesarchiv Berlin, ZC 13267, Bd. 3.

[7]   Sachs, *White Rose history* vol. ii, ch. 44, p. 7.

[8]   Quoted in A. Dumbrach, 'Sophie Scholl: an exploration of a young woman's courage in Nazi Germany', *Life, death and sacrifice: women and family in the Holocaust*, ed. E. Hertzog (New York: Gefen, 2008), p. 222.

[9]   Diary entry, 25 March 1943, *Von Hassell diaries 1938–1944*, p. 266.

[10] Läpple had begun his research before the war, and had written to the Birmingham Oratory about it on 13 May 1939. During his military service he did not lose sight of his topic, and afterwards resumed his studies with new energy and enthusiasm. He was awarded his doctorate at the University of Munich in 1951, based on his thesis, 'The individual in the Church. Fundamental features of a theology of the individual in John Henry Newman'.

[11] When Ratzinger moved to Munich to continue his studies, he was introduced to the *Grammar of assent* by 'my true teacher in theology' Gottlieb Söhngen, who saw Newman as the founder of a true theological personalism in line with intuitions of St Augustine. It was through another theologian Heinrich Fries that Ratzinger encountered Newman's ideas on the development of doctrine; Fries was the first to systematically encourage dissertations on Newman in Germany and helped to integrate him into theological studies, emphasising his personalism as a basis for understanding the dynamics of Revelation and the fundamental role of conscience for a Christian.

[12] Ratzinger quotes from H. Rauschning, *Gespräche mit Hitler* (1940; *Conversations with Hitler*, 1972), p. 19 n25.

[13] Introductory words at the Newman Symposium in Rome, April 1990, *Benedict XVI and Cardinal Newman*, ed. P. Jennings (Oxford: Family Publications, 2005), pp. 33–4. Ratzinger quotes from the 'Letter to the Duke of Norfolk', 1875, *Difficulties felt by Anglicans in Catholic teaching*, vol. ii (London: Longmans, Green & Co., 1900), p. 250.

[14] Introductory words, April 1990, *Benedict XVI and Cardinal Newman*, pp. 34–5.

[15] Written in the wake of the First Vatican Council, the *Letter* was a response to the charge of the Prime Minister William Gladstone that Catholics have 'no mental freedom', being 'captives and slaves of the Pope'. Newman's argument hinged on his understanding of conscience, which he explained at length.

[16] The Chair of Eugenics at London University was renamed the Chair of Sociology after World War I.

17   The Riddell Lectures were delivered on 24–26 February 1943 at King's College, Newcastle, then part of the University of Durham.
18   Vinke, *Short life of Sophie Scholl*, p. 78.
19   Newman, 'The testimony of conscience', *Parochial and plain sermons* vol. v, pp. 252–3.

BIBLIOGRAPHY

Aeschliman, M. D., 'Theodor Haecker', *Crisis Magazine* (9 April 2012).

Arnold, C., 'Newman's reception in Germany: from Döllinger to Ratzinger', Newman lecture at Oriel College Oxford, 2011.

Bald, D. & Knab, J., (eds), *Die Stärkeren im Geiste: Zum christlichen Wilderstand der Weißen Rose* (Essen: Klartext, 2012).

Biemer, G., 'Theodor Haecker: in the footsteps of John Henry Newman', *New Blackfriars* 81:956 (October 2000), pp. 412–31.

Conway, J. C., *The Nazi persecution of the churches 1933–1945* (London: Weidenfeld & Nicolson, 1968).

Donohoe, J., *Hitler's conservative opponents in Bavaria, 1930–1945; a study of Catholic, monarchist, and separatist anti-Nazi activities* (Leiden: Brill, 1961).

Dumbach, A. & Newborn, J., *Shattering the German night: the story of the White Rose* (Oxford: Oneworld, 1986); rev. edn *Sophie Scholl and the White Rose* (Oxford: Oneworld, 2006).

Faulkner Rossi, L., *Wehrmacht priests: Catholicism and the Nazi war of annihilation* (Cambridge Massachusetts: Harvard University Press, 2015).

Fenlon, D., 'From the White Star to the Red Rose: J. H. Newman and the conscience of the state', *Newman Studien* xx (2010), pp. 45–73.

Gill, A., *An honourable defeat: the fight against National Socialism in Germany, 1939–1945* (London: Mandarin, 1995).

Graf, W., *Willi Graf. Briefe und Aufzeichnungen*, ed. A. Knoop-Graf & I. Jens (Frankfurt: Fischer, 1994).

Haecker, T., *Journal in the night*, trans. A. Dru (London: Pantheon, 1950).

—— *Theodor Haecker: Leben und Werk. Texte, Briefe, Erinnerungen, Würdigungen*, ed. B. Hassler & H. Siefken (Esslingen am Neckar: Stadtarchiv, 1995).

Hanser, R., *A noble treason: the revolt of the Munich students against Hitler* (New York: Putnam's, 1979; republished San Francisco: Ignatius, 2012).

Hassell, U. von, *The von Hassell diaries 1938–1944: the story of the forces against Hitler inside Germany* (London: Hamish Hamilton, 1948).

Hartnagel, F. & Scholl, S., *Sophie Scholl/Fritz Hartnagel: Damit wir uns nicht verlieren Briefwechsel, 1937–1943*, ed. T. Hartnagel (Frankfurt: S. Fischer, 2006).

Hildebrand, D. von, *My battle against Hitler: faith, truth, and defiance in the shadow of the Third Reich*, trans J. H. Cosby & J. F. Crosby (New York: Image, 2014).

Hirzel, S., *Vom Ja zum Nein: Eine schwäbische Jugend 1933–1945* (Tubingen: Klopfer & Meyer, 1998).

Kershaw, I., 'Resistance without the people? Bavarian attitudes to the Nazi regime at the time of the White Rose', *Die Weisse Rose: student resistance to National Socialism, 1942–43*, ed. H. Siefken (Nottingham: University of Nottingham, 1991), pp. 51–65.

Klapper, J., *Nonconformist writing in Nazi Germany: the literature of inner immigration* (New York: Camden House, 2015).

Knab, J., ' "Wir schweigen nicht, wir sind Euer böses Gewissen": Die Newman–Rezeption der "Weißen Rose" und ihre Wirkungsgeschichte', *Newman Studien* xx (2010), pp. 21–43.

—— Verhindert das Weiterlaufen dieser atheistischen Kriegsmaschine', *Wider die Kriegsmaschinerie. Kriegserfahrungen und Motive des Widerstandes der Weißen Rose* ed. D. Bald (Essen: Klartext, 2005), pp. 33–56.

—— Fritz Hartnagel: Vom Wehrmachtsoffizier sum Ostermarschierer', *Alternativen zum Wiederbewaffnung. Friedenskonzeptionen in Westdeutschland, 1945–1955*, ed. D. Bald & W. Wette (Essen: Klartext, 2005), pp. 123–37.

Marcusse, H., 'Remembering the White Rose: (West) German assessments, 1943–1993', *Soundings* 22:9 (1994), pp. 25–38.

McDonough, F., *Sophie Scholl. The real story of the woman who defied Hitler* (Stroud: History Press, 2009).

—— 'Sophie Scholl: a woman for all seasons', inaugural lecture, Liverpool Moore University, January 2012: https://www.youtube.com/watch?v=pBeHdtqQHQA.

Melon, R. B., *Journey to the White Rose in Germany* (Indianapolis: Dog Ear, 2006).

Moll, C., 'Acts of resistance: the White Rose in light of new archival evidence', *Resistance against the Third Reich 1933–1990*, ed. M. Geyer & J.W. Boyer (Chicago: University of Chicago, 1994), pp. 173–200.

Newman, J. H., 'The patristical idea of Antichrist', four sermons preached in Advent 1835; publ. as *Tract for the times* 83 (1838); reproduced in *Discussions and arguments on various subjects* (London: Pickering, 1872).

Ratzinger, J., introductory words at the Newman Symposium in Rome, April 1990, *Benedict XVI and Cardinal Newman* (Oxford: Family Publications, 2005), ed. P. Jennings, pp. 33–5.

Rollmann, H., 'Franz Xaver Kraus and John Henry Newman', *The Downside Review* 109:374 (1991), pp. 44–51.

Rowland, T., *Benedict XVI: a guide for the perplexed* (London: Continuum, 2010), pp. 11–12.

Sachs, R. H., *The White Rose history*, vol. i, *Coming together 1933–1942* (Utah: Exclamation, 2002–3).

—— *The White Rose history*, vol. ii, *Journey to freedom 1942–1945* (Utah: Exclamation, 2005).

Scholl, H. & S., *At the heart of the White Rose: letters and diaries of Hans and Sophie Scholl*, ed. I. Jens, trans. J. Maxwell Brownjohn (New York: Harper & Row, 1987).

Scholl, I., *Die Weisse Rose* (Frankfurt: Frankfurter Hefte, 1952); trans. C. Brooks, *Six against tyranny* (London: John Murray, 1955); trans. A. R. Schultz, *Students against tyranny: the resistance of the White Rose, Munich, 1942–1943* (Middletown: Wesleyan University Press, [1970]); rev. edn *The White Rose: Munich, 1942–1943* (Middletown: Wesleyan University Press USA, 1983).

Siefken, H. (ed.), introduction, Die Weisse Rose: student resistance to National Socialism, 1942–1943. Forschungsergebnisse und Erfahrungsberichte: a Nottingham Symposium, ed. H. Siefken (Nottingham: University of Nottingham, 1991), pp. 1–10.

—— Introduction, *Die Weiße Rose und ihre Flugblätter. Dokumente, Texte, Lebensbilder, Erläuterungen* [*The White Rose and their leaflets: documents, texts, biographical sketches, explanations*] (Manchester: Manchester University Press, 1994), pp. 1–11.

Stargardt, N., *The German war: a nation under arms, 1939–45* (London: Bodley Head, 2015).

Stern, J. P., 'The White Rose', *Die Weisse Rose: student resistance to National Socialism, 1942–1943. Forschungsergebnisse und Erfahrungsberichte: a Nottingham Symposium*, ed. H. Siefken (Nottingham: University of Nottingham, 1991), pp. 11–36.

INDEX